MUFFIN TIN MAGIC

pil

Publications International, Ltd.

Louis Weber, CEO
Publications International, Ltd.
8140 Lehigh Ave
Morton Grove, IL 60053

Pictured on the front cover: *(clockwise from top left)* Tortilla Cups with Corn and Black Bean Salad *(page 80),* Chocolate Hazelnut Biscuit Roll-Ups *(page 42),* Eggs Benedict Cups *(page 16)* and Little Potato Gratins *(page 86).*

Pictured on the back cover *(left to right):* Ramen Sliders *(page 70),* Cheesecake Cookie Cups *(page 104)* and Tuna Artichoke Cups *(page 50).*

ISBN: 978-1-68022-700-0

Library of Congress Control Number: 2016945937

Manufactured in China.

8 7 6 5 4 3 2 1

Microwave Cooking: Microwave ovens vary in wattage. Use the cooking times as guidelines and check for doneness before adding more time.

Preparation/Cooking Times: Preparation times are based on the approximate amount of time required to assemble the recipe before cooking, baking, chilling or serving. These times include preparation steps such as measuring, chopping and mixing. The fact that some preparations and cooking can be done simultaneously is taken into account. Preparation of optional ingredients and serving suggestions is not included.

TABLE OF CONTENTS

BREAKFAST
& BRUNCH

Cheesy QUICHETTES

- 12 slices bacon, crisp-cooked and chopped
- 6 eggs, beaten
- ¼ cup whole milk
- 1½ cups thawed frozen shredded hash brown potatoes, squeezed dry
- ¼ cup chopped fresh parsley
- ½ teaspoon salt
- 1½ cups (6 ounces) shredded Mexican cheese blend with jalapeño peppers

1. Preheat oven to 400°F. Lightly spray 12 standard (2½-inch) muffin cups with nonstick cooking spray.

2. Divide bacon evenly among prepared muffin cups. Whisk eggs and milk in medium bowl. Add potatoes, parsley and salt; mix well. Spoon mixture evenly into muffin cups.

3. Bake 15 minutes or until knife inserted into centers comes out almost clean. Sprinkle evenly with cheese; let stand 3 minutes or until cheese is melted. (Egg mixture will continue to cook while standing.*) Gently run knife around edges and lift out with fork.

**Standing also allows for easier removal of quichettes from pan.*

MAKES 12 QUICHETTES

Upside Down PANCAKE MUFFINS

2 cups buttermilk pancake mix

1½ cups water

16 teaspoons maple syrup, plus additional for serving

1 cup fresh or frozen* blueberries, raspberries, blackberries or a combination

Butter

Powdered sugar (optional)

If using frozen berries, do not thaw.

1. Preheat oven to 350°F. Spray 16 standard (2½-inch) muffin cups with nonstick cooking spray.

2. Whisk pancake mix and water in 4-cup measuring cup with spout; let stand 3 minutes. Pour batter into prepared muffin cups, filling three-fourths full. Add 1 teaspoon maple syrup to each cup (do not stir); top with 1 tablespoon berries.

3. Bake 15 minutes or until tops are set and toothpick inserted into centers comes out clean. Loosen bottom and sides of cups with small spatula or knife; invert onto wire rack. If some of berries stick to pan, gently scrape from pan and place on top of muffins. Serve warm with butter and additional maple syrup. Sprinkle with powdered sugar, if desired.

MAKES 16 PANCAKES

Ramen Egg CUPS

- Foil
- 1 package (3 ounces) chicken-flavored ramen noodles
- 6 eggs
- 2 tablespoons milk
- Salt and black pepper
- Chopped fresh parsley

1. Preheat oven to 400°F. Crumple 6 pieces of foil into balls about half the size of standard (2½-inch) muffin cups. Spray 6 muffin cups and foil balls with nonstick cooking spray.

2. Fill medium saucepan half full with water; add seasoning packet and bring to a boil over high heat. Add noodles; cook 1 minute to soften. Rinse and drain under cool running water.

3. Divide noodles among prepared muffin cups, pressing into bottoms and up sides of cups. Place foil ball in each cup to help set shape.

4. Bake 15 minutes. Remove foil balls; return to oven and bake 10 to 12 minutes. Cool in pan 5 minutes. *Reduce oven temperature to 325°F.*

5. Carefully crack one egg into each cup. Top each egg with 1 teaspoon milk; season with salt and pepper. Bake 10 to 12 minutes until egg whites are completely set and yolks are thickened but not hard. Sprinkle with parsley. Serve warm.

MAKES 6 CUPS

Asparagus Frittata PROSCIUTTO CUPS

1 tablespoon olive oil
1 small red onion, finely chopped
1½ cups sliced asparagus (½-inch pieces)
1 clove garlic, minced
12 thin slices prosciutto
8 eggs
½ cup (2 ounces) grated white Cheddar cheese
¼ cup grated Parmesan cheese
2 tablespoons milk
⅛ teaspoon black pepper

1. Preheat oven to 375°F. Spray 12 standard (2½-inch) muffin cups with nonstick cooking spray.

2. Heat oil in large skillet over medium heat. Add onion; cook and stir 4 minutes or until softened. Add asparagus and garlic; cook and stir 8 minutes or until asparagus is crisp-tender. Set aside to cool slightly.

3. Line each prepared muffin cup with prosciutto slice. (Prosciutto should cover cup as much as possible, with edges extending above muffin pan.) Whisk eggs, Cheddar, Parmesan, milk and pepper in large bowl until well blended. Stir in asparagus mixture until blended. Pour into prosciutto-lined cups, filling about three-fourths full.

4. Bake about 20 minutes or until frittatas are puffed and golden brown and edges are pulling away from pan. Cool in pan 10 minutes; remove to wire rack. Serve warm or at room temperature.

MAKES 12 CUPS

Individual Spinach and BACON QUICHES

- 3 slices bacon
- ½ small onion, diced
- 1 package (10 ounces) frozen chopped spinach, thawed and squeezed dry
- ½ teaspoon black pepper
- ⅛ teaspoon ground nutmeg
- Pinch salt
- 1 container (15 ounces) whole-milk ricotta cheese
- 2 cups (8 ounces) shredded mozzarella cheese
- 1 cup grated Parmesan cheese
- 3 eggs, lightly beaten

1. Preheat oven to 350°F. Spray 10 standard (2½-inch) muffin cups with nonstick cooking spray.

2. Cook bacon in large skillet over medium-high heat until crisp. Drain on paper towel-lined plate. Crumble bacon when cool enough to handle.

3. Add onion to skillet, cook and stir 5 minutes or until tender. Add spinach, pepper, nutmeg and salt; cook and stir over medium heat 3 minutes or until liquid is evaporated. Remove from heat; stir in crumbled bacon. Set aside to cool.

4. Combine ricotta, mozzarella and Parmesan in large bowl. Add eggs; whisk until well blended. Add cooled spinach mixture; mix well. Spoon evenly into prepared muffin cups.

5. Bake 40 minutes or until set. Let stand 10 minutes. Loosen sides with small spatula or knife; remove from pan. Serve immediately.

MAKES 10 QUICHES

Apple Cinnamon FRENCH TOAST CUPS

- 1 loaf (16 ounces) challah, egg bread or brioche
- 1 cup milk
- 4 eggs
- ½ cup plus 2 tablespoons sugar, divided
- 1½ teaspoons ground cinnamon, divided
- ½ teaspoon salt
- 1 sweet tart apple, peeled and chopped (about ¼-inch pieces)
- Maple syrup

1. Preheat oven to 350°F. Spray 12 standard (2½-inch) muffin cups with nonstick cooking spray.

2. Cut bread into ½-inch cubes; place in large bowl. Whisk milk, eggs, ½ cup sugar, 1 teaspoon cinnamon and salt in medium bowl; pour over bread. Let stand 10 minutes or until most of egg mixture is absorbed. Stir in apple.

3. Divide bread mixture evenly among prepared muffin cups, filling to top. Combine remaining 2 tablespoons sugar and ½ teaspoon cinnamon in small bowl; sprinkle evenly over top of each cup.

4. Bake 20 minutes or until apples are tender and tops are firm and lightly browned. Cool in pan 5 minutes. Loosen bottoms and sides with small spatula or knife; remove to wire rack. Serve warm with maple syrup.

MAKES 12 CUPS

Eggs Benedict CUPS

- 6 English muffin tops
- 6 thin slices Canadian bacon
- 6 whole eggs
- Salt and black pepper
- 3 egg yolks
- ¼ cup water
- 2 tablespoons lemon juice
- ½ cup (1 stick) cold butter, cut into 8 pieces

1. Preheat oven to 350°F. Spray 6 jumbo (3½-inch) muffin cups with nonstick cooking spray.*

2. Press English muffins into prepared cups. Top with Canadian bacon, pressing down into muffins as much as possible. Crack one egg into each cup. Sprinkle with salt and pepper.

3. Bake 10 to 12 minutes or until eggs reach desired doneness (eggs whites may not look completely set). Remove from pan to serving plates.

4. While eggs are baking, prepare hollandaise sauce. Combine egg yolks, water and lemon juice in small saucepan; cook over low heat about 4 minutes or until mixture begins to bubble around edges, whisking constantly. Whisk in butter, 1 piece at a time, until butter is melted and sauce has thickened. (Do not allow sauce to boil.) Whisk in ¼ teaspoon salt. Serve immediately with egg cups.

**If you don't have jumbo-size muffin cups, standard (2½-inch) muffin cups can be used instead. Prepare as directed; the ingredients will all fit into the cups but it will be a much tighter fit.*

MAKES 6 CUPS

Denver Scramble in HASH BROWN CUPS

- 3 tablespoons butter, divided
- 1 package (20 ounces) refrigerated hash brown potatoes
- 1½ teaspoons salt, divided
- 6 eggs
- 2 tablespoons milk
- ⅛ teaspoon black pepper
- ⅛ teaspoon hot pepper sauce or to taste
- ½ cup diced onion (¼-inch pieces)
- ½ cup diced green bell pepper (¼-inch pieces)
- ½ cup diced ham (¼-inch pieces)
- ⅓ cup shredded Monterey Jack cheese

1. Preheat oven to 400°F. Spray 12 standard (2½-inch) muffin cups with nonstick cooking spray.

2. Melt 2 tablespoons butter. Combine melted butter, potatoes and 1 teaspoon salt in large bowl; toss to coat. Press potatoes into bottoms and up sides of prepared cups (about 5 to 6 tablespoons per cup).

3. Bake about 35 minutes or until bottoms and sides are golden brown. (Insides of cups will not brown.)

4. When hash brown cups have baked 15 minutes, whisk eggs, milk, remaining ½ teaspoon salt, black pepper and hot pepper sauce in medium bowl until well blended. Melt remaining 1 tablespoon butter in large skillet over medium-high heat. Add onion; cook and stir about 4 minutes or until softened. Add bell pepper; cook and stir 4 minutes. Add ham; cook and stir 5 minutes or until bell pepper is crisp-tender. Pour egg mixture into skillet; cook 20 to 30 seconds without stirring or just until edges are beginning to set. Stir around edges and across bottom of skillet with heatproof spatula, forming large curds. Cook 3 to 4 minutes or until eggs are fluffy and barely set, stirring gently.

5. Fill hash brown cups with scrambled egg mixture (about ¼ cup egg mixture per cup); sprinkle with cheese.

MAKES 12 CUPS

Mini Fruit COFFEECAKES

1 package (about 17 ounces) frozen puff pastry (2 sheets), thawed

1 package (8 ounces) cream cheese, softened

1 egg

2 tablespoons granulated sugar

12 teaspoons desired fruit filling (apricot jam, strawberry jam, lemon curd or a combination)

½ cup powdered sugar

2 teaspoons milk

1. Preheat oven to 350°F. Spray 12 standard (2½-inch) muffin cups with nonstick cooking spray.

2. Unroll puff pastry on work surface; cut each sheet into 6 rectangles. Fit pastry into prepared muffin cups, pressing into bottoms and up sides of cups. (Two sides of each rectangle will extend up over top of muffin pan.)

3. Beat cream cheese in large bowl with electric mixer at medium-high speed until creamy. Add egg and granulated sugar; beat until smooth. Spoon heaping tablespoon cream cheese mixture into each cup; top with 1 teaspoon filling. Snip center of each overhanging pastry with scissors or paring knife; fold resulting 4 flaps in over filling, overlapping slightly (as you would fold a box).

4. Bake 20 minutes or until pastry is golden and filling is set and puffed. Cool in pan 2 minutes; remove to wire rack.

5. Meanwhile, whisk powdered sugar and milk in small bowl until smooth. Drizzle glaze over coffeecakes.

MAKES 12 COFFEECAKES

Bacon and Egg CUPS

- 12 slices bacon, crisp-cooked and cut crosswise into thirds
- 6 eggs
- ½ cup half-and-half
- ¼ teaspoon salt
- ¼ teaspoon black pepper
- ½ cup diced red and green bell pepper
- ½ cup (2 ounces) shredded pepper jack cheese

1. Preheat oven to 350°F. Spray 12 standard (2½-inch) muffin cups with nonstick cooking spray.

2. Place 3 bacon slices in each prepared muffin cup, overlapping in bottom. Whisk eggs, half-and-half, salt and black pepper in medium bowl until well blended. Stir in bell pepper and cheese. Fill each muffin cup with ¼ cup egg mixture.

3. Bake 20 to 25 minutes or until eggs are set in center. Run knife around edge of each cup before removing from pan.

MAKES 12 CUPS

Tip: To save time, look for mixed diced bell peppers in the produce section of the grocery store.

Mini Spinach FRITTATAS

1 tablespoon olive oil
½ cup chopped onion
8 eggs
¼ cup plain yogurt
1 package (10 ounces) frozen chopped spinach, thawed and squeezed dry
½ cup (2 ounces) shredded white Cheddar cheese
¼ cup grated Parmesan cheese
½ teaspoon salt
⅛ teaspoon black pepper
⅛ ground red pepper
Dash ground nutmeg

1. Preheat oven to 350°F. Spray 12 standard (2½-inch) muffin cups with nonstick cooking spray.

2. Heat oil in large nonstick skillet over medium heat. Add onion; cook and stir about 5 minutes or until tender. Set aside to cool slightly.

3. Whisk eggs and yogurt in large bowl. Stir in spinach, Cheddar, Parmesan, salt, black pepper, red pepper, nutmeg and onion until well blended. Divide mixture evenly among prepared muffin cups.

4. Bake 20 to 25 minutes or until eggs are puffed and firm and no longer shiny. Cool in pan 2 minutes. Loosen bottom and sides with small spatula or knife; remove to wire rack. Serve warm, cold or at room temperature.

MAKES 12 MINI FRITTATAS

SWEET & SAVORY BREADS

Pumpkin Spice MINI DOUGHNUTS

1 tablespoon granulated sugar
2 teaspoons ground cinnamon, divided
2 cups white whole wheat flour
½ cup packed brown sugar
1½ teaspoons baking powder
½ teaspoon salt
½ teaspoon ground ginger
½ teaspoon ground nutmeg
¼ teaspoon baking soda
2 eggs
½ cup canned solid-pack pumpkin
¼ cup (½ stick) butter, softened
¼ cup milk
1 teaspoon vanilla

1. Preheat oven to 350°F. Spray 36 mini (1¾-inch) muffin cups with nonstick cooking spray. Combine granulated sugar and 1 teaspoon cinnamon in shallow bowl; set aside.

2. Combine flour, brown sugar, baking powder, remaining 1 teaspoon cinnamon, salt, ginger, nutmeg and baking soda in medium bowl; mix well. Beat eggs, pumpkin, butter, milk and vanilla in large bowl with electric mixer at medium speed until well blended. Gradually add flour mixture; beat just until blended. Spoon scant tablespoonful batter into each prepared muffin cup.

3. Bake 12 minutes or until toothpick inserted into centers comes out clean. Cool in pans 2 minutes.

4. Working with one doughnut at a time, roll in cinnamon-sugar to coat. Return to wire racks to cool slightly. Serve warm or cool completely.

MAKES 36 DOUGHNUTS

Greek Spinach-Cheese ROLLS

1 loaf (16 ounces) frozen bread dough, thawed according to package directions

1 package (10 ounces) frozen chopped spinach, thawed and squeezed dry

¾ cup (3 ounces) crumbled feta cheese

½ cup (2 ounces) shredded Monterey Jack cheese

4 green onions, thinly sliced

1 teaspoon dried dill weed

½ teaspoon garlic powder

½ teaspoon black pepper

1. Spray 15 standard (2½-inch) muffin cups with nonstick cooking spray.

2. Roll out dough into 15×9-inch rectangle on lightly floured surface. (If dough is springy and difficult to roll, cover with plastic wrap and let rest 5 minutes.)

3. Combine spinach, feta, Monterey Jack, green onions, dill, garlic powder and pepper in large bowl; mix well. Spread spinach mixture evenly over dough, leaving 1-inch border on long sides.

4. Starting with long side, roll up tightly jelly-roll style; pinch seam to seal. Place roll seam side down on work surface; cut crosswise into 15 slices with serrated knife. Place slices cut sides up in prepared muffin cups. Cover with plastic wrap; let stand in warm place 30 minutes or until dough is slightly puffy. Preheat oven to 375°F.

5. Bake 20 to 25 minutes or until golden brown. Serve warm or at room temperature.

MAKES 15 ROLLS

Peanut Butter and CHOCOLATE SWIRLS

- 1 package (8 ounces) crescent roll sheet
- ⅔ cup semisweet chocolate chips
- 3½ tablespoons whipping cream, divided
- ⅓ cup plus 2 tablespoons peanut butter, divided
- ¼ cup packed brown sugar
- ¼ cup finely chopped roasted peanuts

1. Preheat oven to 350°F. Spray 12 standard (2½-inch) muffin cups with nonstick cooking spray.

2. Unroll crescent roll dough on work surface. Combine chocolate chips and 2 tablespoons cream in medium microwavable bowl; microwave on HIGH 30 seconds. Stir until chocolate is melted and mixture is smooth. Place ⅓ cup peanut butter in small microwavable bowl; microwave on HIGH 20 seconds or just until softened. Spread peanut butter over dough to within ½ inch of edges; sprinkle with brown sugar, pressing sugar lightly into peanut butter. Spread two thirds of chocolate mixture over brown sugar. Sprinkle with peanuts. Roll up dough tightly jelly-roll style; pinch seam to seal. Make sure roll is 12 inches long before cutting crosswise into 1-inch slices. Place slices cut sides up in prepared muffin cups.

3. Bake 12 minutes or until golden brown. Cool in pan 2 minutes; use small spatula or knife to loosen edges and remove to wire rack set over sheet of waxed paper.

4. Add remaining 1½ tablespoons cream to remaining chocolate mixture; microwave on HIGH 10 to 20 seconds or until mixture is smooth and thinned to glaze consistency. Place remaining 2 tablespoons peanut butter in small microwavable bowl; microwave on HIGH 30 seconds or until melted. Drizzle chocolate mixture and peanut butter over rolls. Serve warm or at room temperature.

MAKES 12 ROLLS

Quick Breakfast ROLLS

PREP TIME: 20 minutes **BAKE TIME:** 15 minutes

- **¼ cup sliced almonds, toasted**
- **½ cup packed brown sugar**
- **1 teaspoon ground cinnamon**
- **½ teaspoon ground nutmeg**
- **4 tablespoons butter or margarine, divided**
- **¾ cup DOLE® Frozen Mango Chunks, finely chopped, thawed, drained**
- **1 package (8 ounces) refrigerated crescent rolls**

COMBINE almonds, brown sugar, cinnamon and nutmeg in small bowl. Spray muffin pan with nonstick cooking spray.

PLACE 1 teaspoon butter and 1 tablespoon sugar mixture in each prepared muffin cup.

ADD mango to remaining sugar mixture. Unroll crescent dough from package and pinch seams together. Spread mango mixture over dough. Roll up from long side. Cut into 12 pieces and place each spiral into a muffin cup.

BAKE at 375°F. 12 to 15 minutes. Loosen edges; invert pan onto baking sheet. Serve warm.

MAKES 12 SERVINGS

Punched Pizza ROUNDS

1 package (12 ounces) refrigerated flaky buttermilk biscuits (10 biscuits)

80 mini pepperoni slices *or* 20 small pepperoni slices

8 to 10 pickled jalapeño pepper slices, chopped (optional)

1 tablespoon dried basil

½ cup pizza sauce

1½ cups (6 ounces) shredded mozzarella cheese

Shredded Parmesan cheese (optional)

1. Preheat oven to 400°F. Spray 20 standard (2½-inch) nonstick muffin cups with nonstick cooking spray.

2. Separate biscuits; split each biscuit in half horizontally to create 20 rounds. Place in prepared muffin cups. Press 4 mini pepperoni slices into center of each round. Sprinkle with jalapeños, if desired, and basil. Spread pizza sauce over pepperoni; sprinkle with mozzarella.

3. Bake 8 to 9 minutes or until bottoms of pizzas are golden brown. Sprinkle with Parmesan, if desired. Cool in pan 2 minutes; loosen edges and remove to wire racks. Serve warm.

MAKES 20 APPETIZERS

Prosciutto Provolone ROLLS

1 loaf (16 ounces) frozen bread dough, thawed according to package directions

¼ cup garlic and herb spreadable cheese

6 thin slices prosciutto (3-ounce package)

6 slices (1 ounce each) provolone cheese

1. Spray 12 standard (2½-inch) muffin cups with nonstick cooking spray.

2. Roll out dough into 12×10-inch rectangle on lightly floured surface. Spread garlic and herb cheese evenly over dough. Arrange prosciutto slices over herb cheese; top with provolone slices. Starting with long side, roll up dough jelly-roll style; pinch seam to seal.

3. Cut crosswise into 1-inch slices; place slices cut sides up in prepared muffin cups. Cover and let rise in warm place 30 to 40 minutes or until nearly doubled in size. Preheat oven to 350°F.

4. Bake about 18 minutes or until golden brown. Loosen edges with small spatula or knife; remove to wire rack. Serve warm.

MAKES 12 ROLLS

Jelly Doughnut BITES

- ½ **cup plus 3 tablespoons warm (95° to 105°F) milk, divided**
- 1¼ **teaspoons active dry yeast**
- ⅓ **cup granulated sugar**
- 1 **tablespoon butter, softened**
- 2½ **cups all-purpose flour**
- 1 **egg**
- ½ **teaspoon salt**
- ½ **cup raspberry jam**
- **Powdered sugar**

1. Stir 3 tablespoons warm milk and yeast in large bowl until blended. Let stand 5 minutes. Add granulated sugar, butter and remaining ½ cup milk; mix well. Add flour, egg and salt; beat with dough hook of electric mixer at low speed until dough starts to climb up dough hook. If dough is too sticky, add additional flour, 1 tablespoon at a time. Or knead dough on lightly floured surface until smooth and elastic.

2. Place dough in greased bowl; turn to grease top. Cover and let stand in warm place 1 hour.

3. Spray 48 mini (1¾-inch) muffin cups with nonstick cooking spray. Punch down dough. Shape pieces of dough into 1-inch balls; place in prepared muffin cups. Cover and let rise 1 hour. Preheat oven to 375°F.

4. Bake 10 to 12 minutes or until light golden brown. Remove to wire racks to cool completely.

5. Place jam in pastry bag fitted with small round tip. Insert tip into side of each doughnut; squeeze about 1 teaspoon jam into center. Sprinkle filled doughnuts with powdered sugar.

MAKES 48 DOUGHNUTS

Pepperoni Pizza ROLLS

1 loaf (16 ounces) frozen pizza dough or white bread dough, thawed according to package directions

½ cup pizza sauce, plus additional for serving

⅓ cup chopped pepperoni or mini pepperoni slices (half of 2½-ounce package)

9 to 10 slices fontina, provolone or provolone-mozzarella blend cheese*

**For best results, use thinner cheese slices which are less than 1 ounce each.*

1. Spray 12 standard (2½-inch) muffin cups with nonstick cooking spray.

2. Roll out dough into 12×10-inch rectangle on lightly floured surface. Spread ½ cup pizza sauce over dough, leaving ½-inch border on long sides. Sprinkle with pepperoni; top with cheese, cutting slices to fit as necessary. Starting with long side, roll up dough jelly-roll style; pinch seam to seal.

3. Cut crosswise into 1-inch slices; place slices cut sides up in prepared muffin cups. Cover with plastic wrap; let rise in warm place 30 to 40 minutes or until nearly doubled in size. Preheat oven to 350°F.

4. Bake about 25 minutes or until golden brown. Loosen bottom and sides with small spatula or knife; remove to wire rack. Serve warm with additional sauce for dipping, if desired.

MAKES 12 ROLLS

Chocolate Hazelnut BISCUIT ROLL-UPS

- 2¼ cups all-purpose flour
- ¼ cup granulated sugar
- 1 tablespoon baking powder
- ½ teaspoon baking soda
- ½ teaspoon salt
- ½ cup (1 stick) butter, cut into pieces
- ¾ cup buttermilk
- 1 teaspoon vanilla
- 1 cup chocolate-hazelnut spread
- ½ cup chopped hazelnuts, toasted* (optional)

**To toast hazelnuts, spread on baking sheet. Bake at 350°F 6 to 8 minutes or until lightly browned, stirring frequently.*

1. Preheat oven to 350°F. Spray 12 standard (2½-inch) muffin cups with nonstick cooking spray.

2. Combine flour, granulated sugar, baking powder, baking soda and salt in medium bowl; mix well. Cut in butter with pastry blender or two knives until coarse crumbs form. Stir in buttermilk and vanilla just until blended. Turn out dough onto lightly floured surface; knead briefly to form a ball.

3. Roll out dough into 12-inch square. Spread chocolate-hazelnut spread over dough to within ½ inch of edges; sprinkle with hazelnuts, if desired. Tightly roll up dough jelly-roll style; pinch seam to seal. Roll log back and forth to even out dough. Cut crosswise into 12 slices; place slices cut sides up in prepared muffin cups.

4. Bake 15 minutes or until golden brown. Immediately remove to wire rack to cool slightly.

MAKES 12 ROLLS

APPETIZERS & SNACKS

Almond Chicken CUPS

1 tablespoon vegetable oil
½ cup chopped onion
½ cup chopped red bell pepper
2 cups chopped cooked chicken
⅔ cup prepared sweet and sour sauce
½ cup chopped almonds
2 tablespoons soy sauce
6 (6- to 7-inch) flour tortillas

1. Preheat oven to 400°F.

2. Heat oil in small skillet over medium heat. Add onion and bell pepper; cook and stir 3 minutes or until crisp-tender.

3. Combine vegetable mixture, chicken, sweet and sour sauce, almonds and soy sauce in medium bowl; mix well.

4. Cut each tortilla in half. Place each half in standard (2½-inch) muffin cup. Fill each tortilla cup with about ¼ cup chicken mixture.

5. Bake 8 to 10 minutes or until tortilla edges are crisp and filling is heated through. Cool on wire rack 5 minutes before serving.

MAKES 12 CUPS

Chili PUFFS

- 1 package (about 17 ounces) frozen puff pastry (2 sheets), thawed
- 1 can (about 15 ounces) chili without beans
- 4 ounces cream cheese, softened
- ½ cup (2 ounces) finely shredded sharp Cheddar cheese
- Sliced green onions (optional)

1. Preheat oven to 400°F.

2. Roll out each sheet of puff pastry into 18×9-inch rectangle on lightly floured surface. Cut each rectangle into 18 (3-inch) squares. Press dough into 36 mini (1¾-inch) muffin cups. Bake 10 minutes.

3. Combine chili and cream cheese in medium bowl; stir until well blended. Fill each pastry shell with 2 teaspoons chili mixture, pressing down centers of pastry to fill, if necessary. Sprinkle with Cheddar.

4. Bake 5 to 7 minutes or until cheese is melted and edges of pastry are golden brown. Cool in pans 5 minutes. Serve warm; garnish with green onions.

MAKES 36 APPETIZERS

Tip: Use a pizza cutter to easily cut puff pastry sheets into squares.

Mac and Cheese MINI CUPS

3 tablespoons butter, divided
2 tablespoons all-purpose flour
1 cup milk
1 teaspoon salt
½ teaspoon black pepper
1 cup (4 ounces) shredded sharp Cheddar cheese
1 cup (4 ounces) shredded Muenster cheese
8 ounces elbow macaroni, cooked and drained
⅓ cup panko or plain dry bread crumbs
Finely chopped fresh parsley (optional)

1. Preheat oven to 400°F. Melt 1 tablespoon butter in large saucepan over medium heat; brush 36 mini (1¾-inch) muffin cups with melted butter.

2. Melt remaining 2 tablespoons butter in same saucepan over medium heat. Whisk in flour; cook and stir 2 minutes. Add milk, salt and pepper; cook and stir 3 minutes or until mixture is thickened. Remove from heat; stir in Cheddar and Muenster. Fold in macaroni. Divide mixture among prepared muffin cups; sprinkle with panko.

3. Bake about 25 minutes or until golden brown. Cool in pans 10 minutes; remove carefully using sharp knife. Garnish with parsley.

MAKES 36 CUPS

Tuna Artichoke CUPS

- 1 can (6 ounces) tuna packed in water, preferably albacore, drained, liquid reserved
- ¼ cup minced shallots
- 1 tablespoon white wine vinegar
- ¼ teaspoon ground coriander
- 4 ounces cream cheese
- 1 can (14 ounces) artichoke hearts, drained and coarsely chopped
- 1 tablespoon lemon juice
- ½ teaspoon salt
- ¼ teaspoon white pepper
- Dash ground nutmeg
- 12 (3-inch) wonton wrappers
- 2 tablespoons butter, melted

1. Preheat oven to 350°F.

2. Combine reserved tuna liquid, shallots, vinegar and coriander in small saucepan; bring to a boil over medium-high heat. Reduce heat to low; simmer, uncovered, until liquid has evaporated. Add tuna and cream cheese; cook until cheese melts, stirring constantly. Stir in artichokes, lemon juice, salt, pepper and nutmeg. Cool slightly.

3. Press 1 wonton wrapper into each of 12 standard (2½-inch) muffin cups, allowing ends to extend above edges of cups. Spoon tuna mixture evenly into wonton wrappers. Brush edges of wonton wrappers with butter.

4. Bake 20 minutes or until tuna mixture is set and edges of wonton wrappers are browned.

MAKES 12 CUPS

Tiny Spinach QUICHES

PASTRY

1 package (3 ounces) cream cheese, softened
½ cup (1 stick) butter or margarine, softened
1 cup all-purpose flour

FILLING

5 slices bacon, cooked and crumbled
1 cup grated Swiss cheese
1 can (13.5 ounces) POPEYE® Chopped Spinach, drained
3 eggs
¾ cup light cream
¼ teaspoon ground nutmeg
Salt and pepper to taste

1. **To prepare pastry:** Cut cream cheese and butter into flour. Form into a ball; wrap in plastic wrap and chill 1 hour. Lightly flour rolling pin. Place pastry on lightly floured work surface, roll out to ⅛-inch thickness and cut into 16 circles with 3-inch biscuit cutter. Line sixteen 1½-inch plain or fluted muffin pan cups, or mini-muffin pan cups, with dough circles.

2. **To prepare filling:** Preheat oven to 375°F. Sprinkle bacon, then cheese, evenly over bottoms of unbaked pastries. Squeeze spinach dry and spread evenly over bacon and cheese. In medium bowl, combine remaining ingredients. Pour evenly into pastry cups. Bake 30 minutes or until set.

MAKES 16 APPETIZERS

Note: To serve as a pie, pour filling into one 9-inch frozen ready-to-bake pie crust.

Sesame Chicken Salad WONTON CUPS

- 20 (3-inch) wonton wrappers
- 1 tablespoon sesame seeds
- 2 boneless skinless chicken breasts (about 8 ounces)
- 1 cup fresh green beans, cut diagonally into ½-inch pieces
- ¼ cup mayonnaise
- 1 tablespoon chopped fresh cilantro (optional)
- 2 teaspoons honey
- 1 teaspoon reduced-sodium soy sauce
- ⅛ teaspoon ground red pepper

1. Preheat oven to 350°F. Spray 20 mini (1¾-inch) muffin cups with nonstick cooking spray.

2. Press 1 wonton wrapper into each prepared muffin cup; spray with cooking spray. Bake 8 to 10 minutes or until golden brown. Cool completely in pan on wire rack.

3. Place sesame seeds in shallow baking pan. Bake 5 minutes or until golden brown, stirring occasionally. Set aside to cool.

4. Meanwhile, bring 2 cups water to a boil in medium saucepan over high heat. Add chicken. Reduce heat to low; cover and simmer 10 minutes or until chicken is no longer pink in center, adding green beans after 7 minutes. Drain chicken and beans.

5. Finely chop chicken; place in medium bowl. Add green beans, mayonnaise, cilantro, if desired, honey, soy sauce and red pepper; stir gently until blended. Fill wonton cups with chicken salad.

MAKES 20 CUPS

Quick and Easy ARANCINI

1 package (6 to 8 ounces) sun-dried tomato, mushroom or Milanese risotto mix, plus ingredients to prepare mix*

½ cup frozen peas *or* ¼ cup finely chopped oil-packed sun-dried tomatoes (optional)

½ cup panko bread crumbs

¼ cup finely shredded or grated Parmesan cheese

2 tablespoons minced fresh parsley

2 tablespoons butter, melted

4 ounces Swiss, Asiago or fontina cheese, cut into 12 cubes (about ½ inch)

**Or use 3 cups leftover risotto.*

1. Prepare risotto according to package directions. Stir in peas, if desired. Let stand, uncovered, 20 minutes or until thickened and cool enough to handle.

2. Preheat oven to 375°F. Spray 12 standard (2½-inch) muffin pan cups with nonstick cooking spray. Combine panko, Parmesan, parsley and melted butter in medium bowl.

3. Shape level ¼ cupfuls risotto into balls around Swiss cheese cubes, covering completely. Roll in panko mixture to coat. Place in prepared muffin cups.

4. Bake 15 minutes or until arancini are golden brown and cheese cubes are melted. Cool in pan 5 minutes. Serve warm.

MAKES 12 ARANCINI

Guacamole BITES

- 2 tablespoons vegetable oil
- 1¼ teaspoons salt, divided
- ½ teaspoon garlic powder
- 12 (6-inch) corn tortillas
- 2 small ripe avocados
- 2 tablespoons finely chopped red onion
- 1 tablespoon chopped fresh cilantro
- 2 teaspoons lime juice
- 1 teaspoon finely chopped jalapeño pepper *or* ¼ teaspoon hot pepper sauce

1. Preheat oven to 375°F. Whisk oil, ¾ teaspoon salt and garlic powder in small bowl until well blended.

2. Use 3-inch biscuit cutter to cut out 2 circles from each tortilla to create 24 circles total. Wrap stack of tortilla circles loosely in waxed paper; microwave on HIGH 10 to 15 seconds or just until softened. Brush tortillas lightly with oil mixture; press into 24 mini (1¾-inch) muffin cups. (Do not spray muffin pan with nonstick cooking spray.)

3. Bake about 8 minutes or until crisp. Remove to wire racks to cool completely.

4. Meanwhile, prepare guacamole. Cut avocados into halves; remove pits. Scoop pulp into large bowl; mash roughly, leaving avocado slightly chunky. Stir in onion, cilantro, lime juice, jalapeño and remaining ½ teaspoon salt.

5. Fill each tortilla cup with 2 to 3 teaspoons guacamole.

MAKES 24 APPETIZERS

Spinach-Artichoke PARTY CUPS

36 (3-inch) wonton wrappers

1 jar (about 6 ounces) marinated artichoke hearts, drained and chopped

½ (10-ounce) package frozen chopped spinach, thawed and squeezed dry

1 cup (4 ounces) shredded Monterey Jack cheese

½ cup grated Parmesan cheese

½ cup mayonnaise

1 clove garlic, minced

1. Preheat oven to 300°F. Spray 36 mini (1¾-inch) muffin cups with nonstick cooking spray.

2. Press 1 wonton wrapper into each prepared muffin cup; spray with cooking spray. Bake 9 minutes or until light golden brown. Remove to wire racks to cool completely.

3. Combine artichokes, spinach, Monterey Jack, Parmesan, mayonnaise and garlic in medium bowl; mix well. Fill each wonton cup with about 1½ teaspoons spinach-artichoke mixture. Place pans on baking sheets.

4. Bake 7 minutes or until heated through. Serve immediately.

MAKES 36 CUPS

Tip: If you have leftover spinach-artichoke mixture after filling the wonton cups, place the mixture in a shallow ovenproof dish and bake at 350°F until hot and bubbly. Serve with bread or crackers.

Pepperoni PUFFERS

1 package (3 ounces) oriental-flavored ramen noodles
1 cup (4 ounces) shredded mozzarella cheese
2 eggs, beaten
1 teaspoon Italian seasoning
¼ teaspoon red pepper flakes
¼ cup prepared pizza sauce
2 tablespoons grated Parmesan cheese
24 small pepperoni slices (not mini)

1. Preheat oven to 400°F. Generously spray 24 mini (1¾-inch) muffin cups with nonstick cooking spray.

2. Break noodles into 4 pieces. Cook according to package directions using seasoning packet; drain well.

3. Combine noodles, mozzarella, eggs, Italian seasoning and red pepper flakes in large bowl; mix well.

4. Fill prepared muffin cups evenly with noodle mixture; top each with ½ teaspoon sauce, ¼ teaspoon Parmesan and pepperoni slice.

5. Bake 13 minutes. Cool in pan 10 minutes before serving.

MAKES 24 APPETIZERS

Caesar Salad in PARMESAN CUPS

1¾ cups shredded Parmesan cheese, divided
1 small head romaine lettuce (10 to 12 ounces)
Salt
1 teaspoon Dijon mustard
1 clove garlic, minced
½ teaspoon anchovy paste *or* 1 anchovy fillet, minced
¼ teaspoon ground black pepper
¼ cup lemon juice
⅓ cup grated Parmesan cheese*
⅓ cup extra virgin olive oil
½ cup croutons

**Parmesan used in the dressing should be finely grated to blend properly. Larger shreds of Parmesan work best for the cups.*

1. Preheat oven to 375°F. Line baking sheet with silicone baking mat or parchment paper. Set 12-cup muffin pan upside down on work surface.

2. Place ¼ cup shredded Parmesan in mound on prepared baking sheet; spread into 5-inch circle. Repeat to form 6 circles total, spacing circles at least 1 inch apart.

3. Bake about 8 minutes or until cheese is golden brown and bubbly. Immediately remove from pan with thin metal spatula; place cheese rounds over back of upside-down muffin cups. Press down firmly to mold cheese rounds into cups. Cool completely on muffin pan to set shape.

4. Meanwhile, prepare salad. Cut romaine leaves crosswise into 1-inch pieces. (Cut large leaves in half lengthwise before cutting crosswise.) Place in large bowl; sprinkle with salt. Whisk mustard, garlic, anchovy paste and pepper in medium bowl. Add lemon juice and grated Parmesan; whisk until blended. Gradually whisk

in oil until well blended. Add half of dressing to romaine; toss to coat. Add additional dressing if necessary; reserve remaining dressing for another use.

5. Fill Parmesan cups with salad (about 1 cup salad per cup); top with croutons and remaining ¼ cup shredded Parmesan.

MAKES 6 SERVINGS

Mini Taco CUPS

PREP TIME: 15 minutes **START TO FINISH TIME:** 25 minutes

- **24 wonton wrappers**
- **1 pound lean ground beef**
- **1 packet (1.25 ounces) ORTEGA® Taco Seasoning Mix**
- **½ cup plus 2 tablespoons ORTEGA® Thick & Chunky Salsa, divided**
- **1 cup (4 ounces) shredded Mexican cheese blend**
- **Additional ORTEGA® Thick & Chunky Salsa**
- **Sour cream (optional)**
- **B&G® Sliced Black Olives (optional)**

PREHEAT oven to 425°F. Coat 24 mini muffin cups with nonstick cooking spray. Press wonton wrappers into cups.

BROWN beef in medium skillet over medium-high heat. Drain excess fat and discard. Stir in seasoning mix and 2 tablespoons salsa. Spoon mixture evenly into wonton cups. Top evenly with remaining ½ cup salsa and cheese.

BAKE 8 minutes or until wontons are golden brown. Serve immediately with additional salsa. Garnish with sour cream and olives, if desired.

MAKES 24 APPETIZERS

Tip: For a deliciously different light lunch, press refrigerated rolls or biscuits into regular muffin cups, then fill with the seasoned ground beef mixture. Bake at the time and temperature suggested on the refrigerated roll package.

MAIN & SIDE DISHES

Mashed Potato PUFFS

1 cup prepared mashed potatoes
½ cup finely chopped broccoli or spinach
2 egg whites
4 tablespoons shredded Parmesan cheese, divided

1. Preheat oven to 400°F. Spray 18 mini (1¾-inch) muffin cups with nonstick cooking spray.

2. Combine mashed potatoes, broccoli, egg whites and 2 tablespoons cheese in large bowl; mix well. Spoon evenly into prepared muffin cups; sprinkle with remaining 2 tablespoons cheese.

3. Bake 20 to 23 minutes or until golden brown. Gently loosen edges with knife and lift out with fork. Serve warm.

MAKES 18 PUFFS

Ramen SLIDERS

BUNS

1 tablespoon sesame seeds, toasted*
2 packages (3 ounces each) beef-flavored ramen noodles**
2 eggs
¼ teaspoon garlic powder

BURGERS

1 pound ground beef
½ teaspoon salt
½ teaspoon black pepper
½ teaspoon garlic powder
1 tablespoon vegetable oil

TOPPINGS

3 slices American cheese, each cut into 4 squares
12 lettuce leaves
2 medium plum tomatoes, thinly sliced
12 hamburger dill pickle slices
¼ cup thinly sliced red onion
Ketchup and mustard

**To toast sesame seeds, cook in small skillet over medium-high heat 1 to 2 minutes or until beginning to brown, stirring frequently.*

***Discard 1 seasoning packet.*

1. For buns, preheat oven to 350°F. Lightly spray 24 standard (2½-inch) nonstick muffin cups with nonstick cooking spray. Sprinkle ⅛ teaspoon sesame seeds in each cup.

2. Break each layer of ramen noodles into 4 pieces. Cook noodles according to package directions; rinse and drain under cool running water. Shake off excess water; blot on paper towels.

3. Whisk eggs, 1 seasoning packet and ¼ teaspoon garlic powder in large bowl until blended. Add noodles; toss until to coat. Divide mixture evenly among prepared muffin cups. Bake 10 minutes or until set. Turn buns over in pan; cool completely in pan.

4. For burgers, shape beef into 12 (2½-inch) patties. Combine salt, pepper and ½ teaspoon garlic powder in small bowl. Sprinkle evenly over both sides of patties.

5. Heat oil in large nonstick skillet over medium-high heat. Working in 2 batches, cook patties 2 minutes per side. Remove from heat; top each patty with 1 cheese square.

6. To assemble, place half of "buns" on serving platter. Top with lettuce, patties, desired toppings and "bun" tops.

MAKES 12 SLIDERS

Spanikopita CUPS

6 tablespoons (¾ stick) butter, melted
2 eggs
1 container (15 ounces) ricotta cheese
1 package frozen chopped spinach, thawed and squeezed dry
1 package (4 to 5 ounces) crumbled feta cheese
¾ teaspoon finely grated lemon peel
½ teaspoon salt
¼ teaspoon black pepper
⅛ teaspoon ground nutmeg
8 sheets frozen phyllo dough, thawed

1. Preheat oven to 350°F. Grease 16 standard (2½-inch) muffin pan cups with some of butter.

2. Whisk eggs in large bowl. Add ricotta, spinach, feta, lemon peel, salt, pepper and nutmeg; whisk until well blended.

3. Place one sheet of phyllo on work surface. Brush with some of butter; top with second sheet. Repeat layers twice. Cut stack of phyllo into 8 rectangles; fit rectangles into muffin cups, pressing into bottoms and sides of cups. Repeat with remaining 4 sheets of phyllo and butter. Fill phyllo cups with spinach mixture.

4. Bake about 18 minutes or until phyllo is golden brown and filling is set. Cool in pan 2 minutes; remove to wire rack. Serve warm.

MAKES 16 CUPS

Mini Chicken POT PIES

PREP TIME: 20 minutes **BAKE TIME:** 15 minutes
COOL TIME: 5 minutes

1½ cups cubed cooked chicken

1 can (10½ ounces) CAMPBELL'S® Condensed Cream of Chicken Soup or CAMPBELL'S® Condensed 98% Fat Free Cream of Chicken Soup

1 package (about 8 ounces) frozen mixed vegetables (carrots, green beans, corn, peas), thawed (about 1½ cups)

1 package (12 ounces) refrigerated biscuit dough (10 biscuits)

½ cup shredded Cheddar cheese

1. Heat the oven to 350°F. Spray **10** (2 ½-inch) muffin-pan cups with vegetable cooking spray. Stir the chicken, soup and vegetables in a medium bowl.

2. Roll or pat the biscuits to flatten slightly. Press the biscuits into the bottoms and up the sides of the muffin-pan cups. Spoon **about ⅓ cup** chicken mixture into **each** biscuit cup. Lightly press the chicken mixture down so it's level. Top **each** with **about 2 teaspoons** cheese.

3. Bake for 15 minutes or until the biscuits are golden brown and the cheese is melted. Let the pot pies cool in the pan on a wire rack for 5 minutes.

MAKES 5 SERVINGS

Cacio e Pepe CUPS

8 ounces uncooked spaghetti, broken in half

2 eggs

¼ teaspoon coarsely ground black pepper, plus additional for garnish

¾ cup finely shredded or grated Parmesan cheese, divided

Minced fresh parsley

1. Preheat oven to 350°F. Spray 12 standard (2½-inch) muffin cups with nonstick cooking spray.

2. Cook pasta in large saucepan of boiling salted water until al dente. Drain pasta, reserving about 1 tablespoon cooking water.

3. Meanwhile, beat eggs and ¼ teaspoon pepper in medium bowl. Stir in ½ cup cheese. Add hot pasta and cooking water; stir until well blended and cheese is melted. Divide spaghetti among prepared muffin cups (tongs work best); pour any remaining egg mixture from bowl into cups. Sprinkle tops with remaining ¼ cup cheese and additional pepper.

4. Bake 15 minutes or until tops are set, no longer shiny and lightly browned. Immediately remove from pan. Sprinkle with parsley; serve warm.

MAKES 12 CUPS

Sausage and Kale DEEP-DISH MINI PIZZAS

- 1 tablespoon olive oil
- 4 ounces spicy turkey or pork Italian sausage
- ⅓ cup finely chopped red onion
- 2½ cups packed chopped stemmed kale
- ¼ teaspoon salt
- 1 loaf (16 ounces) frozen pizza dough or white bread dough, thawed according to package directions
- ¾ cup (3 ounces) shredded Italian blend cheese
- ¼ cup pizza sauce

1. Preheat oven to 400°F. Spray 12 standard (2½-inch) muffin cups with nonstick cooking spray.

2. Heat oil in large skillet over medium-high heat. (If using pork sausage, oil is not needed.) Remove sausage from casing; crumble into skillet. Cook and stir about 5 minutes or until no longer pink. Remove to plate. Add onion to skillet; cook and stir 4 minutes or until softened. Add kale; cook about 10 minutes or until tender, stirring occasionally. Return sausage to skillet with salt; stir until blended. Set aside to cool slightly.

3. Divide dough into 12 pieces. Stretch or roll each piece into 5-inch circle; press into prepared muffin cups. Sprinkle 1 teaspoon cheese into bottom of each cup; spread 1 teaspoon pizza sauce over cheese. Top evenly with kale mixture and remaining cheese.

4. Bake about 16 minutes or until golden brown. Cool in pan 1 minute. Loosen sides with small spatula or knife; remove to wire rack. Serve warm.

MAKES 12 MINI PIZZAS

Tortilla Cups WITH CORN AND BLACK BEAN SALAD

3 tablespoons vegetable oil, divided
1 teaspoon salt, divided
½ teaspoon chili powder
6 (6-inch) flour tortillas
1 cup corn
1 cup chopped red bell pepper
1 cup canned black beans, rinsed and drained
1 small ripe avocado, diced
¼ cup lime juice
¼ cup chopped fresh cilantro
1 small jalapeño pepper, seeded and minced

1. Preheat oven to 350°F. Spray 6 standard (2½-inch) muffin cups with nonstick cooking spray. Whisk 1 tablespoon oil, ½ teaspoon salt and chili powder in small bowl until well blended.

2. Stack tortillas; wrap loosely in waxed paper. Microwave on HIGH 10 to 15 seconds or just until softened. Brush one side of each tortilla lightly with oil mixture; press into prepared cups, oiled side up.

3. Bake about 10 minutes or until edges are golden brown. Cool in pan 2 minutes; remove to wire rack to cool completely.

4. Combine corn, bell pepper, beans and avocado in large bowl. Whisk remaining 2 tablespoons oil, ½ teaspoon salt, lime juice, cilantro and jalapeño in small bowl until well blended. Add to corn mixture; toss gently to coat. Fill tortilla cups with salad. Serve immediately. (Tortilla cups and salad can be prepared ahead of time; fill cups just before serving.)

MAKES 6 SERVINGS

Tip: For slightly larger tortilla cups, use the back of the muffin pan instead. Spray the back of a 12-cup muffin pan with nonstick cooking spray. Soften the tortillas and brush with the oil mixture as directed, then fit them between the cups on the back of the muffin pan. (Only about 3 will fit at one time, so 2 batches are necessary.) Bake at 350°F about 8 minutes or until the edges are golden brown.

Meat Loaf CUPCAKES

- 3 medium potatoes, peeled and chopped
- 1½ pounds ground beef
- ½ cup finely chopped onion
- ⅓ cup old-fashioned oats
- 1 egg
- 2 tablespoons chopped fresh rosemary
- ½ cup milk
- 2 tablespoons butter
- 1 teaspoon salt
- Black pepper
- ¼ cup snipped fresh chives

1. Preheat oven to 350°F.

2. Place potatoes in medium saucepan; add water to cover. Bring to a boil; cook 25 to 30 minutes or until potatoes are fork-tender.

3. Combine beef, onion, oats, egg and rosemary in large bowl; mix well. Divide mixture among 10 standard (2½-inch) muffin cups or silicone liners.

4. Bake 25 minutes or until cooked through (160°F). Meanwhile, beat potatoes, milk, butter, salt and pepper in large bowl with electric mixer at medium speed 3 minutes or until smooth. Place mixture in large piping bag fitted with large star tip.

5. Pipe mashed potatoes over meat loaves. Sprinkle with chives.

MAKES 10 SERVINGS

Chipotle Pork TACO CUPS

PREP TIME: 15 minutes **BAKE TIME:** 5 minutes **COOK TIME:** 5 minutes

Vegetable cooking spray

10 whole wheat or flour tortillas (6-inch)

1 container (18 ounces) refrigerated cooked barbecue sauce with shredded pork (about 2 cups)

1 cup PACE® Picante Sauce

¼ teaspoon ground chipotle chile pepper

Shredded Cheddar cheese (optional)

Guacamole (optional)

Sour cream (optional)

Sliced ripe olives (optional)

1. Heat the oven to 350°F. Spray **10** (3-inch) muffin-pan cups with the cooking spray.

2. Wrap the tortillas between damp paper towels. Microwave on HIGH for 30 seconds or until the tortillas are warm. Fold **1** tortilla into thirds to form a cone shape. Press the tortilla cone, wide end down, into a muffin-pan cup. Repeat with the remaining tortillas, rewarming in the microwave as needed.

3. Bake for 5 minutes or until the tortilla cones are golden. Remove the tortillas from the pan and cool on wire racks.

4. Heat the pork, picante sauce and chipotle chile pepper in a 2-quart saucepan over medium heat until the mixture is hot and bubbling, stirring often.

5. Spoon **about ¼ cup** pork mixture into **each** tortilla cone. Top with the cheese, guacamole, sour cream or olives, if desired.

MAKES 10 SERVINGS

Kitchen Tip: You can prepare the tortillas through the baking step up to 24 hours ahead of time and store them in an airtight container.

Little Potato GRATINS

- 1 cup whipping cream
- 1 tablespoon fresh thyme leaves
- 1 clove garlic, minced
- 1 teaspoon salt
- ⅛ teaspoon black pepper
- 2 pounds russet potatoes
- ¼ cup grated Parmesan cheese
- 1 cup (4 ounces) grated Gruyère cheese

1. Preheat oven to 375°F. Spray 12 standard (2½-cup) muffin cups with nonstick cooking spray.

2. Pour cream into small microwavable bowl or glass measuring cup. Microwave on HIGH 1 minute or just until cream begins to bubble around edges. Stir in thyme, garlic, salt and pepper until blended; let stand while preparing potatoes.

3. Peel potatoes and cut crosswise into ⅛-inch slices. Layer potato slices in prepared muffin cups, filling half full. Sprinkle with Parmesan; layer remaining potato slices over Parmesan. Pour cream mixture over potatoes; press potato stacks down firmly. Cover pan loosely with foil; place on baking sheet.

4. Bake 30 minutes. Remove pan from oven; sprinkle potatoes with Gruyère. Bake, uncovered, 30 minutes or until potatoes are tender and golden brown. (A paring knife inserted into potatoes should go in easily when potatoes are tender.) Let stand 5 minutes. Use small spatula or knife to loosen edges and bottoms of gratins; remove to plate. Serve warm.

MAKES 12 GRATINS

Tip: Gratins can be made ahead, refrigerated and reheated for 10 to 15 minutes in a 350°F oven.

DELICIOUS
DESSERTS

Pecan MINI KISSES® CUPS

PREP TIME: 25 minutes **CHILL TIME:** 1 hour **BAKE TIME:** 25 minutes
COOL TIME: 1 hour

½ cup (1 stick) butter or margarine, softened
1 package (3 ounces) cream cheese, softened
1 cup all-purpose flour
1 egg
⅔ cup packed light brown sugar
1 tablespoon butter, melted
1 teaspoon vanilla extract
Dash salt
72 (about ½ cup) HERSHEY'S® MINI KISSES® BRAND Milk Chocolates, divided
½ to ¾ cup coarsely chopped pecans

1. Beat ½ cup softened butter and cream cheese in medium bowl until blended. Add flour; beat well. Cover; refrigerate about 1 hour or until firm enough to handle.

2. Heat oven to 325°F. Stir together egg, brown sugar, 1 tablespoon melted butter, vanilla and salt in small bowl until well blended.

3. Shape chilled dough into 24 balls (1 inch each). Place balls in ungreased small muffin cups (1¾ inches in diameter). Press onto bottoms and up sides of cups. Place 2 chocolate pieces in each cup. Spoon about 1 teaspoon pecans over chocolate. Fill each cup with egg mixture.

4. Bake 25 minutes or until filling is set. Lightly press 1 chocolate into center of each cookie. Cool in pan on wire rack.

MAKES 24 CUPS

Mini TARTES TATIN

- 5 small sweet-tart apples such as Pink Lady or Honeycrisp,* peeled, cored and sliced crosswise into ⅛-inch-thick rounds
- 2 tablespoons granulated sugar
- 1 teaspoon ground cinnamon
- 3 tablespoons butter
- 2 tablespoons packed brown sugar
- 1 refrigerated pie crust (half of 15-ounce package)
- Whipped cream (optional)

**Look for apples that are about the size of standard muffin pan cups, about 2 to 2½ inches in diameter and 5 to 6 ounces each.*

1. Preheat oven to 350°F. Spray 6 standard (2½-inch) nonstick muffin cups with nonstick cooking spray.

2. Combine apple slices, granulated sugar and cinnamon in large bowl; toss to coat.

3. Place ½ tablespoon butter in each prepared muffin cup. Top with 1 teaspoon brown sugar, spreading to cover bottom of cup. Stack apple rings in cups, packing down to fit; fill center holes with broken or small apple slices. (Stacks will be tall and extend about 1 inch above rim of cup.) Place pan on rimmed baking sheet; cover loosely with foil.

4. Bake 25 minutes (apples will sink slightly and be crisp-tender).

5. Meanwhile, let pie crust stand at room temperature 15 minutes. Unroll crust on work surface; cut out 6 circles with 2½- to 3-inch biscuit cutter.

6. Place one dough circle on top of each stack of apples, pressing slightly around apples. Bake, uncovered, 20 minutes or until crust is light golden brown. Cool in pan 3 minutes. Place cutting board on top of pan and invert. Carefully remove muffin pan; transfer tarts to individual serving plates. Serve warm with whipped cream, if desired.

MAKES 6 SERVINGS

Zesty Orange COOKIE CUPS

PREP TIME: 30 minutes **COOK TIME:** 15 minutes

1 cup (2 sticks) butter, softened

½ cup granulated sugar

2 cups all-purpose flour

2 cups (12-ounce package) NESTLÉ® TOLL HOUSE® Premier White Morsels

2 large eggs

1 can (14 ounces) NESTLÉ® CARNATION® Sweetened Condensed Milk

½ to ¾ teaspoon orange extract

1 tablespoon grated orange peel (1 medium orange)

PREHEAT oven to 350°F. Grease 48 mini muffin cups.

BEAT butter and sugar in medium mixer bowl until creamy. Add flour; beat until mixture is evenly moistened, crumbly and can be formed into balls. Shape dough into 1-inch balls. Press each ball onto bottom and up side of prepared muffin cups to form wells. Place *5 morsels* in each cup.

BEAT eggs in medium bowl with wire whisk. Stir in sweetened condensed milk and orange extract. Spoon almost a measuring tablespoon of mixture into each muffin cup, filling about ¾ full.

BAKE for 15 to 17 minutes or until centers are puffed and edges are just beginning to brown. Upon removing from oven, gently run knife around each cup. **While still warm,** top each cup with 8 to 10 morsels (they will soften and retain their shape). Cool completely in pans on wire racks. With tip of knife, remove cookie cups from muffin pans. Top with grated orange peel just before serving. Store in covered container in refrigerator.

MAKES 4 DOZEN COOKIE CUPS

Cranberry Phyllo CHEESECAKE TARTS

1 cup fresh or frozen cranberries
¼ cup plus 1 tablespoon sugar, divided
2 tablespoons orange juice
1 teaspoon grated orange peel
¼ teaspoon ground allspice
6 sheets frozen phyllo dough, thawed
Butter-flavored cooking spray
1 container (8 ounces) whipped cream cheese
8 ounces vanilla yogurt
1 teaspoon vanilla

1. Preheat oven to 350°F. Combine cranberries, ¼ cup sugar, orange juice, orange peel and allspice in small saucepan; cook and stir over medium heat until cranberries pop and mixture thickens. Set aside to cool completely.

2. Lightly spray 12 standard (2½-inch) muffin cups with nonstick cooking spray. Cut phyllo dough in half lengthwise, then cut crosswise into thirds. Spray one phyllo square lightly with cooking spray. Top with second square, slightly offsetting corners; spray lightly with cooking spray. Top with third square. Place phyllo stack into one prepared muffin cup, pressing into bottom and up side of cup. Repeat with remaining phyllo squares.

3. Bake 3 to 4 minutes or until golden brown. Cool completely in pan on wire rack.

4. Meanwhile, beat cream cheese, yogurt, remaining 1 tablespoon sugar and vanilla in medium bowl with electric mixer until smooth. Divide mixture evenly among phyllo cups; top with cranberry mixture.

MAKES 12 SERVINGS

No-Bake Butterscotch SNACK BITES

PREP TIME: 10 minutes **COOK TIME:** 3 minutes

- **3 cups toasted rice cereal**
- **1 cup quick oats**
- **1 cup coarsely chopped walnuts, pecans and/or almonds**
- **1⅔ cups (11-ounce package) NESTLÉ® TOLL HOUSE® Butterscotch Flavored Morsels, *divided***
- **½ teaspoon salt**
- **½ cup light corn syrup**

PAPER-LINE or lightly grease 24 muffin cups.

COMBINE cereal, oats, nuts, *½ cup* morsels and salt in large mixing bowl.

MELT *remaining* morsels and corn syrup in uncovered, microwave-safe bowl on MEDIUM-HIGH (70%) power for 1 minute; STIR. Morsels may retain some of their original shape. If necessary, microwave at additional 10- to 15-second intervals, stirring just until morsels are melted.

DRIZZLE melted morsel mixture over cereal mixture; stir until combined. Working quickly, press ¼ cup of mixture into each prepared cup. Let stand at room temperature for 20 minutes or until firm. Store in tightly covered container(s) at room temperature.

MAKES 2 DOZEN SNACK BITES

Tip: Morsels can also be melted on top of a double boiler following package melting directions, adding corn syrup to melted morsels.

Peanutty Crispy DESSERT CUPS

⅓ cup creamy peanut butter

2 tablespoons butter

3 cups large marshmallows (5 ounces)

3 cups chocolate-flavored crisp rice cereal

Ice cream or frozen yogurt

Chocolate sauce, colored candies and sprinkles, chopped peanuts and/or maraschino cherries

1. Heat peanut butter and butter in large saucepan over low heat until melted and smooth. Add marshmallows; cook until melted, stirring constantly. Remove saucepan from heat; stir in cereal until well blended and cooled slightly.

2. Scoop mixture evenly into 12 standard (2½-inch) nonstick muffin cups; press into bottoms and up sides of cups.

3. Refrigerate 5 to 10 minutes or until set. Remove cups from pan; fill with ice cream and sprinkle with desired toppings.

MAKES 12 SERVINGS

Vanilla Fruit TARTS

PREP TIME: 20 minutes **BAKE TIME:** 10 minutes
CHILL TIME: 15 minutes

1 package (17.3 ounces) PEPPERIDGE FARM® Puff Pastry Sheets, thawed

1 egg, beaten

1 package (3½ ounces) vanilla instant pudding and pie filling mix

1¾ cups milk

½ cup cut-up fresh fruit

Confectioners' sugar

1. Heat the oven to 375°F. Lightly grease 24 (2½-inch) muffin-pan cups.

2. Unfold **1** pastry sheet on a lightly floured surface. Roll the pastry sheet into a 9×12-inch rectangle. Cut into **12** (3-inch) squares. Repeat with the remaining pastry sheet, making **24** in all. Press the pastry squares into the muffin-pan cups. Brush with the egg.

3. Bake for 10 minutes or until the pastries are golden brown. Remove the pastry cups from the pan and let cool completely on wire racks.

4. Mix the pudding mix and milk in a medium bowl according to the package directions. Cover and refrigerate for 15 minutes.

5. Spoon about 1 tablespoon pudding mixture into each pastry cup. Top with the fruit. Sprinkle with the confectioners' sugar.

MAKES 24 TARTS

Kitchen Tip: **To make 12 larger pastries:** Substitute **2 packages** (10 ounces **each**) Pepperidge Farm® Puff Pastry Shells for the pastry sheets. Prepare the pastry shells according to the package directions. Spoon **about 2 tablespoons** pudding mixture into **each** pastry shell. Top with the fruit. Sprinkle with the confectioners' sugar.

Plum-Side Down CAKES

2 tablespoons butter
3 tablespoons packed brown sugar
3 plums, sliced
½ cup granulated sugar
2 tablespoons shortening
1 egg
1 cup all-purpose flour
1 teaspoon baking powder
¼ teaspoon salt
⅓ cup milk

1. Preheat oven to 350°F. Spray 8 standard (2½-inch) muffin cups with nonstick cooking spray.

2. Place butter in small microwavable bowl; microwave on LOW (30%) just until melted. Stir in brown sugar. Spoon evenly into prepared muffin cups. Arrange plum slices in bottom of each cup.

3. Beat granulated sugar and shortening in medium bowl with electric mixer at medium speed until light and fluffy. Beat in egg until well blended. Combine flour, baking powder and salt in small bowl; beat into shortening mixture. Add milk; beat until smooth. Spoon batter into prepared muffin cups, filling three fourths full. Place pan on baking sheet.

4. Bake 20 to 22 minutes or until toothpick inserted into centers comes out clean. Cool in pan 10 minutes. Loosen edges with small spatula or knife; invert onto wire rack to cool completely.

MAKES 8 CAKES

Cheesecake COOKIE CUPS

PREP TIME: 15 minutes **BAKE TIME:** 25 minutes

- **1 package (16.5 ounces) NESTLÉ® TOLL HOUSE® Refrigerated Chocolate Chip Cookie Bar Dough**
- **2 packages (8 ounces *each*) cream cheese, at room temperature**
- **1 can (14 ounces) NESTLÉ® CARNATION® Sweetened Condensed Milk**
- **2 large eggs**
- **2 teaspoons vanilla extract**
- **1 can (21 ounces) cherry pie filling**

PREHEAT oven to 325°F. Paper-line 24 muffin cups. Place one piece of cookie dough in each muffin cup.

BAKE for 10 to 12 minutes or until cookie has spread to edge of cup.

BEAT cream cheese, sweetened condensed milk, eggs and vanilla extract in medium bowl until smooth. Pour about 3 tablespoons cream cheese mixture over each cookie in cup.

BAKE for additional 15 to 18 minutes or until set. Cool completely in pan on wire rack. Top each with level tablespoon of pie filling. Refrigerate for 1 hour.

MAKES 2 DOZEN COOKIE CUPS

Pumpkin TARTLETS

- 1 refrigerated pie crust (half of 15-ounce package)
- 1 can (15 ounces) solid-pack pumpkin
- 6 tablespoons sugar
- ¼ cup milk
- 1 egg
- ¾ teaspoon ground cinnamon, plus additional for topping
- ½ teaspoon vanilla
- ⅛ teaspoon salt
- ⅛ teaspoon ground nutmeg, plus additional for topping
- Dash ground allspice
- 1½ cups thawed frozen whipped topping

1. Preheat oven to 425°F. Spray 12 standard (2½-inch) muffin cups with nonstick cooking spray.

2. Unroll pie crust on clean work surface. Cut out 12 circles with 2½-inch biscuit cutter; discard scraps. Press one circle into each prepared muffin cup.

3. Whisk pumpkin, sugar, ¾ teaspoon cinnamon, vanilla, salt, ⅛ teaspoon nutmeg and allspice in medium bowl until well blended. Spoon about 2 tablespoons pumpkin mixture into each tartlet shell.

4. Bake 10 minutes. *Reduce oven temperature to 325°F.* Bake 12 to 15 minutes or until knife inserted into centers comes out clean. Remove to wire rack to cool completely. Top with whipped topping just before serving. Sprinkle with additional cinnamon and/or nutmeg, if desired.

MAKES 12 SERVINGS

CHOCOLATE DECADENCE

Mini Black and White CHEESECAKES

- 1 cup chocolate wafer cookie crumbs
- 12 ounces cream cheese, softened
- ½ cup sugar
- 2 teaspoons vanilla
- ½ cup milk
- 2 eggs
- ½ cup semisweet chocolate chips, melted and slightly cooled

1. Preheat oven to 325°F. Line 12 standard (2½-inch) muffin cups with paper baking cups. Spoon 1 rounded tablespoon cookie crumbs into each cup.

2. Beat cream cheese in large bowl with electric mixer at medium speed until light and fluffy. Add sugar and vanilla; beat until smooth. Add milk and eggs; beat until well blended. Transfer half of mixture to medium bowl. Stir in melted chocolate; set aside.

3. Divide remaining plain cream cheese mixture among prepared muffin cups. Bake 10 minutes.

4. Divide chocolate mixture among muffin cups; spread to edges. Bake 15 minutes or until centers are almost set. Cool completely in pan on wire racks. Store in refrigerator.

MAKES 12 SERVINGS

Coconut BROWNIE BITES

42 MOUNDS® or ALMOND JOY® Miniatures
½ cup (1 stick) butter or margarine, softened
½ cup packed light brown sugar
¼ cup granulated sugar
1 egg
1 teaspoon vanilla extract
1¼ cups all-purpose flour
⅓ cup HERSHEY'S® Cocoa
¾ teaspoon baking soda
½ teaspoon salt

1. Remove wrappers from candies. Line 42 small muffin cups (1¾ inches in diameter) with paper bake cups.

2. Beat butter, brown sugar, granulated sugar, egg and vanilla in large bowl until well blended. Stir together flour, cocoa, baking soda and salt; gradually add to butter mixture, beating until well blended. Cover; refrigerate dough about 30 minutes or until firm enough to handle.

3. Heat oven to 375°F. Shape dough into 1-inch balls; place one ball in each prepared muffin cup. *Do not flatten.*

4. Bake 8 to 10 minutes or until puffed. Remove from oven. Cool 5 minutes. (Cookies will sink slightly.) Press one candy into each cookie. Cool completely in pan on wire racks.

MAKES 3½ DOZEN COOKIES

Molten Cinnamon-Chocolate CAKES

- **6 ounces semisweet chocolate**
- **¾ cup (1½ sticks) butter**
- **1½ cups powdered sugar, plus additional for serving**
- **4 eggs**
- **6 tablespoons all-purpose flour**
- **1½ teaspoons vanilla**
- **¾ teaspoon ground cinnamon**

1. Preheat oven to 425°F. Spray 6 jumbo (3½-inch) muffin cups or 6 (1-cup) custard cups with nonstick cooking spray.

2. Combine chocolate and butter in medium microwavable bowl; microwave on HIGH 1½ minutes or until melted and smooth, stirring every 30 seconds.

3. Add 1½ cups powdered sugar, eggs, flour, vanilla and cinnamon; whisk until well blended. Pour batter into prepared muffin cups, filling two thirds full.

4. Bake 13 minutes or until cakes spring back when lightly touched but centers are soft. Let stand 1 minute. Loosen sides of cakes with knife; gently lift out and invert onto serving plates. Sprinkle with additional powdered sugar. Serve immediately.

MAKES 6 CAKES

Double Chocolate Chip MINI CHEESECAKES

PREP TIME: 20 minutes **BAKE TIME:** 23 minutes

- **1½ cups NESTLÉ® TOLL HOUSE® Refrigerated Chocolate Chip Cookie Tub Dough or 1 package (16.5 ounces) NESTLÉ® TOLL HOUSE® Refrigerated Chocolate Chip Cookie Bar Dough**
- **2 packages (8 ounces *each*) cream cheese, softened**
- **¾ cup granulated sugar**
- **2 tablespoons all-purpose flour**
- **2 large eggs**
- **1 teaspoon vanilla extract**
- **¾ cup NESTLÉ® TOLL HOUSE® Semi-Sweet Chocolate Mini Morsels, *divided***

PREHEAT oven to 325°F. Paper-line 24 muffin cups. Place 1 level tablespoon of cookie dough (1 square if using bar dough) into each muffin cup.

BAKE for 10 minutes or until cookie has spread to edge of cup.

BEAT cream cheese, sugar and flour in large mixer bowl until creamy. Add eggs and vanilla extract; mix well. Stir *½ cup* morsels into batter. Spoon 2 heaping measuring tablespoons of batter over each cookie in cup.

BAKE for additional 13 to 15 minutes or until just set but not browned. Remove from oven to wire rack. Cool completely in pans on wire rack. Refrigerate for 1 hour.

MELT *remaining ¼ cup* mini morsels in small, heavy-duty plastic bag on HIGH (100%) power for 30 seconds; knead. Microwave at additional 10- to 15-second intervals, kneading until smooth. Cut tiny corner from bag; squeeze to drizzle lightly over each cheesecake just before serving.

MAKES 24 SERVINGS

Chocolate Chip COOKIE DELIGHTS

- 1¾ cups all-purpose flour
- ¾ teaspoon salt
- ¾ teaspoon baking powder
- ½ teaspoon baking soda
- 10 tablespoons (1¼ sticks) butter, softened
- ½ cup plus 2 tablespoons packed brown sugar
- ½ cup granulated sugar
- 1 egg
- 1 teaspoon vanilla
- 1½ cups semisweet or bittersweet chocolate chips
- Coarse salt (optional)
- Vanilla ice cream (optional)

1. Preheat oven to 375°F. Spray 18 standard (2½-inch) muffin cups with nonstick cooking spray.

2. Combine flour, ¾ teaspoon salt, baking powder and baking soda in small bowl; mix well. Beat butter, brown sugar and granulated sugar in large bowl with electric mixer at medium-high speed about 5 minutes or until very light and fluffy. Add egg; beat until blended. Beat in vanilla until blended. Add flour mixture; beat just until blended. Stir in chocolate chips. Spoon scant ¼ cup dough into each prepared muffin cup; sprinkle with coarse salt, if desired.

3. Bake about 14 minutes or until edges are golden brown but centers are still soft. Cool in pans 5 minutes; invert onto wire rack. Turn cookies right side up; serve warm with ice cream, if desired.

MAKES 18 SERVINGS

Easy Chocolate Mousse-Filled TULIP CUPS

24 wonton wrappers (refrigerated in produce department)
2 tablespoons butter or margarine, melted
3 tablespoons sugar, divided
EASY CHOCOLATE MOUSSE (recipe follows)

1. Heat oven to 300°F.

2. Place individual wonton wrappers on wax paper; brush one side with butter. Sprinkle each wrapper evenly with scant ½ teaspoonful sugar; press each wrapper, sugared side up, into ungreased small muffin cups (1¾ inches in diameter) to form flower shape.

3. Bake 15 to 20 minutes or just until crisp and golden brown. Cool completely in pan on wire rack. Pipe or spoon EASY CHOCOLATE MOUSSE into center of each "tulip" cup. Cover; refrigerate. Garnish as desired. Refrigerate leftover cups.

MAKES 2 DOZEN CUPS

Easy Chocolate Mousse: Beat 1 cup (½ pint) cold whipping cream, ½ cup powdered sugar, ¼ cup HERSHEY'S® Cocoa or HERSHEY'S® SPECIAL DARK® Cocoa and 1 teaspoon vanilla extract in medium bowl until stiff. Use immediately.

Chocolate TASSIES

CRUST

2 cups all-purpose flour

2 packages (3 ounces each) cold cream cheese, cut into chunks

1 cup (2 sticks) cold butter, cut into chunks

FILLING

2 tablespoons butter

2 ounces unsweetened chocolate

1½ cups packed brown sugar

2 eggs, beaten

2 teaspoons vanilla

Dash salt

1½ cups chopped pecans

1. For crust, place flour in large bowl. Cut in cream cheese and 1 cup cold butter with pastry blender or two knives; mix until dough can be shaped into a ball. Wrap in plastic wrap; refrigerate 1 hour.

2. Shape dough into 1-inch balls. Place in 60 mini (1¾-inch) muffin cups, pressing into bottoms and up sides of cups. Refrigerate while preparing filling. Preheat oven to 350°F.

3. For filling, melt 2 tablespoons butter and chocolate in medium heavy saucepan over low heat. Remove from heat; stir in brown sugar, eggs, vanilla and salt until well blended and thick. Stir in pecans. Spoon about 1 teaspoon filling into each crust.

4. Bake 20 to 25 minutes or until crusts are golden brown and filling is set. Cool completely in pans on wire racks. Store in airtight containers.

MAKES ABOUT 5 DOZEN COOKIES

Chocolate MINI CHEESECAKES

- CHOCOLATE CRUMB CRUST (recipe follows)
- ½ cup HERSHEY'S® Cocoa
- ¼ cup (½ stick) butter or margarine, melted
- 3 packages (8 ounces each) cream cheese, softened
- 1 can (14 ounces) sweetened condensed milk (not evaporated milk)
- 3 eggs
- 2 teaspoons vanilla extract
- CHOCOLATE GLAZE (recipe follows)

1. Heat oven to 300°F. Line muffin cups (2½ inches in diameter) with paper bake cups or spray with vegetable cooking spray.* Press about 1 tablespoonful CHOCOLATE CRUMB CRUST mixture onto bottom of each cup.

2. Stir together cocoa and ¼ cup butter. Beat cream cheese until fluffy. Beat in cocoa mixture. Gradually beat in sweetened condensed milk. Beat in eggs and vanilla. Fill muffin cups with batter.

3. Bake 35 minutes or until set. Cool 15 minutes; remove from pan to wire rack. Cool completely. Refrigerate. Before serving, spread with CHOCOLATE GLAZE. Allow to set. Serve at room temperature.

**If vegetable cooking spray is used, cool baked cheesecakes. Freeze 15 minutes; remove with narrow spatula.*

MAKES ABOUT 24 MINI CHEESECAKES

Chocolate Crumb Crust: Stir together 1½ cups vanilla wafer crumbs (about 45 wafers, crushed), 6 tablespoons HERSHEY'S® Cocoa, 6 tablespoons powdered sugar and 6 tablespoons melted butter or margarine in medium bowl.

Chocolate Glaze: Melt 1 cup HERSHEY'S® SPECIAL DARK® Chocolate Chips or HERSHEY'S® Semi-Sweet Chocolate Chips with ½ cup whipping cream and ½ teaspoon vanilla extract in medium saucepan over low heat. Stir until smooth. Use immediately. Makes about 1 cup glaze.

Homemade Mini PEANUT BUTTER CUPS

½ cup creamy peanut butter
½ cup powdered sugar
2 tablespoons butter
¼ teaspoon salt
1 cup semisweet chocolate chips
1 cup dark chocolate or milk chocolate chips

1. Line 18 mini (1¾-inch) muffin cups with paper baking cups.

2. Beat peanut butter, powdered sugar, butter and salt in medium bowl with electric mixer at medium speed until well blended and smooth.

3. Place chocolate chips in medium microwavable bowl; microwave on MEDIUM-HIGH (70%) 1 minute. Stir; microwave at additional 30-second intervals until chocolate is melted and smooth.

4. Drop 1 teaspoon melted chocolate into each prepared cup; top with heaping ½ teaspoon peanut butter mixture. Top with about 1 teaspoon chocolate to cover. Gently tap pan on counter to settle chocolate and remove air bubbles. Refrigerate until set.

MAKES 18 PEANUT BUTTER CUPS

Note: If the peanut butter mixture is too sticky to work with, refrigerate 10 to 15 minutes or until slightly stiffened.

INDEX

ACKNOWLEDGMENTS

The publisher would like to thank the companies listed below for the use of their recipes and photographs in this publication.

Allens®

Campbell Soup Company

Dole Food Company, Inc.

The Hershey Company

Nestlé USA

Ortega®, A Division of B&G Foods North America, Inc.

METRIC CONVERSION CHART

VOLUME MEASUREMENTS (dry)

1/8 teaspoon = 0.5 mL
1/4 teaspoon = 1 mL
1/2 teaspoon = 2 mL
3/4 teaspoon = 4 mL
1 teaspoon = 5 mL
1 tablespoon = 15 mL
2 tablespoons = 30 mL
1/4 cup = 60 mL
1/3 cup = 75 mL
1/2 cup = 125 mL
2/3 cup = 150 mL
3/4 cup = 175 mL
1 cup = 250 mL
2 cups = 1 pint = 500 mL
3 cups = 750 mL
4 cups = 1 quart = 1 L

VOLUME MEASUREMENTS (fluid)

1 fluid ounce (2 tablespoons) = 30 mL
4 fluid ounces (1/2 cup) = 125 mL
8 fluid ounces (1 cup) = 250 mL
12 fluid ounces (1 1/2 cups) = 375 mL
16 fluid ounces (2 cups) = 500 mL

WEIGHTS (mass)

1/2 ounce = 15 g
1 ounce = 30 g
3 ounces = 90 g
4 ounces = 120 g
8 ounces = 225 g
10 ounces = 285 g
12 ounces = 360 g
16 ounces = 1 pound = 450 g

DIMENSIONS

1/16 inch = 2 mm
1/8 inch = 3 mm
1/4 inch = 6 mm
1/2 inch = 1.5 cm
3/4 inch = 2 cm
1 inch = 2.5 cm

OVEN TEMPERATURES

250°F = 120°C
275°F = 140°C
300°F = 150°C
325°F = 160°C
350°F = 180°C
375°F = 190°C
400°F = 200°C
425°F = 220°C
450°F = 230°C

BAKING PAN SIZES

Utensil	Size in Inches/Quarts	Metric Volume	Size in Centimeters
Baking or Cake Pan (square or rectangular)	8×8×2	2 L	20×20×5
	9×9×2	2.5 L	23×23×5
	12×8×2	3 L	30×20×5
	13×9×2	3.5 L	33×23×5
Loaf Pan	8×4×3	1.5 L	20×10×7
	9×5×3	2 L	23×13×7
Round Layer Cake Pan	8×1½	1.2 L	20×4
	9×1½	1.5 L	23×4
Pie Plate	8×1¼	750 mL	20×3
	9×1¼	1 L	23×3
Baking Dish or Casserole	1 quart	1 L	—
	1½ quart	1.5 L	—
	2 quart	2 L	—

DogLife ❖ Lifelong Care [illegible] Dog™

YORKSHIRE TERRIER

YORKSHIRE TERRIER

Project Team
Editor: Heather Russell-Revesz
Copy Editor: Joann Woy
Indexer: Ann W. Truesdale
Design: Patricia Escabi
Series Design: Mary Ann Kahn, Angela Stanford

T.F.H. Publications
President/CEO: Glen S. Axelrod
Executive Vice President: Mark E. Johnson
Publisher: Christopher T. Reggio
Production Manager: Kathy Bontz

T.F.H. Publications, Inc.
One TFH Plaza
Third and Union Avenues
Neptune City, NJ 07753

Printed and bound in China

11 12 13 14 15 1 3 5 7 9 8 6 4 2

Library of Congress Cataloging-in-Publication Data
Schimpf, Sheila.
Yorkshire terrier / Sheila Schimpf.
p. cm.
Includes index.
ISBN 978-0-7938-3609-3 (alk. paper)
1. Yorkshire terrier. I. Title.
SF429.Y6S35 2011
636.76--dc22

2010012482

This book has been published with the intent to provide accurate and authoritative information in regard to the subject matter within. While every reasonable precaution has been taken in preparation of this book, the author and publisher expressly disclaim responsibility for any errors, omissions, or adverse effects arising from the use or application of the information contained herein. The techniques and suggestions are used at the reader's discretion and are not to be considered a substitute for veterinary care.
If you suspect a medical problem consult your veterinarian.

Note: In the interest of concise writing, "he" is used when referring to puppies and dogs unless the text is specifically referring to females or males. "She" is used when referring to people. However, the information contained herein is equally applicable to both sexes.

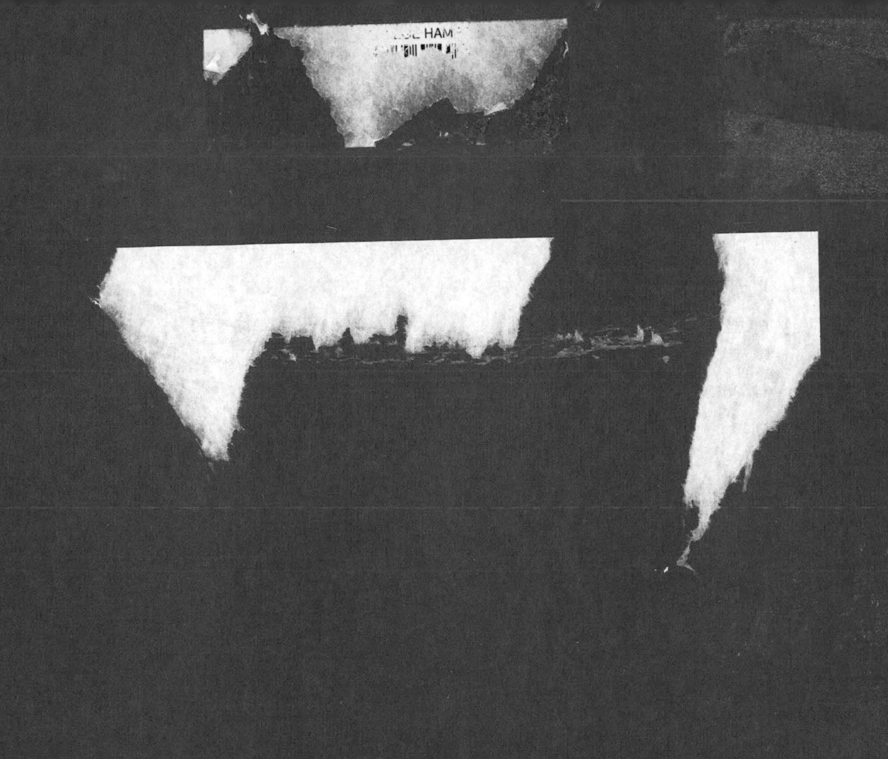

CONTENTS

INTRODUCTION

INTRODUCING THE YORKSHIRE TERRIER

The Yorkshire Terrier is a feisty little dog with a big talent for melting hearts. He is a walking, loving contradiction—funny and fearless. His irresistible merry eyes, blue silky hair, and engaging personality have helped him climb almost to the top of the American Kennel Club (AKC)'s list of most popular dogs. His legion of fans will tell anyone who will listen why their dog is the best. They tell stories of courage, quickness to learn tricks, contentedness at being a lap dog, charming antics, and even portability (Yorkies fit in airplane cabins, shoulder bags, and bicycle baskets). That versatility cinches the Yorkie's popularity. The little dog who once killed rats for sport in English pubs now has the potential to make both city and country people happy. He can be an athletic agility dog, obedience champion, couch potato, and glamorous show dog for those who thrill to the sight of silky hair blowing in a breeze created by a Yorkie's own energy. Most of all, he is a smart, independent thinker who chooses to be with his people and then gives himself to them 110 percent.

A WOLF INSIDE EVERY YORKIE

Weighing less than 7 pounds (3 kg) the Yorkshire Terrier does it all. New owners smitten by such a tiny face surrounded by flowing tresses and hair ribbons may find it difficult to remember that he is a descendant of the wolf, just like any bigger dog. He follows the social rules handed down by his wolf ancestors generations ago. Scientists are rewriting the story of exactly when and where the wolf was domesticated as they make new discoveries in archeology and the canine genome. Currently, scientists are investigating ideas that dog and humankind evolved together. The dog's story probably starts with a human, maybe as many as 100,000 years ago, who took in a wolf and then maybe another one that may have been newborn, sick, hurt, smaller, hungry, or less aggressive than other wolves—wolves who could benefit from a human partnership. Human and wolf worked together over several generations to create a dog. Where this took place is still being debated. Researchers in

It may be hard to believe, but the tiny Yorkie is related to the wolf.

Belgium recently found a Paleolithic dog who dated back 31,000 years, suggesting that the dog could have been domesticated in Europe. Researchers in Africa a short time ago found a wide variety of DNA in village dogs that equaled the variety in Asian dogs, suggesting that both Africa and Asia were home to some very early dogs.

SIZE MATTERS

Researchers in Utah and at several universities are working on another question: Why do some dogs stay small? Their best answer: a mutation in the regulatory sequence next to the gene that controls growth hormone. That happened early in the dog's history, they think about 12,000 years ago. All small dogs have this mutation. Melissa Gray, at the University of Wisconsin Madison, and a team of researchers recently published research in the *BMC Biology Journal* that suggests small dogs evolved from Middle Eastern gray wolves. That puts small dogs in the same evolutionary geography as cats and goats, which also evolved in the Fertile Crescent. The small dogs she tested all had the same differences in the insulin-like growth factor 1 gene, but the big dogs and the gray wolves didn't have those differences. So, she says, big dogs evolved directly from the wolves and the smaller dogs evolved from the big dogs. Archeological remains in the Levant or eastern Mediterranean show small dogs as far back as 10,000 to 12,000 years, she says. "Small size could have been more desirable in more densely packed agrarian societies where dogs may have lived partly indoors or in confined outdoor spaces," her article states.

Once a smaller dog or two appeared, humans bred one to the other until they were able to produce even smaller dogs that carried the mutation. Small dogs were prized right from the beginning.

HISTORY OF THE YORKSHIRE TERRIER

By the time the first Yorkshire Terrier, Huddersfield Ben, came along in 1865, people in Great Britain relied on small dogs to kill mice and rats and even herd livestock. Many histories trace small dog popularity back to feudal days, when British serfs were denied the right to hunt and to own the large hunting dogs that would make poaching possible. Only small dogs that fit through a hoop 7 inches (18 cm) in diameter were allowed—so small dogs became the working dog of the working class.

Creation of the Breed in England

The working class didn't always keep precise records, but enough exist to prove the creation of the Yorkie was not random. He was carefully bred for specific reasons. In her extensive research into the history of the Yorkshire Terrier, breeder Joan B. Gordon found that at least three breeds contributed to the Yorkie: the Clydesdale Terrier (related to the Skye Terrier), the Waterside Terrier, and the Old English Terrier.

Clydesdale/Paisley Terriers

Skye Terriers had been popular for some time, but a rift developed between breeders of silky-haired Skyes and rough-coated ones. The breeders of the harsher coats prevailed and the silky-coated Skye Terriers became known as Clydesdale or Paisley Terriers.

Waterside Terriers

The Waterside Terrier became popular in Yorkshire in the late 18th and early 19th centuries. They had longer hair that was sometimes bluish grey and weighed between

The Yorkshire Terrier was originally developed as a ratter.

During the Victorian era, the Yorkie became a society status symbol.

6 and 20 pounds (3 and 9 kg), averaging about 10 pounds (4.5 kg). They were so good at killing rats, Gordon found, that they were one of several types of terriers used for "sport" in rat pits. In the days before televised sporting events would draw customers, pubs relied on live events. Pub owners built a fight ring that could be filled with rats and set one dog at a time at the rats. Bystanders wagered on their favorite dog, betting how many rats the dogs could kill.

Old English Terriers

Old English Terriers, the third breed in the Yorkie's background, were 20 to 25 pounds (9 to 11 kg) and black and tan; they were dying out at about the time the Yorkshire Terrier appeared.

Scottish Dogs

In Scotland, a group of small terriers emerged about this same time, specially bred by isolated crofters who each had an ideal dog in mind. They were tough little working dogs, skilled at vermin hunting and killing on the croft (a small farm or ranch in the Highlands). When a group of Scottish settlers arrived in Yorkshire looking for work in the mills, they brought their dogs with them, and those dogs were put to work killing rats. The imported Scottish dogs bred with native English dogs.

Huddersfield Ben

The exact combination of terriers that breeders used to produce Huddersfield Ben has been lost, but three dogs are known to be in his pedigree: Old Crab, a Clydesdale or Waterside Terrier; Kitty, a Paisley Terrier; and an Old English Terrier.

In the town of Huddersfield, a breeder named Eastwood bred Ben and, by all accounts, very carefully inbred him. Ben's mother, Lady, was also the mother of his father (whose name has been lost). Eastwood had another dog, Old Ben, who was Lady's father. Old Ben was on both sides of Ben's pedigree, as was another of his dogs, Old Sandy. Before long, Ben belonged to Mary Foster of Bradford, Yorkshire, who decided a dog with a champion ratter heritage could be a show champion as well. His long silky hair and blue-steel color was a natural for the new world of dog shows. His owner embraced the dog show world with enthusiasm, and it turned out to be a winning combination. Ben became famous as a show dog.

During Ben's short lifetime, Yorkshire Terriers were known as broken-haired Scotch Terriers—after the dogs the Scottish mill-workers brought to England. They were probably slightly bigger than the Yorkies we know today. Joan Gordon's history states that they were shown in several categories by weight, and the largest was 9 to 12 pounds (4 to 5 kg).

Ben lived only six years. Small dogs have always been at risk and 1871 was no exception. Ben was run over by a horse-drawn carriage and killed, but not before he won 74 prizes in dog shows. He was also a successful stud, fathering many celebrated show dogs. A newspaper reporter in 1870 writing about Mozart, one of Ben's sons, commented that the name Scotch Terrier no longer fit. They should be called Yorkshire Terriers, he said, because they had been so improved in Yorkshire. And so the Yorkshire terrier now had his name, even if it wasn't widely accepted at first.

The Victorian Love Affair With Yorkies

The 1870s were exciting times to be a dog lover in England. The dog show world, which had existed informally for some years, organized itself into The Kennel Club in 1873. Its first stud book included pedigrees from 40 breeds, including the Yorkshire Terrier, which was still sometimes called the "broken-haired Scotch" or "Toy Terrier, rough and broken-haired." The rat-catching history of the Yorkie was already being downplayed as the breed became a ladies' dog—riding in carriages, groomed with ribbons, sleeping on soft pillows. The rough and tumble crofters' and mill workers' dogs had now become a society status symbol. The Yorkshire Terrier had climbed the social ladder from the bottom to the very top.

WINNING AMERICAN HEARTS

Americans fascinated by Victorian England began importing Yorkshire Terriers, and the little workingman's dog quickly became fashionable in wealthy American circles, too. Mary Foster and her Bradford kennel in England produced several dogs who were imported by Americans and influenced the breed in the United States, such as Ch. Ted, a great-grandchild of Huddersfield Ben on both sides, and Bradford Hero. In 1890, a dog named Bradford Harry was the only Yorkshire Terrier Champion in the United States. He was the great-great-great-grandson of Huddersfield Ben. In 1878, only seven years after Ben was killed, 33 Yorkies showed at the Westminster Kennel Club Show in New York City.

The American Kennel Club recognized the breed in 1885, the year after it was formed.

In her Yorkie history, Joan Gordon found that it is difficult, but not impossible, to trace today's dogs back to Ben and his immediate descendants. The thread is lost usually during World War I, she says. The oldest American strain belonged to Mrs. Fred Senn of New York

In the 1960s, the popularity of the Yorkshire Terrier jumped.

and her dog Little Gem, whose bloodline can be found today in the Petite dogs. Mrs. Senn showed Yorkies for 27 years before she had a champion, Queen of the Fairies, in 1905. She was a granddaughter of Little Gem. Mrs. Senn's kennel was a major contributor to Yorkie development between 1875 and 1909, and she remains a role model for show dog newcomers whose dogs fail to win a championship. She proved that persistence pays off in the show ring.

The Petite name belonged to Goldie Stone, a former vaudeville star who used a Yorkshire Terrier in her act and bought her first show Yorkie, Petite Byngo Boy, after she retired. He became a successful show dog and fathered five champions. She bred Yorkies in Columbus, Ohio, from 1929 to 1954, and made significant contributions to the breed's history.

Yorkies in War Time

World War II disrupted the dog world. In 1940, the AKC registered 91 Yorkies, but the number dropped to 33 in 1943. After the war, in 1949, the AKC registered 173 Yorkies. Soon after, Yorkie registrations steadily rose as the little dog became increasingly popular. Today, registrations for a single month may exceed 2,500 Yorkshires.

The war created a hero in an unlikely candidate, a 4-pound (2-kg) Yorkie named Smoky. GIs found Smoky in 1944 in New Guinea. Her background was a mystery since she didn't seem to understand English or Japanese. Eventually, she ended up belonging to Corporal William A. Wynne of Cleveland. Wynne took her on 12 missions in the Pacific, taught her tricks and visited injured soldiers, entertaining them with Smoky's tricks, and thus creating what some have called the world's first therapy dog. In 1945, when engineers were building an airbase in the Luzon campaign, Smoky helped by carrying a telegraph wire through a 70-foot (21-m) pipe under the airstrip. The pipe was only 8 inches (20 cm) in diameter and dirt had collected in some places, making it even smaller. Because of Smoky, soldiers didn't have to rip up the airstrip to lay the telegraph wire, and the airstrip was allowed

Yorkies are popular dogs for movies and advertising.

to stay in operation. A life-size statue of Smoky was unveiled in Cleveland in 2005 depicting her in a helmet.

Building the American Yorkie Fancy

Since World War II, American Yorkie breeding has been based on 15 dogs imported to the United States from England or Ireland. They are: Buranthea's Doutelle, Don Carlos of Progresso, Finstal Royal Icing, Gleno Credit Card, Golden Fame, Kelpie's Belziehill Dondi, Little Sir Model, Peter of Nordlaw, Pretoria Action, Progress of Progresso, Quarnhill Fusspot, Star Twilight of Clu-Mor, Streamglen Luna Star, Toy Clown of Rusklyn, and Wenscoe's Whizzaway of Tzumiao. All are American, English, or Irish champions except two, Kelpie's Belziehill Dondi and Pretoria Action.

Finstal Royal Icing is recognized as one of the most important of the group.

INFLUENTIAL BREEDERS AND DOGS

Yorkshire Terrier popularity jumped in the 1960s. Several breeders who dedicated their lives to bettering the little dog started with those imported dogs and created the face of the Yorkie world today. Joan Gordon's own kennel, Wildweir, owned Little Sir Model, Golden Fame, and Star Twilight of Clu-Mor whose grandson, Wildweir Pomp N' Circumstance sired 95 champions.

The pedigree of the only Yorkshire Terrier to earn best of show at Westminster Kennel Club, Cede Higgens, who won in 1978, includes Star Twilight and Pomp N' Circumstance. Bill and Barbara Switzer in Seattle bought Cede Higgins in 1973, for their Barbee kennel. He won 33 best in shows before he retired in 1978, after winning Westminster. He fathered at least 34 champions who won numerous groups, specialties, and best in shows, and who can still be found in pedigrees today.

Pomp N' Circumstance is also behind Clarkwyn Debutante, the foundation bitch of Ila Clark's Clarkwyn line in Seattle. She started her kennel in 1958. Two years later, Anne Seranne in Newton, New Jersey, started Mayfair and added a partner, Barbara Wolferman six years after that, when the kennel name became Mayfair-Barban.

Roberta Rothenbach, who died in October 2009, and her Rothby Yorkshires in Elgin, Illinois, were a fixture at Yorkie events for 42 years. Rothby produced many champions who won groups and best in shows for decades. Many Rothby dogs are in the pedigrees of today's winning show dogs.

From Hanover, Canada, Betty Anne Durrer has made a name in the United States by extensively showing and selling her dogs here. Durrer dogs are in top-twenty lists. Durrer's Talk About Bossy, co-bred by Durrer, won the breed competition at the 2009 Eukanuba National Championship. Doreen Hubbard has more than 40 years experience in breeding Yorkies under her Yorkboro name in Marysville, Washington. Marie G. Bradley, of Chattahoochee, Florida, and her Gaelwyn Yorkies bred Ch. Gaelwyn's Celtic Reflection, one of the top Yorkies in 2009. AnnStef, a partnership between Yorkie breeders Anna Stringer and Stephanie Barnes, produces top-twenty show Yorkies, but also made the news by placing several Yorkies with Miley Cyrus and the cast of Hanna Montana.

In Australia, one of most famous Yorkie breeders is Gerri Grieg from Tejada Yorkshire Terriers. Yorkies are now bred around the world and compete internationally.

MEMORABLE YORKIES

- Huddersfield Ben, the original Yorkie, is the ancestor of all modern Yorkies.
- Smoky, the World War II hero, was a well-known ambassador for the breed for many years.
- In Great Britain, Yorkie lovers' hearts still thump at the thought of Ch. Blairsville Royal Seal, who died at age 15 in 1988. "Tosha" won many dog shows and fathered many Yorkies who also had spectacular success in the show ring.
- Only one Yorkie has won Best in Show at Crufts, the British equivalent of Westminster. That happened in 1997, when Ch. Ozmilion Mystification took the prize.
- Only one Yorkie has won Best of Show at Westminster—Cede Higgens, in 1978.
- One Yorkie has lived in the White House—Pasha, who belonged to Tricia Nixon Cox.
- A long list of celebrities have owned Yorkies, including Amy Tan (Bubba and Lilli), Justin Timberlake (Bella and Bearlie), Bruce Willis (Wolfie), Donny Osmond (Spike), Orlando Bloom (Frankie), Whitney Houston (Doogie), Audrey Hepburn (Mr. Famous, Assam of Assam), Britney Spears (London), Paris Hilton (Cinderella), Natalie Portman (Whizz), and Vanessa Williams (Enzo).
- Yorkies have been in a few movies: *Funny Face* with Audrey Hepburn, *Meet the Fockers* with Ben Stiller, *A Fish Called Wanda* with Michael Palin, *High School Musical 2* with Sharpay Evans, and *Daltry Calhoun* with Beth Grant.

PART I

PUPPYHOOD

CHAPTER 1

IS THE YORKSHIRE TERRIER RIGHT FOR YOU?

Yorkshire Terrier puppies are calendar cute. With their shaggy hair and inquisitive eyes, Yorkie puppies inspire that "Ahhhhh" reaction. Who can resist falling in love with a Yorkie puppy? But loving the look and living with the real dog are two different things. The Yorkshire Terrier is not the right breed of dog for every dog lover. Their size and temperament require special handling. Their coat and teeth require regular maintenance. They just don't fit into every household. Yet many people rush right in at the first irresistible toss of a Yorkie head, plunk down the money, and take home a dog they know very little about. They would be surprised to know that the Yorkie's ancestors were renown for killing rats in mines, mills, and pubs. "Most people do not research a breed," says Sue Walters, Michigan Yorkie owner of agility and rally champions. Owners have to manage that energetic hunting ability and toughness in everyday life. Yorkies are full grown before their first birthday but do not get their mature coat until they are almost two years old. Yorkies can be considered puppies until they are 18 to 24 months old, says Illinois breeder Vicki Meadows, and prospective owners should take that long puppyhood into consideration.

WHAT MAKES A YORKIE A YORKIE?

A Yorkie is a small terrier with a huge personality and a magnificent coat that has an unusual steel blue color. But once you get to know a Yorkie, you may not even see his beautiful blue coat—his personality overshadows everything. A Yorkshire Terrier is attitude with four feet. His size, his personality, and his coat are what make a Yorkie a Yorkie.

Size Counts

The almost-too-obvious first thing to consider about getting a Yorkie is his size. The Yorkshire Terrier is one of the smallest breeds, and Yorkie puppies are even smaller. Calendar shots often do not show just how tiny Yorkie puppies are. Breeders in the Yorkshire Terrier Club of America pledge not to sell their puppies until they are twelve weeks old for a number of reasons—and size is at the top of the list. Even at three months, Yorkies are only about half the size they will be as adults (four to seven pounds [2 to 3 kg]) and taking on the responsibility for such a small life is a serious undertaking. Tiny puppies need to be protected from weather, disease, and accidents even more than larger puppies. There is little margin

Yorkies love to be the center of attention.

for error. Breeders almost always discourage families with small children from getting a Yorkshire Terrier. It is just too easy for Yorkie puppies to get stepped on, injured, or killed when things fall on top of them. They break bones when dropped short distances or if knocked off the back of a couch.

Personality Plus

Then there's the unique Yorkshire Terrier temperament—bigger than most new owners can imagine. Yorkies, experienced breeders will tell you, don't know they are so small. They live life large and expect a lot. They come with a big helping of intelligence that some owners also might not be expecting. Who wants to admit a four-pound (2 kg) dog can outsmart them? But time after time, a Yorkie does outsmart unsuspecting owners and ends up running the house. He gets the good chair, the treats when he wants them, and pretty much decides when things are going to happen.

As an extra bonus, Yorkies have their tiny feet planted firmly in two worlds. Yorkies are terriers through and through—determined, independent, and self-assured—but right from the beginning, the American Kennel Club (AKC) classed them as toy dogs—contented companions. That dual personality can mean two things—your Yorkie can be a charming lap dog like his fellow toys one minute and a strong-willed terrier the next. Or, a litter may include some of each—contented little toy dogs and feisty terriers. A breeder can help a prospective owner choose a puppy who matches her personality. Even by twelve weeks, breeders have a good idea which puppies are more active and confident and which are quieter and happier to curl up on the couch. But even quieter Yorkies should never be underestimated. This is a breed that likes to be the center of attention, thinks the world revolves around them, and is full of courage. It has the rat-killing ancestors to prove it.

"I love their spirit," says Julie Howard, a Yorkie breeder in Kokomo, Ind. "This is a fearless little toy dog that is a wonderful companion, that has the spirit of a larger dog. They don't realize they are small."

Top Dog Attitude

In the words of the Yorkie standard: "The dog's high head carriage and confident manner should give the appearance of vigor and self importance." That is because, down deep, Yorkies are brimming with vigor and feelings of self-importance. It is their very real state of mind. So owners need to be able to live with a dog who thinks he is in charge without actually letting him run the show. That's why obedience classes are a good idea for Yorkie owners, especially first-timers. Obedience training establishes the foundation of a relationship that can last 15 years, and that relationship should be based on one clear rule: The people are in charge. A dog who sees himself at the center of the world can be hard to live with, some even snapping and growling to get their way. More than a few Yorkies who have become impossible to live with end up in rescue. So, in obedience classes, the Yorkie owner can learn ways to teach cooperation

Your Yorkie can be a charming lap dog one minute and a strong-willed terrier the next.

A Word About Teacups

"There is no such thing as 'teacup,'" says Sharon Griffin, president of the Yorkshire Terrier Club of Southeastern Michigan. "We hate that word. It's just a small Yorkie. It's a marketing ploy for people to get more for their dogs."

The smaller the dog, the more some breeders charge—trying to make its very smallness desirable. They advertise tiny dogs at 2 1/2 or 3 pounds (1 or 1.5 kg). These tiny lives are designed to inspire the nurturing urge in some people. Some buyers can't resist the perpetual babyness of such a tiny dog. They see themselves cuddling such a dog forever.

Instead, they may be buying into serious health issues and hefty vet bills. Some very real reasons exist for avoiding dogs weighing less than 4 pounds (2 kg) at adulthood. Smaller dogs have more health problems, starting with hypoglycemia or low blood sugar in puppyhood. All Yorkie puppies must eat often, and smaller puppies must eat even more often or they may succumb to hypoglycemia. Symptoms include extreme sleepiness, uncoordination, seizures, and unconsciousness.

The Yorkshire Terrier Club of America warns that health problems in dogs under 4 pounds (2 kg) can continue into adult life: "Special circumstances often come with extra tiny dogs. They are extremely susceptible to both hereditary and nonhereditary health problems, including birth defects that may go undetected for a long time. Other common problems may include, but are not limited to, diarrhea and vomiting, along with extra and expensive tests prior to routine teeth cleanings and surgeries. Small ones are more likely to have poor reactions to anesthesia and die from it. Tiny dogs are more easily injured by falls, being stepped on, and being attacked by other dogs. These health problems nearly always result in large veterinary bills."

and get professional training support. Plus, the puppy can improve his socialization skills and manners. This is truly a case when an ounce of prevention is worth way more than a pound of cure.

Difficulties With Housetraining

When it comes to housetraining, Yorkie owners need high levels of patience and persistence. That adorable little puppy may not be as easy to housetrain as some other breeds. Yorkie puppy bladders are tiny and need to be emptied frequently. "It takes patience, repetition," breeder Howard says. "People have to have a commitment." Failures sometimes occur when some owners decide it is just easier to clean up a tiny puddle than work with their dog—and the dog never learns. Yet housetraining can be done. Whether you want your puppy to go outside or use an indoor relief station, Yorkies *can* be housetrained. It just takes effort, and more time than you might think . . . weeks . . . even months, sometimes.

Built-In Alarm System

Some Yorkies like to bark more than other dogs. They are, after all, terriers, and terriers as a group bark more. They are hard-wired to bark as they chase a rat, to keep their owner informed of their progress. As a breed, Yorkshire Terriers have the reputation of being yappy and, because of that, sometimes are recommended as good watchdogs. A Yorkie will alert you to anything out of the ordinary, and that can be a very good thing. But if barking dogs bother you, look elsewhere for your breed. Yorkies can be trained to bark less and some breeders will tell you yappiness isn't a problem in their line, but it is an issue that new owners must be prepared to face. Yorkies can be very verbal dogs.

THAT YORKIE LOOK: PHYSICAL CHARACTERISTICS

Before they discover the playful Yorkie personality or legendary courage, many people fall in love with the Yorkie look—the long silky hair, the blue sheen, the black eyes, and the ears cocked to see what's happening next. Yorkies are agile toy dogs with a smart look in their eye and unusually beautiful hair—steel blue with tan markings. The hair can be long and silky, puddling on the floor or, when cut, can be short and wispy, almost rakish. Whichever style you choose, it is a great look. In addition, the breed comes in a portable package that can go many places bigger dogs can't.

Height and Weight

According to the breed standard—which is the blueprint for a winning show dog—adult Yorkies should weigh less than 7 pounds (3 kg), and (according to the AKC) more than 4

When it comes to housetraining, Yorkies need a high level of patience.

Yorkie's are known for their unusually beautiful hair—steel blue with tan markings.

pounds (2 kg). Some breeders advertise teacup or miniature Yorkies who weigh less than four pounds (2 kg) but officially, neither exists (see box, "A Word About 'Teacups.'") Although most people focus on the weight of Yorkies, height is also important. The height and the weight have to be in proportion. Long spindly legs do not belong on a Yorkie. No height is specified in the Yorkie standard—it calls for a compact dog. Yorkies range in height, with many topping out at the 6 or 7 inches (15 or 17 cm) mark.

The Crowning Glory: The Coat

The standard spells out in great detail specifications for the Yorkshire Terrier coat, calling it of prime importance. The breed standard calls for a coat that is straight, trimmed at the floor, long at the muzzle, and trimmed at the tip of the ear. But that's for a show dog. Pet dogs and pet owners have chosen short coats, sometimes called *puppy cuts*, for years. It is much easier to care for and that can be good for dog and owner. Owning a pet dog should be all about quality of life, yours and the dog's. The puppy cut is a cute look that some owners actually prefer. It is a look that can change slightly with each haircut—shorter, longer, even shaved in spots to look more like a Schnauzer.

Yorkies born with a cottony, rather than a silky coat, don't fit the breed standard; these dogs are destined for pet homes—their coat does not affect their personality, just their look.

Color

Puppies are born black and tan, but adult dogs have a dark steel-blue coat, with tan that is darker at the roots than on the tips. Hair on the tail should be darker blue, especially at the tip. A show dog who is any solid color or any combination of colors other than steel blue and tan will be disqualified. A small white mark on the chest is allowed.

Body Type

Yorkies should have a compact look, with front and back at the same height. The front legs should be straight, but the back legs should have a slight bend at the stifle or knee. The top line should be level, and the dog's back should be short rather than long. It should not have a long look like a Dachshund.

Head

Although round "baby doll" heads have become popular with some buyers, the official Yorkie standard calls for heads that are slightly flat on top, with a black nose and a muzzle that is not too long. Baby doll heads are not recognized by the Yorkshire Terrier Club of America. Breeders who advertise them are adding a feature to raise the price.

Eyes

Eyes should be dark and medium in size, not too prominent, and rimmed in black.

Ears

The small ears should be triangular and erect. Floppy ears are another marketing gimmick some breeders use to sell dogs, but these ears do not belong to the true Yorkie look. The hair should be trimmed at the tips of the ears.

Tail

In the United States, most Yorkies have docked tails. In Europe, tail docking is against the law, so Yorkies there have natural tails. Some Yorkie fanciers think originally Yorkies had docked tails to eliminate a target for rats—if the dog had no tail, the rat couldn't bite it. Others think the original purpose was cleanliness, because docking the tail eliminates some long hairs that are easily soiled when the dog defecates. A third reason that is impossible to ignore is that, back then, people liked the look of a short tail on such a small dog, so it got written into the standard. It became part of the Yorkie look. The U.S. standard today calls for a tail docked to a medium length and carried slightly higher than the back. If your puppy's tail was not docked in the first few days of life, docking it as an older puppy or adult is major surgery and requires anesthesia.

An Ideal, Not a Reality

Of course, no dog matches the standard perfectly. And a Yorkshire Terrier who is sold as a pet most likely has a fault that the breeder thinks will be held against him in a show ring. The good news is that most of these faults are cosmetic. Ask your breeder for a quick analysis of your dog—conformation, temperament,

Multi-Dog Tip

Two Yorkie puppies may seem like twice the fun, but think carefully before you get two dogs from the same litter. It is harder to bond with each dog when two have each other to play with. Training sessions, vet bills, and grooming will double. It might be better to wait six months or a year before adding a second dog.

and size. Most faults based on the standard will have no effect on his life with you. In fact, when it comes to the 7-pound (3 kg) limit for show dogs, too big can be a plus for some families. Some people prefer slightly larger Yorkies, hoping for a little more robust playmate for their older children. And whether your Yorkie's eyes are the right shape, or his teeth have a perfect bite, or his ears flop a little makes no difference in the way he will love you.

WHAT A YORKIE NEEDS

Before you sign on the dotted line and carry your new Yorkie home, think about what he will need for a long and happy life. His bigger-than-life personality comes with some very definite requirements and desires. The best matches between owner and puppy are those that pair two like souls who want the same things.

Home

The first thing a Yorkie needs is a safe home. The good news is that it can be anywhere. Yorkies successfully live in urban apartments, suburbs, and rural areas. They can travel in small cars or giant RVs or under an airplane seat. But wherever you live, the safety issue is a serious one and must be met. Yorkies need to be protected from traffic, marauding predators, bad falls, poisons, drowning, and even getting lost. Obedience training, fences, puppy-proofing your home and yard, and vigilance are all things a Yorkshire Terrier owner must be prepared to take on. Baby gates and exercise pens are standard equipment in a Yorkie home. You may need two of each. Pools must be fenced, and fences must be tightly woven and go all the way to the ground.

By the Numbers

Puppies less than five months old are more inclined to get hypoglycemia or low blood sugar. They should be fed four or five times a day. Owners should have on hand a simple sugar, such as corn syrup, for emergencies. Rub it on the puppy's gums in case of an attack.

Exercise

All dogs need exercise, and Yorkies are no exception. They may be little but they have vast reserves of energy. If you live in a one-room apartment, your Yorkie may need leashed walks twice a day. But if you live in a two-story house with stairs, several rooms on each floor, and a fenced yard, your Yorkie may get enough exercise without daily leashed walks.

Somewhere in between no walks and several a day would be best for most Yorkies. One walk a day with you would make him very happy. A Yorkie needs less exercise than many breeds, but running and exploring is good for his physical and mental health. He came from sturdy farm dog stock that hunted rats in fields and barns, and every so often he should be allowed to sniff the ground and follow a trail. Besides, it is so much fun to walk a Yorkie—don't be too quick to give it up. He will be the center of an adoring public wherever you go. Walks can also be an important bonding time for you and your dog, as well as training time and socialization. Although you might be tempted, don't carry him everywhere. Teach him to walk on a leash, and take him places he will find curious and challenging. Let him

Yorkies may be little but they have lots of energy.

learn to pay attention to you and go where you want to go. He will be a more agreeable companion if he learns this major lesson.

However, if the weather outside is inhospitable, relax. Your Yorkie can get the minimum exercise he needs in the house, at least for a few days.

Sociability

Yorkies are terriers—they bark first and negotiate last. But Sue Swanson, who has owned four pet Yorkies, says it isn't that simple. "They all have different personalities," she says. So, the way your Yorkie responds to vacuums, children, strangers, or other dogs in some part depends on his personality: Some will attack the vacuum, others will just move to a quieter room; some will be happy to play with other dogs, others will challenge every one they spot.

You can improve his sociability by exposing him to many different things right from the beginning. If he learns that noise and commotion sometimes happen, if he learns that other dogs and strange people are just a part of everyday life, he will be able to take them in stride. If he sees that other dogs sometimes walk on the same sidewalk he does and no one gets hurt, he will be able to pass by the next one without causing a scary ruckus. The goal of socialization is to help your dog learn that life is an adventure, and going places with you is fun. He should be confident without being dominant. He should be able to watch the world go by if you stop to chat, and walk through a crowd without bothering dog or human. Socialization balances fear and aggressiveness.

Yorkies and Children

Most breeders discourage families with small children from getting a Yorkie because it is too dangerous for the dog. But Yorkies and slightly older kids can co-exist happily. Sharon Griffin, breeder at Majestik Kennels, says, "They are wonderful with kids if they are raised with kids. You just have to worry about the size of the dog. The biggest killers of Yorkies are slamming doors and lounge chairs (recliners) that go down." Kids may slam doors or put a reclining-type chair down without thinking to look for the dog first.

Yorkies do best in households with older children who understand how to handle them.

Vicki Meadows, Illinois breeder, does not sell Yorkie puppies to families with children younger than 10. It's too dangerous for the puppy and no fun for the child, Meadows says. She believes children should have a puppy they can play with. "It's not so much getting along with small children. Small children can't actually play with them easily," she says. "If they drop them, we have a broken leg."

Because Yorkies usually don't live with babies or small children, they sometimes have trouble adjusting to them when visiting. They have not been socialized to the quick movements and unpredictability of children. This requires a vigilant owner.

You can help your Yorkie adjust to children by staging short, supervised visits with one or two children who are willing to follow your instructions. They can talk to the dog, offer him treats, and even play controlled games. Gradually, the Yorkie learns that people come in all sizes.

Yorkies and Strangers

According to Meadows, properly socialized Yorkies are great with children and strangers of all ages—as long as they greet them correctly on the street. "With my Yorkies, it's all about me. Pet me first," she says. "No Yorkie in this house runs from people coming in the door." Meadows tries to intercept strangers who are rushing to pet her Yorkies on the street by saying, "Please do not ever touch a dog without asking permission. Always give the dog the back of your hand. Don't stick your fingers out. A kid could have chocolate on his fingers. The dogs like it." But the child may not appreciate a dog licking his hand.

A bigger problem, Meadows says, is a stranger who suddenly puts her face directly in the Yorkie's face, hoping for a kiss. "The problem

When introducing a Yorkie to a larger dog, make sure you stay close by and keep a close eye on the situation.

I have is, they are kissers," Meadows says. "The worse thing people can do is come in and put their face in a dog's face. You don't know what that human is giving off to that dog. The human could be thinking, 'I hate dogs but I am going to pretend to like this one because everyone expects that.' Dogs know that." You can't fool a dog and Yorkies are no exception. So if your Yorkie reacts loudly or violently to one person, pay attention, Meadows says. It may just be better to remove the Yorkie from the scene.

Other Dogs and Pets

Tales of tiny Yorkies attacking larger dogs are legion. Every Yorkie breeder has one. These tales of courage stir the heart and make good conversation, but small dogs who attack big dogs get hurt. This is where socialization comes in. The Yorkshire Terrier Club of America requires member breeders to keep puppies with the litter and their mother until they are 12 weeks old to allow puppies to learn how to play with other dogs, and especially to learn the limits of roughhousing. Fellow littermates will yelp and quit playing with a brother or sister who has suddenly gotten too rough. If he wants to play, a puppy has to stay within the limits his littermates set. He learns self-control.

Taking your puppy to obedience class, where he can learn to work with other dogs nearby, continues that process. He has to practice his self-control in order to get the treats you offer and to make you happy, even though he wants to play with the other dogs.

Finding other dogs to play with yours is another good idea, but start slowly and watch to see if the dogs accept each other as playmates. Start with dogs that are a similar size or only slightly larger. Stay close by and keep an eye on the dogs. Keep sessions short and end them before the dogs get tired and start losing their new self-control.

In multi-dog families, Yorkies have been known to live with dogs of all sizes. Terriers can be feisty around other dogs but at home, they may make an exception. The size of the other dogs is not as important as whether those particular dogs like each other.

Yorkies can get along with cats and even birds, Yorkshire Terrier Club of America president Carl Yochum says. "It depends on the dog. I had one that let a parrot ride around on his back."

Yorkies were bred to kill rats, so keeping small animals such as hamsters or gerbils in the same house with Yorkies is not a good idea. At the very least, it would require extra vigilance and baby gates.

Grooming

The good news is that Yorkshire Terriers have hair that is similar to human hair, with no undercoat. They do not shed as much as other long-coated dogs. The challenging news is that all that hair needs regular attention. If brushing hair flummoxes you, a shorthaired breed might be better for you—unless you are willing to commit to getting your Yorkie a regular haircut. At one extreme, the long Yorkie show coat requires daily brushing. Breeders wrap sections of the long show coats in paper to protect it when the dog is playing. They also worry about the dog rolling in dead leaves.

But all that changes with a haircut. That long hair just does not lend itself to everyday life, and many pet owners rely on professional groomers to trim the coats every couple months—either in a puppy cut or a Schnauzer cut (some shaving that makes the dog look more like a terrier). But even trimmed, your Yorkie's hair needs to be brushed and bathed

regularly between groomer visits. Sue Walters, who does agility and rally with her Yorkies, bathes her dogs every week.

Even with a haircut, some Yorkie owners like to keep enough hair on top of his head to create a topknot. With rubber bands and bows, the hair is pulled up so it can't fall in the dogs' eyes. Topknots should be redone often—daily if possible. All show dogs wear topknots with bows on their heads selected to set off the color of the coat. A popular choice is red, since it looks smart against the tan head.

Yorkie teeth should be brushed often. Tooth and gum disease are common in Yorkies, and oral care must be added to the list of owner responsibilities. Teeth must be kept clean and checked by a vet regularly. Yorkies frequently have their teeth cleaned every year, a process that requires anesthesia.

Health Issues

The Yorkshire Terrier as a breed has a number of potential health issues owners should learn about, both before getting a dog and as the dog matures. Breeders work conscientiously to reduce potential health problems by breeding individual dogs who have been tested and cleared of major health problems. When a Yorkie is healthy, he is very healthy and can live to an advanced age, even 16 or 17 years old.

But unscrupulous puppy mills will breed any dog. And as Yorkies rose in popularity, so did puppy prices, making it a very attractive breed to sell. Some puppy mills bred any two Yorkies they could find without getting health clearances. Some backyard breeders also do not know enough about genetics to understand what the results could be of simply breeding the only two dogs they have. When you are looking for a puppy, ask the breeder what health clearances both parents have. Some test results to ask for are a bile acid test for liver malfunctions, patellas (kneecaps), eyes (CERF), and hips (OFA). Well-cared-for Yorkies without major genetic defects are a joy to live with, and you should be able to look forward to a long relationship with your dog.

Training Tidbit

Some Yorkie owners prefer to use a harness rather than a collar when leash-training their puppies. Yorkies have very thin necks and tracheas that are subject to collapse. Your dog should have a collar with an identification tag in any case.

Eyes

The Canine Eye Registration Foundation (CERF) tests dogs for genetic eye disease and certifies them if they are free of such disease. Certification is only good for 12 months, and then a dog must be retested. Yorkies can get cataracts, dry eye, distichiasis (extra eyelashes that are abrasive to the cornea), and occasionally progressive retinal atrophy. But, in general, Yorkies have fewer eye problems than many breeds. Breeding stock should have a CERF clearance within the last year.

Want to Know More?

For a detailed look at what grooming a Yorkie entails, see Chapter 6: Yorkshire Terrier Grooming Needs.

Hips

Yorkies sometimes get hip dysplasia or Legg-Calve-Perthes

disease, two abnormalities of the hips. In hip dysplasia, the abnormal formation of the hip leads to crippling arthritis in severe cases. In Legg-Calve-Perthes, the femoral head is cut off from its blood supply, and bone cells die. The Orthopedic Foundation for Animals (OFA) tests for both conditions and can certify whether breeding stock is free of them.

Liver

One of the most serious, life-threatening health issues Yorkies can have is a liver shunt or congenital portosystemic shunt. A blood vessel that bypasses the liver before a Yorkie puppy is born—when the mother's body is cleansing the puppy's blood—does not close after birth, continuing to carry the puppy's blood around (or bypassing) the liver. So the toxins in the puppy's blood do not go through the liver to be processed. Both physical and behavior issues can result. In Yorkies, this shunt is usually outside the liver, which is important in purifying the blood. Puppies with a shunt accumulate toxins. Puppies can be tested at 18 weeks of age for liver bile acid, and breeding stock should have passed this test. Veterinarian Karen Tobias at the University of Tennessee College of Veterinary Medicine found the Yorkshire Terrier is 36 percent more likely to have a liver shunt than other breeds.

Liver shunts can be passed on to offspring as a recessive trait. This is why it is important to buy your Yorkie from a responsible breeder. In a litter, one puppy may have a serious liver shunt. The other puppies, healthy, still may be carriers of the recessive gene and should not be bred. Dogs who are carriers but do not have shunts are sometimes bred and produce

Luxating patellas can affect small breeds as early as eight weeks.

puppies with shunts. Many liver shunts can be corrected with surgery, but it is major, expensive surgery. Responsible breeders have been working hard to eliminate liver shunts in Yorkies. Talk to your breeder about the issues she has faced with both shunts and carriers.

Patella

Luxating patellas or slipping kneecaps on the rear legs affect small breeds as early as eight weeks. As the kneecaps slip in and out of place, the dog may feel pain and extend a rear leg, hoping it will slip back in. Slipping in and out wears down the ridge the kneecap belongs in and the condition gets worse. Surgery may help.

The Orthopedic Foundation for Animals tests for luxating patellas. It found that Yorkies were fourth in all breeds to have luxating patellas, after the Pomeranian, Boykin, and Cocker Spaniels. Of 119 Yorkies tested who were older than one year, 17.6 percent were affected.

Trainability

Just how trainable Yorkies are depends on whom you ask. The first-time Yorkie owner trying to housetrain a six-month-old puppy may answer, "Not very trainable." Experienced breeders and Yorkie owners may answer, "Trainable enough to win obedience and agility titles."

The fact is, Yorkies have a mind of their own. Training them requires a slightly different technique that recognizes this fact. And then there's the size difference. "Training is totally different," Sue Walters, agility champion trainer, says. "A Yorkie's head is so low they are focused on your knee," she says. "You have to bend very low to give them treats." Walters has turned to clicker training, a type of training that uses the sound a clicker makes to tell the dog when he has done a good thing. "I get the dog to respond so much faster," she says. Clicker training is known for its precision. But if you are thinking of clicker training, look for an obedience class that can teach you how to do it properly. Walters used clicker training to quickly get a Yorkie to stand on a skateboard and to put his head in a bucket. She has a wall of ribbons won by Yorkies in obedience and agility. How did she do it? "Baby steps," she says. She tries to teach only one thing at a time, and allow a lot of time for the dog to learn it—a lot of time.

When training a Yorkie it's important to understand he has a mind of his own.

CHAPTER 2

FINDING AND PREPPING FOR YOUR YORKSHIRE TERRIER PUPPY

Every family has an image of the perfect dog for them, but finding that dog requires hard work and an investment of time. The effort pays off when your puppy is happy and healthy and matches your lifestyle. If you can resist impulse buying and do your homework, you can increase your chances of being rewarded with a true companion. Besides, going to dog show, visiting kennels, and talking Yorkies with breeders can be a fun and educational experience.

WHY A PUPPY MAY BE RIGHT FOR YOU

For some people, a three- to six-month old puppy is the only new dog they will consider. They love that puppy cuteness. These are the people who are excited about watching their puppy grow into an adult dog, who want to be there for all their puppy's milestones. They want an adult dog whose background is no mystery. They want to know exactly what their puppy has lived through and what his socialization and nutrition has included. They want to guarantee that their puppy gets the best right from the start. They want to be the person the puppy bonds with and learns to trust. They want to teach the puppy their way of doing things from Day One. Housetraining a puppy does not intimidate them. Cleaning up accidents is no problem for them. Teaching a puppy not to chew is a challenge they take in stride.

Pet or Show?

Just as a puppy's history has no surprises, his future is unknowable. For pet owners, a puppy, with his unpredictable future, may be exciting. They feel no pressure to have a dog that conforms to a standard. No one knows for sure what kind of coat or look that ten- or twelve-week-old puppy will ultimately have. Pet owners are more concerned about temperament and trainability, and breeders can give them a pretty good idea what type of Yorkie a three-month-old puppy will grow into. Breeders who belong to the Yorkshire Terrier Club of America will not sell a puppy younger than that because of size and socialization concerns. The puppy should stay with his mother and littermates to learn certain skills that only another dog can teach, such as bite inhibition in play. Some breeders take that even further. Vicki Meadows, Illinois breeder, does not sell a puppy younger than four months. "I want them to be able to use piddle

Two puppies are cute, but twice the work!

pads without mistakes. I want them to know the word 'come' for their own safety. Most are taught to sit and stay," she says of her four-month-old puppies.

Owners of potential show dogs take a big chance with a three- to six-month-old puppy, no matter how good his pedigree is. At three months, a puppy is just too young to exhibit winning show dog attributes, such as the coat. But a six-month-old puppy may have enough markers to convince experienced breeders that he has potential in the ring. Carl Yochum, president of the Yorkshire Terrier Club of America and a longtime Yorkie breeder, says he can tell if a puppy from one of his lines has show potential. "If you stick with your bloodlines, you know what you've had through years and years. You can pretty much tell what you have," Yochum says. But if you're interested in a show puppy, be wary of a first- or second-time breeder who claims a six-month-old or younger puppy has show potential. It just too early for most inexperienced breeders to tell, Yochum says.

However old your show puppy is when you get him, be sure your breeder agrees that the puppy has show potential, and be prepared to keep his coat long. The long coat requires daily maintenance, so teach your puppy to stand on a grooming table right from the beginning. He must be kept intact, not neutered (or spayed if the puppy is a female), and taught to walk on a leash and stand for examination. Show puppies are usually not taught to sit as a default behavior but to stand for a treat. Conformation classes at dog shows start at six months, so buying a six-month-old puppy means you can jump immediately into the show dog world, learning with your puppy.

That is, if you can find a six-month old show puppy. Breeders who will sell a six-month-old puppy as a show prospect are unusual. Ask yourself: Why is the breeder parting with such a hot prospect? If you want more certainty, wait three or four more months. The Yorkshire Terrier Club of America advises show dog homes to wait until a puppy is nine or even ten months old before buying a Yorkie meant for the show ring. By then, the silky texture and color of the coat will be obvious. Meadows sometimes shows her own six-month-old puppies but does not sell them to show homes that young. "I had one bitch at six months and she won a major. But a good breeder will not sell a show dog that young. They are going to know at nine, ten, or eleven months old."

HOW TO FIND A YORKIE PUPPY

The best way to find a happy, healthy puppy is research, research, research. And that is just fun, fun, fun. Immerse yourself in the world of the Yorkshire Terrier, breeders, websites, shows, and magazines, and let your imagination go. Imagine yourself with a dog from each breeder you visit. When you are buying a puppy, you should follow that old carpenter's adage: measure twice, cut once. Plan, prepare, and research before you bring home a puppy. After all, how many puppies do you buy in a lifetime? It's worth it to take your time and talk to a lot of people before you make a decision.

Do Your Research

Read about Yorkies until you know what questions to ask. Talk to people at dog parks or vet offices, who already own Yorkies, and ask them where they got their dogs and if they are pleased. Ask about temperament and health. Go to dog shows if you are interested in a show dog or even a puppy from show dog lines that may be cosmetically not suited for the ring. Talk to people at shows who are grooming or waiting for their Yorkie's turn. Collect business cards, go home, and study their web pages.

Yorkies are also shown in agility and obedience rings at bigger dog shows, so if you are interested in a Yorkie who can participate in performance sports, ask competitors where they got their Yorkies.

Consider finding a breeder through the Yorkshire Terrier Club of America and its local or regional affiliates. They all must agree to a code of ethics. Ask a local vet or two for breeder recommendations.

Avoid sending for a puppy from an out-of-state breeder you ran across online. It is harder to gauge the quality of a puppy and the socialization skills of such a breeder. "If people want to meet you on the side of the road or in a parking lot, avoid them," Yochum says. "You want to go to their home and inspect how they keep their dogs and what type breeder you are buying from. Get some kind of health guarantee."

By the Numbers

The best age to get a Yorkshire Terrier depends on a number of things, but a puppy younger than 12 weeks is harder to care for. Look for a puppy between 12 and 16 weeks who has been allowed to stay with his mother and littermates.

This six-week-old puppy is far too young to leave his mom. A breeder should wait until at least 12 weeks to allow you to bring a puppy home.

Since Yorkies spend so much time with the breeder as puppies, the type of socialization the breeder offers is a key factor and a question you should ask. A Yorkie who has been taken away from his mother and littermates early and placed in a cage by himself with little human contact is going to be harder to live with, at least at first. Puppy mills that do that can hide online behind statements of excellence and photos of pretty puppies that may not even be theirs. If you don't ask enough questions, they don't have to prove anything.

Visit the Breeder

Visit two or three Yorkie breeders if you can. Breeders should be able to tell you what kind of experiences a three-month-old Yorkie has had—going to the vet, learning to walk on a leash, potty training, playing with different toys, playing outside, playing with more than one person, playing with other dogs. At the breeder, find out the following:

- Ask to see the mother and father. The mother should have been at least 18 months old when she gave birth.
- Ask to see where the litter was raised.
- Ask for a feeding schedule, the type of food your puppy is used to, a vaccination record, and any other health information on the puppy.
- Ask for a pedigree, health clearances for both parents, and American Kennel Club (AKC) status (registered litter or not).
- Ask if the breeder will be available to help you after you take the puppy home.
- Avoid breeders who suddenly raise the price when you show an interest in one puppy. ("Oh, that one is special and costs $500 more.")
- Be sure the breeder offers you a signed contract that allows you to bring the puppy back within a few days if you take him to a vet for a preliminary exam and the vet discovers a major health issue.
- Ask for the names and contact information for some previous puppy buyers. When you get home, contact them.

It sounds like a lot to ask—and it is—but it is better than spending the next 15 years wishing you had asked more questions. People with soft hearts have fallen for a cute Yorkie puppy only to find some months later that their "Yorkie" grew to 15 pounds (7 kg) and is obviously a mixed breed. Or, that the love of their life has a liver shunt and needs major surgery.

In return, you can expect more than a few questions from the type of quality breeder you are seeking. Breeders will want to know if you have a vet and what your plans are for dog care when you are on vacation. Breeders will want to know if you have ever had a small dog, if you have ever raised a puppy, if you have a fenced yard, if you have other dogs or small children, and whether you will contact the breeder first if, for any reason, you can no longer keep the dog. The type of breeder you are looking for does not want her dogs ending up in rescue. She has invested time and money in producing the best puppy she can, and she does not want someone abandoning him at a shelter. She is looking for a buyer who cares for the dog as a living creature, not as an ornament or status symbol.

BEFORE PUPPY COMES HOME

While you are searching for the perfect puppy, you can start to assemble some basic equipment and begin to puppy-proof the house and yard.

Puppy-Proofing

You'll need to puppy proof indoors and out.

Inside

In the house, decide which rooms the puppy will be allowed to use. Your puppy is a baby, not yet the dog he will be someday. He needs to be protected as you would any baby. A three-month-old puppy does not need access to the entire house right away. He may not need to go upstairs, for example, if you have a two-story house. A baby gate at the bottom of the stairs will keep him out of trouble upstairs. If the basement has a door, it should be kept closed, and you can start practicing that as soon as you decide to get a puppy. Count how many baby gates you will need. Dog catalogs sell them at various heights, so you can buy shorter ones than those used for children.

Puppies chew everything they find, so crawl through your house at puppy level and see what he will see. Shoes should be locked behind closet doors. Wet gloves or socks should dry up on a counter. Dirty clothes should be out of reach. The kitchen and bathrooms should have a wastebasket with a lid. Cans of soda or beer should be stored off the floor, out of puppy reach. The mail should be kept in a drawer. Even a magazine basket may be trouble, at least at first. Dogs like to chew on both paper and wicker. Electrical cords should be eliminated if possible, or covered. Any large pieces of art or sculpture that can tip over and crush a small dog should be removed from the floor. If you can't eliminate a hazard, use a baby gate to keep puppies out of bathrooms, home studios or offices, and laundry areas where soaps are stored. Even a paperclip can cause problems.

Visit the Yorkie breeder, and be prepared to ask lots of questions.

Make sure shoes are put away, or your Yorkie puppy is sure to find them irresistible.

Outside

Outside, in the yard, fences should be tightly woven and extend to the ground or even under the ground. Puppies squeeze through surprisingly small spaces, and they can dig. Prizewinning roses or other plants should be fenced off. Swimming pools and duck ponds should be fenced and separate from the dog's area. Birdbaths should be sturdy enough so that a dog cannot knock them over and high enough so that a puppy can't fall in. Garbage cans should be outside the puppy area. Raised decks should be enclosed by a fence with posts close enough together so that no puppy can squeeze through.

An exercise pen, a portable plastic or wire pen that every Yorkie owner should have, may be used at first to keep the puppy in a safe space, inside and out.

As your puppy grows, and as you gain confidence in his ability to listen to you, you may allow him access to the entire yard or a room when you are nearby. Older dogs frequently give up chewing, and you may be able to add many things back into your home then.

The Puppy Schedule

A three-month-old puppy cannot be left alone for nine or ten hours. Think of him as a baby. At the beginning, his bladder can only hold on for roughly as many hours as his age —three hours for a three-month-old, four hours for a four month old. Neither can he go all day without food. If everyone in the house works all day, someone will have to come home for an early lunch to let him out and feed him.

Someone else may have to let him out and feed him again in the late afternoon. Yorkie puppies need to eat every few hours or they face the threat of hypoglycemia, a serious medical emergency caused by low blood sugar. Friends, neighbors, and even pet sitters can be pressed into this duty. Visiting dog caregivers can help to socialize your dog, but the most important thing to realize is that your puppy cannot be left alone all day at first.

Like most living creatures, Yorkies thrive on routine. Routines are familiar and give puppies a sense of security. Puppies appreciate being able to anticipate what you have in store. They learn faster on a routine. Housetraining and all other puppy manners are easier to teach if you set up a schedule and stick to it, more or less. For example, if you wake up at 7 a.m. every day, wake up the puppy, carry him outside or to his potty place, and wait until he has relieved himself before feeding him. Do not feel obligated to play with him now. After he eats, take him outside again, watch to see if he has to eliminate again, and then you can play if you want. That kind of routine will quickly etch itself on the puppy's brain. He will know what to do first thing in the morning. When it is time for you to leave the house, establish a similar routine and stick to it. Take the puppy outside and wait until he relieves himself. Bring him inside and put him in his safe place, whether it is a crate or an exercise pen. Offer him one treat and leave quietly without a melodramatic departure.

The puppy's day should be anchored around several meals and trips to his potty place, at least one outside play time (two or three is better), time alone with you, and reasonable expectations as to what he should and should not do. When he bites or chews something he shouldn't, it helps him if you react firmly the same way every time.

Shopping for Puppy Things

Your puppy will need several things you might not have lying around the house.

Baby Gate

Baby gates are useful when you want to leave your Yorkie in a room or keep him out of a place that could be dangerous. Baby gates can be bought at major retailers, both in the infant and in the pet departments, or through dog catalogs and websites. Look for a gate that has mesh or posts close enough together so even a puppy can't squeeze through. If you want to move the gate from room to room during the week, buy one that is pressure mounted and can easily be removed. If you have a designated dog room, mount the gate on the doorway with more permanent installation. Some specialty businesses offer free-standing dog gates that are attractively finished in furniture stains.

Clothes

If you are housetraining your puppy to eliminate outside and it is cold, he may need two sweaters or coats to stay warm—one to wear and one for backup in case the first one gets wet or muddy. Even if you intend for him to use an indoor potty, he will need to wear

Multi-Dog Tip

If you already have a dog, he may or may not like the idea of a new puppy in the house. Pay extra attention to your first dog, one-on-one. Take just your first dog in the car if he likes car trips. Feed the dogs separately, so you can tell which dog is eating how much.

a sweater or coat for leash training when it is cold. Yorkies lack the undercoat that keeps some breeds warm in cooler weather. Coats can be cute, but most importantly they should cover enough of your dog to keep him warm. Yorkies get cold fast.

Collar/Harness/Leash

He will need a puppy collar (that he'll eventually outgrow) and then an adult collar. You might also consider a harness. Yorkies are prone to tracheal collapse, and a harness helps avoid that, especially in the beginning. He will also need a leash. Buy a medium- or lightweight leather or nylon straight leash that feels good in your hands. Avoid metal chains always and retractable leashes—at least at first. Your puppy should learn to walk on a 6-foot (2 m) leash before you try a retractable leash.

Crate/X-Pen

Every puppy should have a safe place where he can go when the world is overwhelming. This can be a crate with the door left open when you are home or an exercise pen in a quiet corner. The crate should be just big enough that he can stand up and turn around. Until your puppy shows he is not interested in shredding a cloth or fleece bed, put a towel or small inexpensive fleece in the crate. When he is past the teething stage, add a crate pad or soft rug. You might want an additional dog bed in the TV room or kitchen, to give your dog another place where he can relax.

An exercise pen is a handy tool some Yorkie owners use when they can't be with their Yorkie every minute but prefer that he be out in the house. The pen can be set up in the kitchen while you are cooking or out in the yard where you can see him from a window. An indoor and an outdoor ex-pen work well.

Your Yorkie will need to wear a sweater or coat when it is cold.

Floor/Carpet Cleaner

Housetraining accidents are guaranteed to happen. Buy a floor or carpet cleaner that is specially designed to remove the smell of urine, feces, and vomit. Dogs have very sensitive noses, and puppies are inclined to urinate where they smell urine. Their inner voice tells them this must be the place to go. Discourage that by eliminating the smell as well as the color and moisture.

Food

It is a good idea to buy a small bag of food before you pick up the puppy. Research the options and choose a food before your puppy comes home. A small bag is best for two reasons: It might not agree with your puppy, and you may have to switch foods after a week or two. Second, fresh food is very important. Only buy enough food that your puppy can eat in a short time, about two months.

Food and Water Bowls

Your dog will need two bowls, one for water and one for food. Bowls that go in the dishwasher are best. Avoid thin glass that could break. Avoid plastic. Plastic bowls, especially cheap plastic, can be chewed by your dog or dragged around the house. Some dogs are allergic to plastic and can get skin irritations from daily contact. All plastic scratches eventually, and those scratches hold bacteria. Some research has shown that toxins leach out of plastic, especially plastic that has been heated repeatedly in the sun or dishwasher. If you use plastic bowls replace them frequently.

Since dogs need a quiet place to eat, the best place for his bowls is in his crate or ex-pen.

Grooming Tools

Even if you intend to have your dog professionally groomed, you'll need some basic grooming tools, such as a soft brush for his coat and one for his teeth. Toenail clippers are a good thing to have and serve two purposes: keeping his nails short and getting him used to having someone handle his feet.

Identification

Your dog needs to carry some identification with him. Many breeders microchip puppies before they leave the kennel. Be sure to ask your breeder if your puppy has been microchipped and leave with his number written down. Some dogs have been tattooed with identifying information that does not require a special reader, such as microchips do. All dogs should wear a tag on their collar with enough information to ensure a lost dog could be returned. If you travel a lot or own a second home, consider putting your cell phone or e-mail address on the tag, or having separate tags made with information unique to each home or trip. Inexpensive ID tags can be made while you wait at major pet products stores.

A small crate is the best training investment you can make. It should be hard-sided, metal or plastic, with a door that latches. Every time you take your puppy out of the crate, immediately take him to his potty place. Feed him in his crate and let him sleep there as long as he is a puppy.

Toys

Toys may seem like a frivolous purchase but in reality, high-quality dog toys are important and a necessity. Cheap toys don't last and may have dangerous materials that your puppy can choke on, such as the eyes that can come off stuffed animals. Toys come in a wide variety that encourage different types of play and interaction with people. Balls are a good way to teach your Yorkie to fetch and to have fun. Be sure the ball is big enough that it cannot be swallowed. Tug toys can be used by you and your dog or by two dogs. Tug toys can be bought or even made by tightly braiding and knotting sturdy fabric. Chew toys encourage your puppy to chew on only approved objects. Nylabone makes a wide variety of chew toys that are safe and long lasting.

COMING HOME

Imagine bringing your puppy home. Run

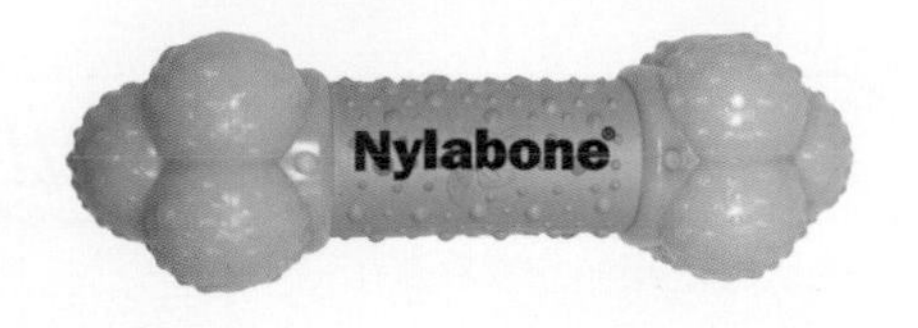

through all the steps before the day arrives. You have puppy-proofed the house and yard, and bought a crate or exercise pen. You have a sweater, collar, and leash. You have a plan for potty training. You walk in the door with the puppy in your arms and…What do you see that still has to be done? Or, are you all set?

Once you know when you are picking up the puppy, call your vet and make a new puppy appointment. It should be the day you pick him up or the next day, if possible.

When homecoming day arrives, ask someone to drive you to the breeder's so you can hold the puppy on the way home. Take things that will keep the puppy warm if it is cold outside. You might want to take a camera. Plan enough time so you can ask the breeder any questions you've thought of since you agreed to buy the dog. Be prepared to sign a contract and pay.

Look at the dog carefully to make sure it is the puppy you agreed to buy—gender, color, size. Look him over to see if there is any evidence of diarrhea or smelly ears or running eyes. These are probably not enough to make you change your mind at this point but you should ask the breeder why these things are happening and what to do when you get home. Be sure you have a return clause in the contract. Pack up whatever the breeder gives you (food sample, folder with AKC papers and contract, book or information about Yorkshire Terriers, a phone number to call if you are concerned, vaccination records, health clearances of parents if you don't already have them, pedigree). Pick up your puppy and get in the back seat. Keep the puppy warm.

When you get home, put the puppy on the grass or outside potty place in the fenced-in area and wait to see if he has to relieve himself. Then you can play with him. If he appears sleepy, take him in the house, offer him some water, then put him in his safe place. He has had a lot of excitement and may welcome a rest.

THE FIRST FEW WEEKS

Life with a new puppy is a chaotic roller coaster ride that is insanely funny and happy, while at the same time being exhausting and frustrating. Be sure to take time to sit on the floor with your puppy and just be together.

Potty Training Supplies

Think through the way you want to housetrain your puppy and acquire whatever supplies you need. If yours is going to be a dog who goes strictly outdoors, a stock of small plastic bags and two or even three dog sweaters may be a good idea (in case one gets wet). If you are opting for indoor house training, research the different systems that are available and choose one before your puppy arrives. Possibilities include puppy pads (similar to hospital blue pads), boxes of real sod or artificial grass, and puppy litter boxes. Each has pluses and minuses. Talk to your breeder. Many use puppy piddle pads because they are portable. The dog does not have to go out in bad weather, he can use the pad when no one is home, and he can use the pad on trips, in airports or hotel rooms.

Enjoy him. Laugh at his antics and love his affection. Take pictures. Before long, he will be a full-grown dog.

Veterinary Exam

One of the important things to do the first day or the next is to take your puppy to a vet for a new puppy examination. This is a thorough physical that may include vaccination. Be sure to take the health record the breeder gave you. Ask ahead of time if you should bring a stool sample. The vet should be able to tell you if the puppy's heart and lungs are sound, if he has worms, or an ear or eye infection or fleas. The vet will set up a vaccination schedule based on the information from the breeder. You can ask about heartworm prevention, puppy food, and any supplements.

If there is a major medical issue, think carefully about keeping the puppy. It is not too late to take the puppy back to the breeder.

Stick to the Schedule

Once the puppy passes a veterinary inspection, the next biggest job is to put in place the schedule you have already thought through. It is tempting to spoil your puppy, but your job is to enforce a few rules right from the beginning, so the puppy knows who is in charge. The puppy should be taken to a potty place often, praised when he performs, and ignored when he has an accident, unless you catch him in the act. Then he should be taken to the potty place. He should be discouraged from biting people. He should be denied the chance to bother people or beg while you are eating. He should be fed on a schedule every few hours and sometimes left alone in his safe place so he learns that you will come back. He should sleep in his safe place—a warm secure spot that is just his, and where no other housepet, dog or cat, can bother him.

Establish Rules

Things that are cute once or twice in a three-month-old puppy—like begging at the dinner table—lose their attractiveness after a few weeks or when the dog is an adult. But once the puppy has learned it is okay to beg for food from the dinner table, teaching him not to do it becomes a chore when you would rather spend the time teaching him to fetch a ball. So, in the first few days, establish the rules that are important to your family and stick to them.

Encourage visitors to come in small numbers after the first week. Give the puppy a chance to learn who is in his new family and that he can trust them before you deluge him with visitors.

It is too soon to take him for a walk, so play with him in the house or in the backyard. Sit down on the grass and take a few cues from him. Life is fun and puppies should be enjoyed.

Want to Know More?

For information on how to properly socialize your puppy, see Chapter 4: Training Your Yorkshire Terrier Puppy.

CHAPTER 3

CARING FOR YOUR YORKSHIRE TERRIER PUPPY

Watching a new life unfold is exciting. What will your puppy be like? What will he look like? The answers to all those questions start in the day-to-day care you provide. Puppies need food, water, sleep, exercise, safe play, and humans to interact with. Watching your puppy respond to all these things will give you the first clues as to who he really is. You'll see for yourself if he attacks life with vigor, or if he prefers to sit back and watch it unfold. Being responsible for a puppy round the clock gives you the inside track into the way his mind works. That's helpful when it comes to training.

FEEDING A PUPPY

When you take over the care of a puppy, you assume the job his mother Yorkie did naturally and successfully. Since you are not biologically equipped to feed the puppy, you must figure out another way to be just as successful. This new job requires thought and responsibility. It should be your priority for the next few months. A puppy has to be fed several times a day, in a clean safe place, and he has to be fed a high-quality diet. He is relying on you.

What to Feed

Dog food today is in the midst of a sea-change. As pets replace children in many homes, as we expect our canine friends to live longer, we are willing to buy better and better dog food. But the question remains: What is the very best food for my Yorkie puppy? Science can hardly keep up with our demand for information about dog food and for better-quality foods. We want the best, but nutrition experts are still doing long-range studies to determine exactly what that is, and if that changes from breed to breed. Scientists and dog breeders sometimes disagree on what is best.

Dog owners from fifty years ago would be amazed at the science and the ingredients that now go into a bag of puppy food. They would also be flabbergasted at the number of choices and the price sticker on each one. But the proliferation of choices makes it more difficult for today's dog owners. More choices mean more research for the average owner.

Manufacturers have responded to the consumer demand for better-quality dog food in different ways. Some offer high protein, others went with "natural," still others attempted raw diets—all mostly unregulated by the federal government. Whether those are right for your Yorkie puppy is another question. Just because it's for sale does not mean it's a good buy for you and your puppy.

The choices today for puppy food start with dry, canned, semi-moist, raw, and homemade. Picking one of those can be a complex task, but any one of them is better than simply offering your dog leftovers from the table. Leftovers do not contain the balance a puppy needs to stay healthy and grow strong. Leftovers may also contain a higher percentage of fat, sugar, salt, and foods that are not good for dogs, such as onions.

Commercial dog foods or foods you prepare at home specifically for your dog are made from formulas and recipes that have balanced ingredients that include exactly what your dog needs. Dogs cannot live on meat alone.

Picking a commercial dog food is made more confusing when friends, breeders, show dog mentors, and advertising all insist their food is the best choice—or even the only good choice.

It is important to take a deep breath and remember that puppies will survive and be healthy on many foods. Many commercial foods are better today than they were in previous generations. But, it's also true that some cheap foods out there are not worth the money saved. That conundrum makes it important that you do your homework and find a food you are comfortable with.

Changing Food

Your Yorkie puppy should come from the breeder with a small sample of the food he is used to eating. Even if you have decided to change food, you should start off feeding your puppy what the breeder gave you, mixed with a small amount of your new food. Gradually decrease the breeder's food. Spread the change over several days. Give the puppy's system a chance to adjust gradually to the new food to reduce gastric upset.

Dry Food/Kibble

Many new Yorkie owners choose to feed their puppies a high-quality puppy kibble, and some even select one specifically designated for small or toy breeds. Dry food is a very popular choice. Nationally, more dry foods are sold than any other type.

A dry food that the Association of American Feed Control Officials (AAFCO) has determined is complete and balanced contains everything your puppy needs to grow into a strong healthy dog: protein, fat, carbohydrates, vitamins, and minerals. No supplements are necessary. And because Yorkies eat tiny amounts, even the most expensive dog food may be affordable. Look for the AAFCO label on bags of food.

Several premium foods that cost more are on the shelves, and here's where your research is important. Your puppy will probably do fine on any one of them, but one may be slightly better for him. Start with your breeder. Ask why she chose the food she fed your puppy. Has she had trouble with corn allergies? Does she have dry-skin issues she is trying to avoid? Read the dog food label. Look at the first five ingredients and count how many are corn, wheat, or other grains. Dogs are omnivores—they eat a lot of different foods—but meat is the mainstay of their diet. The first ingredient on a bag of high-quality kibble should be chicken, beef, or lamb. Some dogs can live on high quantities of corn—it has protein—but it can cause problems in other dogs. Most dog experts think dogs do better on diets that have corn in a secondary role to meat or not included at all.

Whatever you decide to feed your puppy, make sure it is fresh.

Ask any friends who have Yorkies what they feed and why. Keep an open mind. Some people have had dogs who are allergic to one ingredient and sought brands that left out that one ingredient. Others are overly impressed with labels such as "natural" without being able to explain exactly what that means.

Keep it Fresh

Choose a puppy food that is reliably available. Fresh food is important, so you should buy dry puppy food in smaller quantities. Dry foods do go stale and lose vitamins and nutrients. Pass up an opportunity to buy several large bags of puppy food, even if they are an unbeatable price. Think twice before choosing a food you have to order online and have delivered. Can you be sure the food will be delivered before you need it? How much is the delivery charge? Are you required to buy large amounts that might go stale?

Store the dry food in the bag it comes in to preserve moisture and vitamins. Keep the bag in an airtight container that is also puppy-proof.

Life Stages

Nutritional experts at the Michigan State University (MSU) College of Veterinary Medicine say commercially prepared complete and balanced dog foods typically have an AAFCO claim for all life stages, adult maintenance, or for growth (puppy food). "Fifteen to twenty years ago, there were distinct differences between puppy and adult foods, but the lines have blurred significantly in

Many new Yorkie owners choose to feed their puppies a high-quality puppy kibble.

the past five to ten years," the MSU experts say. "What is typically recommended is that puppies be fed a growth-type food until they reach 90 percent of their skeletal maturity. For toy and small-breed dogs, this might be when they are eight to nine months old." Or, another logical time to switch puppies from puppy to adult food is when the dog is spayed or neutered, for example at six months.

Commercial dog foods have more similarities than differences, the MSU experts say, and pet owners should focus on how they feed rather than what they are feeding. How should they feed? Just enough to avoid obesity, the MSU experts say. Obesity is the biggest problem your dog faces today. It affects every system in his body, as well as his willingness to play.

Canned Food

Canned dog foods contain a high percentage of moisture and usually come in second to dry foods with dog experts because of cost. Others believe canned food is bad for teeth. Yorkies have more dental problems than many breeds, and some experts recommend staying away from anything that can promote tooth decay. Canned foods can be useful as appetite stimulants or occasional treats.

Semi-Moist

Semi-moist foods in pouches have higher quantities of additives—chemical and otherwise—and are not as beneficial as dry and canned. Check the amount of sugar and salt on pouches. They are generally a poor choice.

Raw/BARF Diet

Raw food or the BARF diet—bones and raw food—is the favorite diet of some very passionate dog owners. They believe dogs should eat a diet that mimics what they would eat in the wild. Raw food has less processing, cooking, and additives, and some studies have shown animals get fewer degenerative diseases when on a raw diet. The danger in a raw diet is the lack of balance. It takes skill and patience on your part to work out a raw diet so that it covers all the nutritional needs of your Yorkie. Your vet can help you with this. A major veterinary college can also analyze your pet's diet and make recommendations. A dog on a raw diet should be on some vitamin and mineral supplements.

Homemade Diet

A homemade diet for dogs is human food you cook from dog recipes designed to provide the balance Yorkies need. Typically, it includes meals such as chicken and rice or beef stew that have all the food groups represented, including fruit and vegetables. The advantages are that the dog gets fresh food with less processing and that is tailored to his needs. The disadvantages are the cost, the time involved in shopping and cooking, and the effort required to guarantee a balanced diet. A homemade diet should also be analyzed by a major veterinary college for balance. Dogs eating a homemade diet should also be on vitamin and mineral supplements.

Feeding Schedule

Puppies should eat several times a day in the beginning—four or five times a day if you have a very young or very small puppy. Eventually, adult Yorkies should eat twice a day. For many people, one advantage of dry food is the convenience of leaving a bowl of kibble out for the puppy all day without it spoiling. This practice—free feeding—is not recommended by most dog experts. Its success depends on your dog and whether you have another pet that might eat the puppy food. Some dogs will overeat if allowed to eat as much as they want. The reverse is also true—some dogs will not eat enough, especially if a cat or another dog is competing for the food. You must keep track of how much your puppy is eating and be sure he eats enough to avoid low blood sugar (hypoglycemia). Some Yorkie puppies—often those who are very small, very young, or likely to develop a major health issue later—may have bouts of hypoglycemia if they do not eat often or enough food. So, feed your puppy in his crate at first, away from distractions and other animals, and watch carefully to see how much he eats.

Spread your puppy's meals over as many hours as you can: 7 a.m., noon, 6 p.m., 11 p.m. As the puppy adapts to your house and grows, drop one feeding and then another so your healthy adult Yorkie is being fed two meals roughly 12 hours apart.

Vicki Meadows, Illinois breeder, who sells her

By the Numbers

Yorkshire Terriers, like other toy dogs, reach their full size before they are one year old. A Yorkie's coat, however, has not matured until he is at least 18 or even 24 months old.

Once your puppy gets a little older you can start brushing him on a table.

puppies at four months of age, recommends to her buyers that they feed puppies three times a day at distinct mealtimes to encourage puppies to eat. "They get it put down for 15 or 20 minutes then I take it up," she says. "By the next feeding they are thinking, 'I better eat.' It does not make for picky eaters."

GROOMING A PUPPY

It's true that your puppy does not have a full coat but he still needs to be groomed.

In fact, grooming a puppy is very important. An adult Yorkie's life includes frequent—sometimes daily—grooming, and puppies should learn to relax and accept grooming as just another part of the day. His coat will look better for it, and you will be able to stop mats before they start. Grooming a puppy is your chance to get him used to people handling him. The puppy learns he must stand or sit still and let people touch his feet. He may even learn to like the attention. Your groomer and your vet will appreciate your dog's ability to stand still and be examined without a fuss.

Bonding Time

Grooming is the time when you and your puppy can bond. He will learn to trust you, and you will learn to admire his good points. He will also learn that you are in charge and that he will have to practice some self-control—both good lessons for a Yorkie. As you groom his whole body, brushing hair under his legs and on his stomach and ears, he will come to enjoy your touch. During grooming, the puppy will have your undivided attention and that alone is enough to make most puppies deliriously happy. Talk to your puppy and admire his coat while you brush it. Massage his shoulders and between his toes. Sing to him if you want to. He won't know if you are off-key but he will love hearing your voice. He will feel loved and very special.

While you are grooming and consciously looking for hair mats or cutting toenails, you are also looking for skin irritations, sores, lumps, hot spots, ear infections, eye infections, and other health issues. Concentrating on your puppy enables you to do a quick health check.

When the job is done, you'll have a great sense of satisfaction. The results will be a noticeable improvement. The two of you did this project together, and other people will admire it.

Grooming Supplies

At the very beginning, you won't need a great many grooming tools.

- A soft brush will get the puppy used to brushing.
- A nail clipper.
- A pair of dog scissors, possible with blunt ends, to cut out mats and trim ears and the bottoms of feet.
- Puppy shampoo.
- Soft towels and a hair dryer.
- Possibly a ribbon for a topknot and some tiny rubber bands.
- Soft toothbrush and dog toothpaste.

How to Start Grooming Your Puppy

Your job is to make this early grooming fun. Talk to your puppy in a friendly voice, even if he wiggles. Your tone of voice is very important. You should be firm and matter-of-fact, happy not angry or frustrated, even if at first he does not cooperate.

Brushing

Start out by holding the puppy in your lap and, using a soft brush, gently stroke his head and back. Keep your voice encouraging and affectionate. Offer tiny treats every so often. Make the first sessions short. When he is a little older, you can try brushing him on a table covered with a towel. Be careful to hold him securely with one hand. Keep these first table sessions very short.

Toenails

The next job is to cut his toenails. Using a nail clipper, trim the tip off each toenail. If he resists, clip just one toenail and stop for the day. Tomorrow, try for two toenails. Do not attempt to overpower the puppy or make nail cutting a do-or-die confrontation. Of course you would win. You are bigger. But what we want is for the puppy to learn to cooperate. He should learn that grooming is an ordinary occurrence that can even be fun. Teaching that lesson can be a slow process but well worth it.

Later in the day, when you have the puppy on your lap while you are watching television or talking on the phone or reading, handle his feet almost in a distracted way, as if it weren't that important to you. Pick up a foot and rub the bottom. Then rub the top of his foot. Scratch it. Massage it. Make sure that within a day or two, you have handled all four feet in this way, casually and as if it were no big deal. Keep handling his feet this way until cutting his toenails is also no big deal.

Use a nail clipper to trim your puppy's toenails.

Brushing the Tummy

The desensitization technique used for getting your puppy used to having his feet touched also works if brushing his stomach proved difficult. Start massaging his stomach, gently, softly when he is sitting on your lap or lying next to you at a time of day when you are not set up for grooming. Use your fingers to comb through his hair. You are just a dog and a person, having fun together. Make it seem like a good thing but again, not a big deal. Send the dog a message: This is just what we do here.

Bathing

Occasionally you may have to bathe your puppy, even if you use a professional groomer. Puppies will find the only mud puddle in the backyard, or they will manage to knock over a can of soda and play in the sticky mess. In any home emergency, a sink with warm water and a small bit of dog shampoo will soon put things right.

It is a good idea to fill the sink with an inch or two of warm water and splash a little with one hand while holding the puppy with the other. His curiosity will soon take over and he will want to feel the water. Lower him gently into the sink and continue to hold him with one hand. Use a cup or hose to gently wet his hair, scrub a little shampoo into his hair, then rinse. Be sure to rinse all the shampoo out. Talk gently to your puppy, and work quickly. Hold him securely so he feels safe, and do not pour water over his head.

If just his feet and belly are muddy, try a soapy bath: put a little shampoo in the sink while the warm water is running. Put the puppy in the soapy water and massage his feet and belly until the mud has dissolved. Then pick the puppy up and rinse with lukewarm water from a cup or hose until all the shampoo is gone.

Be sure to keep your puppy as warm as possible. Dry him as quickly as possible. Use soft towels and pat him dry, so you do not rub mats into his hair. Then, always use a hair dryer on low heat, so he won't get chilled.

Hair Trimming

Some people like to tie a topknot on their Yorkie's head with a rubber band and cover it with a ribbon. Puppies, of course, do not come with enough hair to make that necessary but as your puppy gets a little older, it can be a cute addition—even if strictly speaking, the hair isn't ready to fall in his eyes yet.

As your Yorkie gets a little older, hair may grow unsightly around his feet. You can trim away that shaggy look with an ordinary scissors or a blunt-ended scissors if your Yorkie cooperates by standing still.

Another area that may need occasional trimming is the ear tip. The ears of a Yorkshire Terrier should be upright and free of long hair

Teach your puppy to like teeth cleaning by making it fun. Start by wrapping your index finger in a thin cloth or piece of gauze. Spread some dog toothpaste on your finger and talk in a soft but excited voice to your puppy. Be sure to rub his gums as well as his teeth.

for the top third. If your Yorkie's ears are folded over, it may be from the weight of hair. Hold the ears upright with your fingers along the edges. Trim the hair close to your fingers with a scissors. Go slow. It may take two days to do both ears. And remember, hair grows fast. If you have trouble cutting a straight-line at first, you can count on lots of practice to improve your scissors skills.

Teeth

Yorkies are one of the many small breeds that have issues with their teeth. A soft toothbrush and dog toothpaste will help you keep your puppy's teeth clean. Do not use human toothpaste. Dog toothbrushes can look like human brushes, or they can look like a ribbed rubber thimble that fits over your index finger. This toothbrush has knobs that rub the teeth and gum. Some dog owners use gauze pads. You can rotate them or find the one you like and use that. See "Training Tidbit" box on this page for how to get your puppy used to having his teeth brushed.

HEALTH

It's important for you to learn to do a few health procedures, such as taking a dog's temperature and giving a pill. You will also develop a sixth sense about your Yorkie's general health, being able to predict when he is coming down with something. But in the end, you should rely on your vet for major medical advice and treatment. It's best to leave some things in the hands of professionals. Your vet has both the education and the experience to help your Yorkie live his life in the best of health.

Finding a Veterinarian

Your vet is really one of the most important allies you can have in your quest to raise a healthy puppy. A good veterinarian is one who not only supplies timely and accurate medical care but one who also supports you and takes your concerns seriously. A vet is someone who can help you in a medical crisis, but also at well-puppy checkups with advice and dog wisdom. A good vet for you and your Yorkie may not be the same good vet who takes care of your friend's giant working dog or your sister's cat. Trust your instincts and pick a vet you can talk to and call, even when you are not sure anything is wrong.

Start selecting a vet even before you get your puppy. Ask Yorkie owners or owners of other toy dogs what veterinary care they have and how they like it. Visit a couple vet offices before you get your puppy. Ask at the desk if they are taking new patients, what is the fee for an ordinary office visit, if they have more than one vet in the office, or what they do for patients when the vet goes on vacation or gets sick. Ask if they can do x-rays, teeth cleaning, and other basics, such as run some blood tests.

Sit in the waiting room and watch people check in with animals. The desk staff should like animals and respond to the various ones who come in, especially dogs who are obviously sick. The waiting room should not be chock full of people and animals who

Multi-Dog Tip

If you have an older dog and a puppy, let the puppy watch as you cut the older dog's nails. Then say, "Puppy's turn," pick up the puppy and start cutting his nails. He may accept it faster as just something dogs do in this house.

Your vet is one of the most important allies you can have in your quest to raise a healthy puppy.

have been waiting an hour or more. No smell should be obvious. No sounds of animals in distress or fighting should be heard. The office should have veterinary technicians who can answer some of your questions.

The vet's office should be close enough to your house that you can get there in relatively good time if your Yorkie gets sick. Out-of-town vets may be useful as specialists, but for every day animal care, you need someone close by.

If you are interested in health insurance for your Yorkie, ask if the office staff will help you when it's time to file a claim. Forms have to be filled out and signed. Sometimes receipts have to be sent in and extra copies are required. Busy vet offices have to make time for something that didn't exist when many vets were in school. Ask to find out how they would react to this inconvenience.

Vets' offices should have free community information available to pet owners, such as training classes, order forms for identification tags, and flyers about local fund-raisers for rescue or pet health. Vets are a big part of the pet community, and local involvement is a good sign.

New Puppy Physical

Make an appointment for your new puppy's physical examination as soon as you know when you are getting the puppy, but before you actually have him, if possible. Try to go the same day you get the puppy or the next day. On the day you go, collect a stool sample from the puppy in a sealable plastic bag with your name written on it. Take any health papers the breeder may have given you, especially any record of vaccinations and microchip numbers. Put a collar and a leash on your puppy but carry him into the vet's office, either in your arms or in a carrier. Unvaccinated puppies should not walk on floors where sick dogs may have been. Hand the stool sample in to the desk as soon as you get there; they can start processing it so the results are ready before you leave.

Your puppy will be weighed. The vet will listen to his heart and lungs, move his legs, feel his belly, look into his eyes, ears, and mouth. His stool will be checked for worms. No blood test will be done for heartworm because the puppy is too young to have developed it. You may, however, leave with some heartworm preventive to give your puppy immediately, in case he has worms and to prevent heartworm.

Then your puppy will be vaccinated or a vaccination schedule will be set up.

Now is when you should ask all the questions that keep you awake at night. At a new puppy exam, almost no question is foolish. Ask about heartworm preventive, vaccinations, food, water, fleas, worms, teeth, biting, dog sweaters and when to use them,

Make an appointment for your puppy's first physical before you bring him home.

Lyme disease vaccination is only recommended for a few dogs in very highly infested areas.

liver shunts, neutering, temperament. Most vets will answer behavior questions and then offer you names of local trainers.

The first question you should ask is: Is the puppy healthy enough to keep? You may have fallen in love with your puppy already, but a seriously sick Yorkie puppy is a challenge to raise and very expensive. If the vet finds evidence of a serious genetic defect, at least consider taking the puppy back to the breeder.

The second question to ask yourself when you get home is: Do I like this vet and the way this office runs, or should I find another right away? Did I feel comfortable talking to the vet tech? Can I afford this vet?

Vaccinations

Your puppy probably had one or even two sets of vaccination shots at the breeder's. One set is not enough. Puppies should be vaccinated every month until they are at least four months old. Diseases puppies may be vaccinated against include:

- Adenoviruses that cause respiratory infections and infectious viral hepatitis.
- Bordetella or kennel cough, a bacteria that

invades the respiratory system.

- Coronavirus, a virus that affects the intestines.
- Distemper, a virus that attacks several systems in the dog at the same time (respiratory, gastrointestinal, central nervous system).
- Leptospirosis, a bacterial disease that can damage the liver or the kidneys.
- Lyme disease, which is caused by bacteria from a tick, usually a deer tick.
- Parainfluenza, a virus that causes an upper respiratory infection.
- Parvovirus, a virus that causes an intestinal infection.
- Rabies, a virus that affects the nervous system.

Core Versus Noncore

Veterinarians divide vaccines into *core vaccines* that no puppy should go without and *noncore vaccines* that are given at the discretion of the vet and the dog owner. The American Veterinary Medical Association (AVMA) classifies rabies, parvovirus, distemper, and adenovirus-2 for hepatitis as core vaccinations.

Some of the vaccines have been combined to reduce the number of injections your puppy will get. The DHLPP shot protects your puppy against distemper, hepatitis, leptospirosis, parvovirus, and parainfluenza—all the core vaccines except rabies. The rabies shot is always a separate shot and given when your puppy is a little bit older.

The noncore vaccines vary by geography and the type of things your dog does. Only your veterinarian knows what diseases are in your community this year and what noncore vaccinations you should use. Vaccinations against bordetella, for example, are common for dogs who spend time with other dogs, such as at dog parks, dog shows, or boarding kennels. The disease is highly contagious. The vaccines do not prevent 100 percent of kennel cough cases, but one puppy barking with the unique sound of kennel cough may convince you to have all your puppies vaccinated in the future. Plus, bordetella bacteria in a puppy's respiratory system can result in pneumonia. The bordetella vaccine can be given as a few drops dripped into your puppy's nose or it can be injected.

Lyme disease vaccination is only recommended for a few dogs in very highly infested areas.

Vaccination Controversy

Vaccinations, tested and used for generations of dogs, are considered safe for most puppies, but they may have side effects. Dogs may have an allergic reaction to the vaccine that can be fatal in a small number of cases. Other dogs that have allergies may have more severe symptoms after a shot. The injection site may be painful and swollen. Some dogs may have a slight fever and loss of appetite.

The controversy surrounding vaccinations has grown in recent years. Vaccinations successfully prevent and have almost eradicated some diseases in dogs, such as rabies. But dogs still need rabies vaccinations because every year rabid animals, such as feral cats, bats, squirrels, or skunks, bite dogs. If that

Vaccines are divided into core and noncore.

Hypoglycemia affects mostly puppies younger than four months, but it can be seen in smaller dogs a month or two after that.

dog then bites a human, the result is serious and can be fatal if treatment is not started quickly.

The debate is over how often dogs need a vaccination booster. Some tests seem to indicate that protection against disease from vaccination lasts longer than originally thought. In 2009, Alabama became the last state to drop its annual rabies booster requirement. Dogs in Alabama can now get a booster every three years if the owner prefers, but also can get the old annual booster. Some advocates of fewer vaccinations suggest owners talk to their vets about testing for effectiveness by measuring blood titers instead of routinely scheduling boosters every year. A blood titer will show how much immunity the dog has against a disease and whether a booster is necessary that year. This is recommended especially for dogs who have had routine boosters for several years.

But this debate does not affect your puppy. He needs his puppy shots now. Be prepared to return to the vet on a regular schedule until he has finished them.

Puppy Ailments

Puppies are susceptible to a wide variety of diseases. They are born with a certain amount of immunity that they get from their mothers, but this only lasts a few weeks, depending on when the mother was vaccinated.

Most experts suggest unvaccinated puppies stay away from dogs we can't be sure are vaccinated until the puppies have had all their shots. But, and this may sound surprising, unvaccinated puppies should also stay away from empty places that are heavily used by dogs, such as dog parks and even some sidewalks used by dogs who no one picks up after. Puppies can get diseases from dog urine and feces they lick off their feet or off a toy like a tennis ball that rolls through one or the other.

Demodectic Mange

Demodectic mange is a skin condition puppies can get from their mother. Healthy dogs carry an unknown number of mites (demodex) on their skin but, in some dogs, the number of mites gets out of control. The dog's immune system for some reason can't control them. The dog's skin becomes inflamed, and he may lose some hair, usually in patches. A vet should scrape some cells from the skin and determine if it contains mites. Sometimes demodectic mange goes away by itself as the puppy grows and his immune system gets stronger. In those cases, nutrition and supplements become even more important to boost the immune system. In severe cases, treatment is available.

Hypoglycemia

Hypoglycemia or low blood sugar is something owners of young Yorkshire Terrier puppies should be on the lookout for every day. Because Yorkies are so little, they have small reserves of energy, and this sometimes run out before mealtime. This may happen sooner in cool temperatures. Hypoglycemic puppies become listless and, in severe cases, can have seizures or become disoriented. Experienced Yorkie breeders keep a simple sugar, such as corn syrup, on hand. Emergency treatment is to rub corn syrup on the puppy's gums. If he recovers in a few minutes, feed him. If he does not seem better in a very short time, call a vet. When you get home, shorten the time between meals for a while. Be sure your diet is appropriate for a toy puppy and is high enough in carbohydrates, proteins, and fats. Make sure your training treats are not replacing a balanced meal.

Other causes of hypoglycemia in puppies are exhaustion from too much play, an upset stomach, and chilling. All use energy reserves the puppy may not have.

Hypoglycemia affects mostly puppies younger than four months, but it can be seen in smaller dogs a month or two after that.

Kennel Cough

Kennel cough is a respiratory ailment that can be caused by a virus and a bacteria your puppy gets from other dogs. It is highly contagious. Puppies with kennel cough have a honking cough and other respiratory symptoms that can last 10 days. Sometimes kennel cough is very mild and needs little or no treatment. In other cases, a vet will prescribe an antibiotic. A vaccine that comes in the form of nose drops protects against some but not all causes of kennel cough. Because

Roundworm is a common parasite that affects puppies.

kennel cough is so contagious, dog facilities, such as boarding kennels, frequently require dogs be vaccinated against it.

Parvo

Parvovirus can be especially deadly to a small puppy. First identified in the early 1970s, parvo affects dogs of all ages. Sick dogs vomit and have bloody diarrhea that is highly contagious. A puppy who comes in contact with contaminated feces and licks it off his feet or hair may come down with symptoms a week or two later. The AVMA says no medicine can cure parvo, but its symptoms can be managed to reduce the chance of fatality. Hospitalization is common because puppies with parvo are frequently dehydrated. Vaccination can prevent parvo but not all the time. If you have had parvo in your house, clean contaminated areas with a bleach solution. Parvo is very hardy and tough to kill.

Roundworm

Roundworm is a common parasite that affects puppies. It causes diarrhea. Puppies who have diarrhea when they come from the breeder should have a stool sample checked for roundworms. Roundworms are spread when puppies eat contaminated feces or other things off ground that has been contaminated. The contamination can come from other dogs or even mice that share a yard or basement with puppies. Your vet can effectively treat roundworms with two doses of worming medicines repeated to cover the entire roundworm life cycle. Some heartworm medicines are effective against roundworms. Extra sanitation is required to avoid contaminating the puppy's environment and reinfecting the puppy later. Roundworm eggs can live outside the puppy in the soil for a long time. If your puppy has roundworms, pick up his contaminated feces immediately and seal them in a plastic bag. Scrub solid surfaces, such as cement patios, with a bleach solution. Indoors, feces should also be picked up immediately, and floors should be cleaned. In extreme cases, contaminated soil may have to be removed or turned under. Wash your hands after cleaning the puppy's area, because roundworms can be passed to people.

Spaying and Neutering

If you bought a Yorkie puppy as a pet, your breeder may have required you to sign a contract promising to spay or neuter your dog. Breeding Yorkshire Terriers and raising a litter are highly specialized occupations that require extensive knowledge and experience. A breeder has to be able to look at the pedigree of a breeding dog and know whether that dog would be right to breed to hers. Decisions have to be based on genetic information, size, and appearance. Even after years of experience, breeders sometimes whelp puppies with serious health issues or lose a mother dog during delivery and have to raise the puppies themselves. There are no guarantees in dog breeding, and it is no place for the underinformed.

Spaying and neutering have several advantages to a pet owner. Females will no longer spot the carpet when they are in season twice a year, or have hormonal fluctuations that cause their coat to fall out. Each season lasts three weeks, and during that time the dog must be kept confined or under supervision, and must wear "pants" when in the house. These pants are secured with Velcro strips—like a baby diaper—and include a pad that catches the seasonal bloody discharge. The pads are washable or disposable. Neutered males may have less need to mark a

Breeding dogs requires specialzed knowledge and experience—it's best left to the experts.

room with urine or roam outside your yard, looking for a mate.

Spay Surgery

In a spay surgery, the vet will remove the ovaries and uterus. It is major abdominal surgery. When the puppy comes home, she will have a shaved area on her belly and an incision. Dogs who want to lick the incision must be discouraged by an Elizabethan collar (a big cone of plastic or stiff fabric) or some other device that she wears over her own collar. Once she has recovered from the anesthetic and the pain medication and the incision heals, her personality will return. Spaying does not affect a dog's personality, except to even it out. She loses the seasonal highs and lows. Spayed bitches are not fat or lazy unless they eat too much and don't get enough exercise.

Neutering Surgery

In neutering surgery, the vet will remove the dog's testicles. The male will come home with enough pain medication for a few days and also must be discouraged with an Elizabethan collar or some other device from obsessively

Spaying and neutering have many advantages to pet owners.

licking the surgery site. He must be kept on leash when outside to prevent running and opening the wound.

Some breeders believe that the earlier you neuter a male, the less likely the chances are that he will spray urine in the house, to mark his territory. Neutering is also recommended as a partial solution for some male-on-male dog aggression. But the puppy's basic personality remains the same.

How Old?

Some Yorkie breeders and shelters now spay or neuter a puppy before placing it in a pet home to ensure that these puppies are never used for breeding. This means tiny puppies—only a few pounds (kg)—are undergoing surgery, a still-controversial idea. "Some people spay them at twelve weeks," Carl Yochum, president of the Yorkshire Terrier Club of America, says. "I think that's too young." Yochum prefers to wait to spay a bitch until right before or right after her first season but in any event, before she is one year old. But he doesn't have an issue with neutering a male dog at twelve weeks. "It's not as major a surgery," he says. Males should be neutered before they start lifting their leg to urinate, he says. Pet owners who buy a puppy who has not been spayed or neutered should talk to their vet, Yochum says.

Several things may affect your decision on when to spay or neuter your Yorkie. Traditionally, dogs were spayed and neutered at six months of age. Research has shown that females who are spayed before their first or at least their second heat season have greatly reduced rates of mammary gland cancer. Many females come into season for the first time at seven or eight months, so spaying her at six months makes sense from that point of view. But waiting until seven or eight months has an additional advantage for Yorkie puppies. While your puppy is under anesthesia, the vet can also pull any baby teeth that are left in your puppy's mouth, a common experience with Yorkies. Baby teeth that are left in must be pulled while a puppy is under anesthesia and anesthesia for tiny dogs is always riskier than it is for large dogs. Doing two procedures for the risk of one anesthesia is a very good idea.

Expect to have more than the usual office-visit blood work done before any surgery. Recovery should be relatively quick and uncomplicated. Your dog will come home with some pain medication and reduced exercise instructions. The hardest part may be to keep your dog from running too soon.

Want to Know More?

For more information about health issues affecting the Yorkie, see Chapter 8: Yorkshire Terrier Health

CHAPTER 4

TRAINING YOUR YORKSHIRE TERRIER PUPPY

You've researched the breed. You've found your puppy. You've brought him home. And now you just want to love him and protect him. He's so little, you think. He's too little for anything as serious as training.

Well, he may be little. He may need to be loved and protected. But he also needs training. It's right up there on the list of things he really can't do without.

Poorly behaved dogs have a greater chance of ending up in a rescue or shelter. They are the cause of friction between dog owner and guests, especially extended family members who come for holidays. They also get stuck at home more because they can't be trusted not to snarl at people out in society.

So, be kind to your puppy. Start training, right from the beginning.

WHY TRAIN?

Why is training so important? It will make your Yorkie easier to live with and improve your relationship with him. Just as food nourishes your puppy's body and helps him grow into a strong healthy dog, training helps his personality develop into one that likes people and can live with them easily and anywhere. It teaches him a default behavior that keeps him out of trouble (sit) and makes people happy (shake or rollover). When people are happy, good things happen to dogs. They are included more often in human activities. Training teaches your puppy the language of people—words he can't live without. Puppies aren't born understanding human words. They have to be taught. Teaching your puppy words is training. It is as simple and unstructured as that. Stanley Coren, a scientist who researches the dog–human bond, estimates that dogs learn about 165 words. Dogs who don't learn human words and what is expected of them are hard to live with and often end up in rescue. They stay home alone instead of going out and about with their people. These are the dogs who people shy away from at the dog park or sidewalk café because they are so unpleasant. All of that can be avoided with consistent, daily training.

Consistency is one of the most important things you can practice when you train a dog. Set up a routine for a command and follow it every time you say the command, so the dog knows exactly what he is supposed to do to make you happy. Expect your dog to follow the command, and he will absorb that

Find a trainer who uses positive, fun training methods.

message and be more eager to comply. If you are half-hearted or don't really care, the dog will absorb that message, too, and not try very hard to comply. Yes, they are that smart, even as puppies.

POSITIVE TRAINING

Training today is called *positive training* because it reinforces the positive things the dog does and ignores most of the negatives. The idea is to catch your dog doing something good and praise him. Positive training does not include punishment for bad behavior. It can include picking up a puppy who is urinating on the carpet, saying "no," and putting him in his potty place; it does not include hitting him or rubbing his nose in anything or shaking him by his scruff. It can include saying "no" when your puppy tries to bite you; it does not include any kind of physical or verbal punishment.

Pat Miller, a dog trainer, wrote in the classic, *The Power of Positive Dog Training,* "Positive reinforcement training opens the door to your dog's mind. It gives you and your dog the keys to understanding each other's alien cultures."

With that kind of communication, it is only natural that positive training cements the bond between owner and dog. It affords the dog the respect that a living creature is entitled, and encourages the dog to respect you in return. Since dogs are hard-wired to respect their people anyway, training can help forge the bond even faster.

Positive trainers work *with* the dog, not against his natural instincts. In positive training, trainers sometimes allow the dog to offer different behaviors. If you say, "down," the dog may sit. If you don't respond, the dog may offer a paw to shake. If you don't respond, the dog may roll over on his back, exposing his stomach. But eventually the dog may offer the down. Then, when you reward the down with praise and treats, your puppy is on the road to learning a new word and learning how to solve a problem.

Positive trainers usually advertise they are positive trainers. They will mention that in any introductory conversation or class. If not, you should ask about their training philosophy. Avoid any trainers who talk about making the dog see who is dominant in the relationship. Positive trainers talk about leadership.

FINDING A TRAINER

Because training is so important, finding a trainer is also important—especially if this is your first puppy or your first small-breed puppy. It is also important if you have not had a puppy in some years—a decade or more—and need a refresher course. Finally, it is important if you have never worked with the principles of positive training, since dog training has changed in the past few years.

Word of mouth is still the best way to find a trainer. Ask people you know who have small dogs if they have a trainer. Ask friends with bigger dogs if their trainer works with small dogs and uses positive training methods. Ask your vet for help you find a trainer. Check out vet offices for flyers on dog training classes. Trainers sometimes leave class information at vet offices or pet supply stores. Some trainers work through community education centers or animal shelters. Big pet supply stores now offer puppy classes in the store. Call for information on small dogs in classes.

This adds up to a variety of options. Choose one that fits your family, whether the classes are every day for two weeks or 90-minute or 45-minute classes once a week. Choose a trainer you can work with, someone who allows family members to observe and who seems to genuinely like dogs. And choose a trainer who likes small dogs and can work with them. Sit in on classes before your puppy comes. See if you like the approach the trainer takes. Check if toy dogs are in the class and if the instructor seems to know how to train a small dog.

You may be surprised to find most of the class is aimed at the people. The puppies may spend half of the class sitting while the instructor talks to you or demonstrates what she is teaching with her own dog.

A couple reasons are behind that. First of

By the Numbers

Your puppy is never too young to start socialization and training. Whether you get your puppy at 8 weeks or 16 weeks, start training and socializing your dog right away. Offer him new experiences, ask him to sit before he gets a treat, and just expect him to be a good dog. Dogs live up to our expectations.

all, you are the one really training the puppy. The trainer should be able to explain to you what to do at home. A dog trainer who is good with dogs but not with people is not what you want, at least for a class. Second, a puppy can't concentrate for an hour. It's too exhausting. Your puppy needs some down time between exercises.

You may wonder why the dog can't stay home. But learning to relax in a stressful situation, surrounded by other dogs and strangers, is a good socialization experience for your puppy. A professional dog trainer can train a dog in much less time than you can—or in much less time than she can teach you to train him—but the purpose of going to class with your puppy is to learn more about each other. A training class is a shared experience you have with your puppy. The puppy has to learn to cooperate with you, not just the dog trainer.

SOCIALIZATION

A well-socialized dog is a joy to live with. That should be your goal. Getting there takes some effort. Puppies have to be socialized almost from the beginning with other dogs, other pets, children, men, women, cars, and other places you are likely to go. Puppies need to learn that life holds different types of experiences and most of them are fun. Just because your dog is little doesn't mean you can skimp on socialization.

Having your puppy meet a toy dog who you know is vaccinated and healthy is an excellent way to start socialization.

Take him everywhere you possibly can. Give him as many different experiences as you can think of. Let him see and smell things he can't at home.

He should meet the world on his own four feet and learn that, basically, it's a good place. Dogs who are afraid of new experiences frequently withdraw, bite, or destroy whatever they can get their teeth on, such as crate blankets or your pants leg.

Socialization can produce a happy, confident dog who takes life's surprises in stride.

How to Socialize Your Yorkie

"They should take them—once they've had all their shots—to a pet store and let them learn life, especially if they just have one dog," Carl Yochum, president of the Yorkshire Terrier Club of America, says. Most pet stores allow vaccinated dogs on leashes inside. People who work in pet stores will usually make a fuss over your puppy and even offer him a treat. So, the puppy has a positive experience outside his home and feels good about going out the next time you say, "Let's go!"

Contrast that to the dog who never goes anywhere but to the vet. He is terrified of getting in the car because he thinks bad things will happen.

Yochum says puppy owners should also take their puppy on walks, to the mall, to meet other people and dogs. "It just makes a better dog," Yochum says. "You don't want one who is scared of the world. People protect them, and they don't ever see anything. If you socialize them, they will be happy no matter where they are. You want a friendly dog."

People are inclined to protect Yorkies more than say, a German Shepherd Dog, because Yorkies seem so small and vulnerable. They also can get the exercise they need in a large house or a big yard. But socialization is not about the exercise. It's about mental stimulation and confidence building.

Meet and Greet

Before your puppy is completely vaccinated, as well as after, invite people to your place to meet your puppy. Someone with another toy dog who you know is vaccinated and healthy would be an excellent idea. But people—especially people who are not like you in size, age, or gender—are the best idea. Invite your friends in ones and twos to play with the puppy and offer him a small treat. Again, the puppy has a good time with a stranger and learns he doesn't have to be afraid or bite a stranger. He learns people can come into his home without disaster striking. That is an important lesson for a dog with a terrier's territorial instinct.

Be sure to include a child or two in your puppy's world. Children have a different sound to their voices and a different way of moving that can startle dogs who have never had experiences with children. Allow children to give your puppy a treat or play with a new toy with them.

After he is vaccinated, take him to a puppy kindergarten class that is just for fun. Let him play with other puppies. Take him places where he has to walk on different textures. Some parks have grass, gravel, sand, wood chips, wooden bridges over creeks, and even metal grates. Don't avoid places

A group training class can help socialize your Yorkie

just because they are loud or busy. Your puppy should learn that sometimes the world is loud and busy, but he can trust you to take him through it safely. Don't coddle him if a train goes by and scares him. Just matter-of-factly say something like, "Well, there goes the train," and act like it's no big deal. Your Yorkie is looking to you for clues to this big new world. If you act like he shouldn't be afraid, he won't be.

Puppy Kindergarten

The first training class your puppy will be eligible for is puppy kindergarten. When to take the class depends on the requirements of your trainer, but most will require some vaccinations and the paperwork to prove it. Photocopy the health records the breeder gave you and whatever records the vet gave you at your first appointment. It is handy to have spare copies you can carry to classes and not worry about losing.

Take a puppy kindergarten class as soon as your local trainer allows. Your puppy may be too young to concentrate on lessons but the experience of going somewhere fun with you and coping with other dogs and people is invaluable. This is socialization that cannot be duplicated when the puppy is an adult. Now is the time to show him what life is like so he can learn not to fear it.

Socialization at three, four, and five months of age comes when the puppy is most open to new things and can make them a part of his adult self. It is easier and more appropriate than socialization at seven or eight months, but if you got your puppy at eight months, don't give up. Your puppy will learn to accept new things because he trusts you. Dogs can learn behavior at any age.

In a puppy kindergarten class, all the dogs are healthy and have had at least some of their shots, so it is considered safe for puppies who have not finished their vaccinations.

Your puppy should be used to a leash and collar, although walking nicely on a leash may be some ways off. The trainer will most likely work on a few basic commands, such as "Sit," and talk about puppy behavior problems, such as chewing. The trainer can be a helpful resource for specific issues you may be having. Other dog owners may also be a resource. Compare notes, and sometimes you will be happy to go home with the dog you have rather than the dog next to you.

Finding the Right Puppy Kindergarten

Finding the right puppy kindergarten for you and your dog is important. Ask if the trainer has small-dog experience and if there are any other toy dogs in the class. Ask how many dogs are in the class. If there are more than a handful, the trainer should have a helper. Find a class not too far from your home and in a clean and safe place, including the parking lot. The trainer should have cleaning supplies on hand in case one of the puppies has a housetraining accident. This happens regularly, and no one should react angrily. It is a fact of life with young puppies. If it happens to you, ask where the cleaning supplies are and quickly clean up. No excuses are necessary.

Bring your own high-quality soft treats—crunchy biscuits are not a good idea since they take so long to eat—and be prepared to go through more treats than you do at home. Hot dogs cut into small pieces or leftover chicken make good training treats. The trainer may also have treats she offers your puppy. She wants your puppy to learn that a stranger can be a good thing.

At the end of the class, she may offer a playtime for the puppies. This is an off-leash opportunity for your puppy to play with others. Most puppies will run excitedly from puppy to puppy. Some may start a chase game. Others may wrestle. Some may prefer to meet the people in the class, going from person to person looking for affection. Watch your puppy carefully during this time. Yorkies are terriers and do not know how small they are. They may take on the biggest puppy or one that may not know how to wrestle with a three-pound puppy.

After this much excitement, your puppy should be given potty time before you get in a car. He should sleep well.

When you are searching for a puppy kindergarten, be sure to ask if the class includes training or just socialization and if it is set up for young toy puppies. Ask your Yorkie-owning friends or your vet if they know of any puppy kindergartens good for small puppies.

Turning your back on a puppy who is misbehaving can sometimes stop the behavior. Any attention—even displeasure—is better than none to a puppy. So turn around, cross your arms, and don't say a word. Praise your puppy if he stops what he was doing.

CRATE TRAINING

Some people have an aversion to crates. They think of them as cages or prisons. But many experienced dog owners tell stories of puppies choosing to spend time in their crate. Overwhelmed by too many new things in a day, these puppies took refuge in a crate whose door was left open, curled up and went to sleep, safe and happy.

Dogs tend to think of a crate as a den. It's their bed, their safe place. Puppy owners can take advantage of this. A crate becomes a good thing.

It is also a safe place where you know your puppy can't get into trouble or get hurt. Sometimes that is the most important thing.

What Is Crate Training?

A crate is a tool that puppy owners use in successful housetraining. Dogs are hard-wired to avoid soiling their nests. So, if a puppy sees the crate as his nest, he will try to hold his urine while he is in it. He gets used to the idea of holding it for longer and longer periods.

In order for crate training to work, several things have to happen.

The Crate

The crate itself should be just big enough for the puppy to stand up and turn around. If the crate is too big, the puppy may end up using a far corner of it as his potty place. Wire crates can be purchased with an adjustable insert that can reduce the size of the crate the puppy is allowed to use. Later you can remove the insert and allow the full grown dog use of the entire crate. To increase the feeling of a den, some owners put a blanket or towel on top of a wire crate and drape it down one or both sides. At first, you should use an old blanket or towel because puppies may pull part of the towel into the crate and chew on it. The crate can also be placed up against a wall or in a corner to increase the puppy's sense of security.

Small plastic crates, like those Nylabone makes, are easy to carry from room to room and have solid sides that make the puppy feel like he is in a safe den.

Soft-sided crates or purse carriers should not be used for crate training. Puppies like to chew fabric and may be able to chew their way out.

Location

Whether you have a wire crate or a plastic carrier, put it in a quiet place not too far from the sounds of the household. A basement or upstairs bedroom is not a good place because it is too far from the activity center of the family. A first-floor bedroom or laundry room near a kitchen or a corner in a large kitchen or family room is a better place.

How to Crate Train

Life with a dog is easier if the puppy likes his crate. This may seem counterintuitive to first-time crate users but it can happen. In fact, it most probably will happen with just a little help from you. Start off with a clean crate in the middle of a room that the puppy uses. Put a new toy in the crate. Leave the door open. Let the puppy sniff around and go in the crate and come out with the new toy. Play with the puppy and his toy. Then show him a treat and toss it in the crate, still with the door open. Let the puppy retrieve a few treats from the crate. Then, after you toss a treat in, shut the door for a few seconds. Talk matter-of-factly to your puppy. Do not say things like, "Poor puppy, stuck in a crate." Your tone of voice will convey the message to the puppy even if he can't understand the words. Open the door. Repeat this a few times. Play with the puppy until you know he is very tired. Take him to his potty place, then put him in the crate with a small blanket or towel and shut the door. Offer him a treat through the door and leave. He should go right to sleep because he is tired.

Crates can be used for successful housetraining.

Don't stay where the puppy can see you, and don't let him out if he cries. He is most likely surprised and not sure of himself. Never open the crate when the puppy is crying. Always wait until he has been quiet for at least a few seconds before you let him out.

Feed your puppy in his crate, so he learns that good things happen in the crate. Put the puppy in his crate several times during the day, but only when someone is not available to watch him. In the crate, the puppy is safe and can sleep. But puppies need to do many other things, so crate training only works if the crate is used along with generous play time.

Praise your puppy after he eliminates in the correct spot.

When you are home, play with your puppy near his crate. Leave the door open. He should be able to go in and out when he wants to. Soon he will see it as his bed, a safe and comfortable place where he can go when things get overwhelming. You can help this happen by never using the crate as a place of punishment.

Schedule

Crate training only works if you devise a schedule and stick to it. A young puppy can only be left in the crate for a few hours in the daytime. If you wait too long and the puppy has an accident in the crate, it sets back the whole idea of training.

Every time you open the crate door to let your Yorkie out, carry him to his potty place immediately. Before you put the puppy back in his crate, be sure to take him to his potty place and then throw a small treat in the crate ahead of him.

HOUSETRAINING

Housetraining means teaching your dog to use the potty place that you have selected. He is not allowed to go just anywhere. Teaching Yorkshire Terriers to use a potty place, indoors or out, is challenging, especially for some Yorkies who learn more slowly than others.

"If they get it, they get it," says Carl Yochum, president of the Yorkshire Terrier Club of America. "And if they don't, they don't. They are probably one of the hardest breeds to housetrain as far as you can find."

How to Housetrain

Yorkies can be housetrained. Housetraining any dog requires consistency, patience, and a schedule. With a Yorkie it just may take twice as much of everything . . . or not. It depends on the Yorkie and the breeder he lived with as a newborn.

Timing Your Praise at the Potty Place

Praising a dog who uses the potty place is an art. Timing is everything. As soon as the dog squats down, say, "Good dog" or "Yes" or "Yay!" Don't wait until he's finished and you are picking him up. Dogs live in the moment, and this is one of those moments that has to be pointed out to him as good while he is doing it. Be overly demonstrative, at least at first. Pretend you are in acting class and your grade depends on emotion. Put on a performance your dog will remember.

Before your puppy came to live with you, he lived with his mother in a whelping box. She cleaned up after him. She cleaned the floor. She cleaned him. If she missed anything, the breeder cleaned it up. Life was easy for him.

Then he discovered the world outside the whelping box.

Vicki Meadows, Illinois Yorkie breeder, says that's when she starts training puppies—very early. "At five weeks to six weeks is when my puppies start crawling out of their whelping box," she says. She puts a piddle pad on the floor next to the box and the mother dog uses the piddle pad. The puppies crawl out of the box onto the piddle pad. "They will tinkle right where their mama tinkles," Meadows says. "By the time they are 12 weeks old, they are housetrained. I don't care what anybody says. It's a proven fact with me."

What if your puppy didn't have a breeder like Meadows, and you don't have a mother dog to show the puppy the approved place?

A little equipment can help. Get a crate that is just big enough for your puppy to lie down and turn around. Get some puppy pads that come treated to smell like a potty place (only to the dog. You won't be able to smell anything).

Put your puppy in the crate for an afternoon nap. After an hour or two, open the crate door, pick him up and carry him to the piddle pad or out on the grass. Watch carefully to see if and when he does something. Then praise your puppy. Really praise him. Jump up and down if you want.

Here comes the hard part for some people: If he poops outside, leave it where you want him to poop the next time. Inside, leave the soiled piddle pad in place. Cleaning up may be your first instinct, but puppies come with an urge to go where other dogs—including themselves—have gone before. Smell is how they know that this must be an approved place. Remember that mother dog on the piddle pad? She didn't really show her puppies how to use a piddle pad. She left a scent trail that even five-week-old puppies could read and act on.

Play with your puppy for a while. If he starts to circle around, smelling the ground, pick him up and take him to his potty place. If he goes, praise him and then pick him up and put him in the crate for another nap. Put a treat in the crate before you put the puppy in.

Repeat this process all day every day for several weeks. Housetraining a dog is not a fast one-step project. It takes time—weeks, and for some Yorkies, it may take months.

Yorkie puppies have very small bladders. They need to go to the potty place every time they wake up, finish playing, or eat. At first your puppy will not be able to go six or eight hours between potty breaks during the day, when he is playing and eating. Someone will have to be available to get a very young or very small puppy to the potty place every couple hours. If you remove the water dish an

Hold a treat above your puppy's head to get him to sit.

hour or two before bedtime, it may help your puppy make it through the night. He may be able to go eight hours at night because his metabolism slows while he sleeps. But at the very beginning, he may not make it through the night. You may have to get up and take him to his potty place in the middle of the night.

When Accidents Happen

If your dog has an accident on the carpet or the kitchen floor while you are watching, say, "No" or "oops" or "Uh oh" and pick him up and put him in his potty place. Clean up the accident right away with a special cleaner that removes odors. Don't say anything to him while you are cleaning up. Ignoring bad behavior is one step on the long road to making it go away.

Dogs understand housetraining at different ages. Some pick it up right away. Others may take a few months. It is easier to housetrain a puppy if you have another dog in the house who is already trained and has a potty place. The puppy will follow the older dog to the potty place, smell all the right smells, and imitate what the bigger dog does.

Yelling at a puppy for having an accident doesn't work, especially if the accident happened some time ago. The puppy will look guilty but he really is just upset that you are upset. He won't have a clue why you are upset.

If you catch the puppy having a housetraining accident in the house, say "No!" This is a word that will have the most effect if you use it sparingly. Save it for important things, like when you catch your puppy having a housetraining accident in the house or discover him doing something unsafe, like chewing electrical cords. Other times, use a word like "oops" or "uh oh." The puppy will understand that you are not pleased but it does not have the total shut-down effect a "No!" can have.

When he is urinating on the carpet in front of you, say "No!" Pick him up and put him in the potty place. That's all.

BASIC OBEDIENCE COMMANDS

Right from the beginning, you can work with your puppy on basic obedience. He will come to see your expectations as part of his everyday life. His obedience training may have started with a breeder who has taught him to sit before she feeds him dinner. Yorkshire Terriers are smart enough to pick up basic obedience at a very young age and very quickly if they are happy and learning is fun.

"They are so stinkin' smart," says breeder Vicki Meadows. "Anybody who has a dumb

Yorkie has a Yorkie who's bored to death. They are very intelligent."

But a Yorkie is a terrier, and terriers have minds of their own. Once again, patience and repetition will get you what you want faster than scolding or hitting. And the best tip to remember as you embark on a training goal: A tired Yorkie is a happy Yorkie, and a happy Yorkie is easier to teach. Give your Yorkie enough exercise.

Use tiny treats as a reward. Something your dog can swallow quickly is better than a crunchy biscuit. Try bananas, banana bread, cooked meat, lunchmeat such as bologna, hot dogs, or commercial training liver bits.

The Sit

The sit is the first and easiest command to teach. Your puppy may have learned this from the breeder.

How to Teach Sit

With your puppy standing in front of you, offer him a treat. Put the treat right up to his nose and then move it upward and backward. The puppy will sit in order to keep track of the treat. Praise your puppy and give him the treat.

Be sure to end by saying "Okay" or "That's all" or some other word that tells the puppy it is all right if he stands up. This is the release command and should be used when you are finished with any exercise, not just the sit.

Repeat the sit several times before you actually start using the word. Then say, "Sit" as your puppy's bottom hits the ground.

Keep sessions short, but practice several times a day. Praise your puppy when he does it right and ignore him when he gets distracted. Don't yell or say, "No," if doesn't get it. Just end the session without giving him the treat.

When your puppy has reliably learned to sit when you say, "Sit," work the command into everyday life. Expect him to sit before you put his food dish down, before you open the door to go out, and when guests first enter the house. It will become his default behavior. When he doesn't know what to do, he will sit and look to you for help.

Come (Recall)

The recall—calling your dog and having him come to you—is perhaps the most important command you can teach your puppy, and it may take some time for him to learn. This is a command you should practice even when he is no longer a puppy because it is so important it could save his life someday. If you spot danger, even in the backyard, and call, a dog who comes quickly may avoid injury or even death. If your dog gets loose and runs into the street, the recall may be the only thing that saves him from getting hit by a car or running off and getting lost. Besides, just having a dog that comes in from the yard when you call him the first time makes life easier for you.

One rule: Never call your dog to scold him. Always praise him when he comes. Make him feel he did the right thing by giving up

Multi-Dog Tip

Teaching a puppy "Come" can go faster if you have more than one dog. Put the older dog and the puppy in a room or yard and call them from a distance. The puppy will follow the older dog when he comes. Eventually, you will have to work with the puppy by himself, but he may already understand the command by then.

whatever he was doing to be with you. At least in the beginning, reward him with a treat.

How to Teach Come

Start by putting your puppy on a leash. Step back as far as you can, squat down, open your arms and say his name and the word, "Come." Say it in a happy, higher than usual voice. He will catch the excitement and run toward you. Praise him and offer him a treat. If he does not come right away, call his name again and use the leash to guide him gently to you. Practice several times a day for several days. Then try calling him without squatting down. He should come when you are standing at the end of the leash.

Then find a longer leash or something you can tie to his collar, such as twine or a thin rope. Step back 15 feet (4.5 m) or more and call him. Keep practice fun. Use your voice to keep him excited and reward him with some special treats. Then move to a hallway in the house and try it without a leash. Stand at one end and call your puppy at the other end. Once your puppy will come to you when he is off leash in the house, ask someone to help you. Ask them to stand in a room at one end of your house with a treat your puppy really likes. Move to another room where you can't see that person and call your dog. When your dog comes to you, reward him with lots of praise and a treat. Then ask the second person to call the dog. She should also reward him with lots of praise and treats. Take turns calling your puppy until he comes quickly and reliably every time. He will like this game—two people paying attention to him! Two treats! When your puppy has mastered the indoor off-leash recall, take him outside in a fenced area and repeat all the steps, starting with the puppy on a six-foot (2-m) leash.

If your puppy comes almost every time you call, add a distraction to his training. Ask someone to talk to the puppy while you call him. Wait until he is playing with a toy and then call him. The idea is to teach him to come to you no matter how interesting life seems to be someplace else. Be sure to reward him with lots of praise and a treat he likes.

All this effort will pay off the day the door opens too wide and he slips out.

The Down

Once your puppy sits reliably on command, you can introduce the down. The down is a good command to have when you are out and need to wait, maybe at the vet's office. It is useful at dinnertime. Instead of begging or becoming a nuisance, a dog in the down waits patiently for the people to eat first.

How to Teach Down

You can use food to lure a puppy into a down from a sitting position. Sit on the floor in front of your dog and say, "Sit." Then hold a treat that you know he likes and let him sniff it. Slowly lower the treat to the ground. Be sure not to lean back or pull the puppy out of the sit. Lower the food as close to the puppy as you can get, forcing him into a

Once your puppy sits reliably on command, you can introduce the down.

Yorkies can pick up on housetraining at a young age.

down in order to see the treat. Once his elbows hit the ground, let him have the treat and praise him.

Again, practice a few times before you say the word, "Down." At first, say it when his elbows hit the ground. After he seems to understand, try standing in front of him and repeating the exercise, then saying the command before he does it.

Remember to say your release command when it is okay for your dog to stand up.

Some dogs resist the down more than others. Practice and patience are the only solutions. Extend the down into your regular routine. Tell your dog to "Down" before you give him dinner.

To vary your practice routine, add puppy push-ups after you have taught your dog both "Sit" and "Down." The puppy push-ups reinforce both commands.

Sit or kneel on the floor in front of your puppy with a treat in your hand. Hold the treat up and over his head until he sits. Praise him and give him the treat. Then with another treat immediately lure him into the down, praise him and give him the treat. One sit and one down is one push-up. You can do several in a row without a release command. . . this is a great way to burn off that excess puppy energy!

Walk Nicely on Leash

All obedience training leads to walking on a leash. It is one of the ultimate dog–human activities. A dog comes when you call him, and it is time for a walk. He sits or goes into a down while he waits for you to put the leash on his collar and get yourself ready. Then you go out together on a walk and have an adventure. If he

After a few leash walking sessions in the backyard, move the training to a sidewalk.

walks nicely on the leash, you might walk more often or take longer walks. It is to your dog's advantage that you teach him how to walk on a leash. When you are sick or out of town, friends or dog walkers will take the other end of the leash. Your dog will benefit even more by being a sociable and mannerly walking companion if he can walk on a leash for other people..

How to Teach Walk Nicely

Start with a regular buckle or snap collar, or, if you prefer, a harness. Your dog should already be comfortable wearing a collar or a harness when you start leash training. A 6-foot (2-m) leash is ideal for training but a 4-foot (1 m) leash will do. Pick something lightweight and comfortable for you to hold. Do not use a retractable leash for leash training. Save it for later, when your dog already knows how to walk on a leash.

Start in the house. Put the leash on your puppy's collar and follow him around the house a bit. Then offer him a treat and take a few steps, encouraging him to follow you. Pick a phrase such as, "Let's go" or "This way" to indicate to him that you are ready to walk and lead the way. If the puppy bolts away from you, say, "Let's go" again and walk in the opposite direction. When he starts to follow you, praise him and offer him a small soft treat he can swallow easily. Keep the session short. After a few sessions in the house, move the training to a fenced area.

The idea is to make the puppy understand that

he does not get to pick where you walk but, if he stays with you, he will get treats and praise. What if he wants to go in a different direction, for example, after that squirrel he sees? Trainers offer two ways to teach the dog he has to stay by your side—turning and walking in the direction opposite from where the dog is pulling or simply stopping and waiting until he stops pulling. Either can work. Turning away can get dizzying but it is very demonstrative to the dog. Stopping every time the dog pulls can mean you don't actually walk very far, and the dog may not be sure why you stopped. Either way, for the first week or maybe three, you should not consider leash training an actual walk. This is not time you can count as exercise either for you or the puppy. This is a training session.

When you are ready to try walking outside, start with the puppy and a leash on your left side. This is the universal dog-walking position. If you already have a dog trained to walk on your left side, and you are not training the new puppy for obedience, the show ring, or any other performance activity, consider training him to walk on your right. Then you could walk one dog on the left and one on the right. But Yorkies are so small, many people walk both dogs on the left anyway, with both leashes held in one hand (or on a *brace lead,* which is made for two dogs).

Walk a few steps with the leash in your right hand and a treat in your left. Praise the puppy if he follows you and lean down and give him a treat while you keep walking. If he tries to run off to the left, make a sharp right turn and keep walking. If he runs to the right, turn left and continue walking.

If you choose to just stop when he veers away, start walking again when the leash is slack and he is looking at you, wondering what happened. Say, "Let's go" and keep going in the direction you were heading.

When you want to stop, say, "Stop." After a few times, the puppy will associate that word with actually stopping. Eventually, you can add, "Sit," and before you know it, your dog will sit when you stop. But that is several steps away.

After a few sessions in the backyard, move the training to a sidewalk. The distractions will increase, and you may have to start over. But the puppy should catch up quickly. He is already familiar with the commands and what you expect. Now he has to learn to cooperate, even though something in that bush is distracting him. Use attractive treats, so that you are more exciting than the bushes. Some puppies may be startled or frightened by loud cars or trucks passing by. Keep walking matter-of-factly, saying "Let's go!" in a cheerful voice so your puppy understands that you are not afraid of the cars. Don't pick him up when he is afraid. That reinforces his fear and tells him he was right to be afraid, and you may end up carrying him everywhere. Offer him a treat if he moves with you through his fear. He needs to learn to walk on a loose leash no matter what distractions are out there. Pulling is bad for a Yorkie's trachea.

After you have walked the sidewalk in front of your house, increase the challenge by moving to a sidewalk on a busy street, at an outside shopping mall, or a downtown area. Rushing into the next level, though, is not the goal. The idea is to convince your dog that fun and adventure lie at the end of the leash next to you. This is an exercise in team building, not a race to the finish.

Want to Know More?

For advanced training commands, see Chapter 9: Yorkshire Terrier Training.

PART II

ADULTHOOD

CHAPTER 5

FINDING YOUR YORKSHIRE TERRIER ADULT

Some people who are looking for a Yorkie realize halfway through the search that an adult dog fits best into their family. Puppies are not for everyone. Housetraining, teething, and obedience training just do not appeal to every dog owner. Since Yorkies routinely live to be 13 or even 15 years old or more, adopting a two-year-old means you will have many years together. Adopting an adult dog just feels right to many people. Yorkies are fully grown by the time they are a year old, but some breeders consider them still adolescent and puppyish at eighteen months. By the time they are two, they are adults.

WHY ADOPT AN ADULT

The reasons why people want an adult Yorkie are as numerous as there are adopters. Some don't want the responsibility of a tiny puppy, the worry about hypoglycemia, and the regimen of three or four meals a day. Some want a dog who is already housetrained and past the chewing age. Some want to know what their dog will look like, especially his coat, and Yorkies don't always have a mature coat until they are two years old. Some want a Yorkie who has already passed all his health clearances and has been spayed or neutered. (A dog has to be two years old before the Orthopedic Foundation for Animals will certify his hips are free of dysplasia.) Some want a dog who knows basic obedience commands. Some are touched by homeless or special-needs dogs, and want to rescue one or two.

Whatever your reason for looking for an adult Yorkie, bypassing the puppy stage can be a good thing for many families with children or senior citizens. Adult Yorkies are sturdier and more reliable than three- or four-month-old puppies. They are past the chewing stage, and so the house does not have to be as thoroughly stripped of items dangerous if

By the Numbers

An adult Yorkie of six of seven still has half his life to live and would make a good pet for many people. Senior citizens especially have been found to do well with slightly older dogs.

chewed, such as electrical cords. As one rescue volunteer put it, the dogs are turn-key dogs; all you have to do is turn the key, and they are ready to start a new life with you.

Waiting until a dog is fully grown means his temperament is also a known quantity. It is possible to find a dog that matches your needs—couch potato or firebrand, easily trainable or terrier independent, healthy or with special needs.

ADOPTION OPTIONS

If you are looking for an adult Yorkshire Terrier, you have three options: Yorkie breeders, Yorkie rescues, and all-breed shelters.

Breeders

Yorkie breeders sometimes have adult dogs they are willing to place in pet homes. These dogs have finished their show or breeding career and have been retired. But, unlike people, many show dogs retire at a fairly young age, especially a dog who just wasn't cut out to be a show dog. Some may be only two or three years old. Slightly older dogs may have had a few litters and are ready to be spayed and retired from a breeding program. Some dogs may have been returned to a breeder after their owner died, got divorced, or had a baby.

Although cost should not be a deciding factor, Vicki Meadows, Illinois breeder who sometimes places older dogs, says her adults always cost much less than puppies. All she wants for the older dogs is a good home. Whatever you pay for the dog up-front is only a fraction of what the dog will cost over the years, so it is more important to find a dog who matches your lifestyle, not your price range.

Adults from a breeder may vary in socialization and life experiences. Some may have lived on the road in a crate during show season and may not know how to live in a house. Others may have lived a privileged life with someone who really understands Yorkies. It depends on the breeder, how many dogs she has, and her philosophy. If you are thinking of getting an adult from a breeder, start with the Yorkshire Terrier Club of America website and find one of their members near you. Ask questions and look for signs of a well-socialized dog who will fit in to your lifestyle, one who is house-trained and up to date on vaccinations. The dog should not be afraid of strangers or nip at people.

Multi-Dog Tip

Add an adult dog to your existing household by introducing the dogs on a walk. Neutral ground can reduce some territorial aggression. When you get home, put the new dog in an ex-pen in the middle of the house and let the other dogs get used to him before you let them play. This may take a day or two.

Yorkie Rescue

Across the country, a network of volunteers stand ready to rescue Yorkies who have been abandoned or whose families surrendered them. The reasons why people give up their Yorkies are numerous. In many cases, the families really cared for them and surrendered the dogs reluctantly. But sometimes a dog owner who didn't do enough research ended up with a dog who was a poor match, and the dog was never socialized or even taken to the vet. Sometimes the economics of keeping a dog prove too much for families who have lost

Adult Yorkies are sturdier and more reliable than puppies.

income. Sometimes the owner died and no one could take the Yorkie. Sometimes a health issue—human or canine—forced a family to give up a dog. Many dogs are surrendered when families face an extraordinary vet bill, such as broken bones or a genetic flaw like a liver shunt.

Connie Kramer, director of a Yorkshire Terrier rescue called RetroDoggy Rescue, says the number one reason people give up a Yorkie is difficulty between the dog and young children. "Many times people have gotten a Yorkie, and it's so cute, and they treat it like a little baby," Kramer says. "The Yorkie does not learn its place in a pack situation, and it starts to rule the household." But things stumble along, she says, until the couple has a baby, or the baby starts to crawl and toddle around. "The advent of a small child can frighten a small dog—its quick movements and lack of gentle touching. The dog may become terribly intimidated, snappy, or injured through an accident," Kramer says.

And, so she says, the dog ends up in rescue, and volunteers start the process of finding him a new home.

Rescue workers evaluate the Yorkies and place them in foster homes with volunteers who understand Yorkies. Their medical treatment is started—even the expensive things like surgery. Their socialization proceeds. When the foster family thinks a dog is ready for adoption, he is placed on a list or website for people to consider.

People who wish to adopt from a rescue should be prepared to answer at least as many questions as a breeder would ask.

Prepare to be Scrutinized

Those cute faces sometimes attract many callers who say they want to adopt a Yorkie. But people who wish to adopt from a rescue should be prepared to answer at least as many questions as a breeder would ask. After saving a dog's life, rescue volunteers don't want to place a dog in another situation that may not last. They are looking for a permanent, stable home for a dog who has already been uprooted at least once. They will want to know everything about you and your dog history. What skills do you have for handling your new dog? What dogs have you had in your life, and what happened to them? If the new dog is healing from a broken leg or surgery, are you prepared to assume the recovery? Can you afford a dog? Do you have a fence? Have you ever had a toy dog? Do you have any small children?

"We have some very tough criteria," Kramer says. "We require previous Yorkie experience, a current vet reference, some type of safe enclosure outside (ex-pen). We do not adopt to families with small children (under six years old) unless they have an existing small dog. We do home visits, and interview everybody in the family. We do a reference check with veterinarian, reference checks with others. Every adopter is interviewed at least twice."

But there's a payback for all that scrutiny, Kramer says: "The benefit of rescuing from a credible rescue is that the dog will have been medically checked out. If someone adopts from my rescue, the dog has had a complete checkup, a full blood profile run with emphasis on possible liver issues, spayed or neutered, shots. You are getting a turn-key dog in terms of health. Most dogs that come to us are with us a minimum of two months. We are able to assess behavior and the pluses and negatives of every dog. We can give a true picture of the dog they are adopting, what the dog's needs are, and the best match."

After the dog has been adopted, rescue volunteers are available to offer help. Dogs may have housetraining accidents in the first few days in a new situation. Kramer recommends a crate. She also recommends holding off on the welcome-home party. A newly adopted dog may be confused at first if a number of people come and go. The dog needs to learn who is in his new family before visitors descend, Kramer says.

Rescue dogs are not free. They come spayed

or neutered and up to date on vaccines, but depending on the age of the dog and other factors, the adoption fee can range from a couple hundred dollars to almost $1,000.

Special-Needs Adoptions

Olga Fireman, who is one of the online moderators at the DogLiverDisease group at Yahoo! Groups, says sometimes people abandon a Yorkie at the vet's office because they can't afford the bill. Many of these Yorkies have liver disease. Fireman has rescued and cared for dogs with liver disease for several years. She has negotiated reduced fees from several vets. She has researched liver disease and the connection to nutrition, and has developed a diet and supplement regimen. She does not recommend adopting a sick Yorkie for your first toy dog. The regimen for treatment and recovery is very arduous. "I want this dog on four meals a day forever and using the supplements, vegetarian protein," she says. "No store bought treats. No rawhide. No flea and tick products. Heartworm preventive at a reduced dosage." All of those things stress a tiny liver that is already disadvantaged by a birth defect, she says.

Fireman says rescue groups have to be careful not to place a puppy in an inappropriate home. She once had a two-pound (1 kg) Yorkie whose spine was damaged when someone sat on her. She was then surrendered to a rescue group. The rescue group fitted her in a cart so she could walk without using her back legs. Fireman was appalled when someone volunteered to adopt this dog so her 10-month-old baby would have a dog. Fireman thought this was inappropriate because of the age of the child and the frailness of the dog. She set out to discourage this family from getting any Yorkie, but especially a tiny Yorkie in a wheelchair.

"As a rescue, we are very tough on adopters," Fireman said. "We are not going to put them [rescued Yorkies] in a situation where the dog is going to come back. We are not in a hurry to adopt them."

All of this checking can take at least two weeks, so be prepared to wait a little longer.

Shelters

Yorkies sometimes end up in animal shelters run by the city or county government or by a nonprofit organization. These shelters take in a wide variety of animals, such as cats and rabbits, in addition to dogs. The shelter dogs live in kennels while they are being evaluated, treated for some medical issues, and await adoption. Sometimes shelters have limited space and run out of kennels, especially if they have to take in a lot of animals in an emergency situation, such as a police raid on a puppy mill or a hoarding situation. Some shelters euthanize animals if they run out of space or if an animal has not been adopted after a specified time.

Fees for shelter dogs usually include at least one series of vaccinations. Puppies usually cost

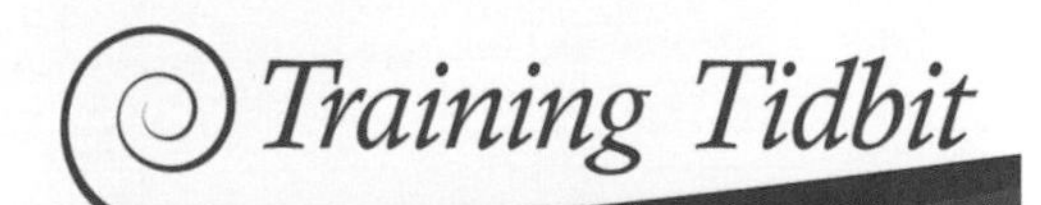

Dogs are never too old to learn new tricks or even a new name. If you don't like the name your new adult Yorkie came with, you can change it. Say the old name and then the new name together for a few days and then just drop the old one. Reward your dog generously for a few days when he responds to the new name.

It may take up to two weeks to adopt your Yorkie.

more than adults, and adults cost more than senior dogs.

The Michigan Humane Society, one of the biggest in the country with about 100,000 animals of all kinds each year, sees mostly adult dogs, Jennifer Robertson, spokeswoman, said. It gets very few puppies. It operates three centers that all try to help people keep their pets rather than surrender them, she said, so even in the bad economy, the number of animals surrendered has not increased.

Anyone who comes in looking for a dog to adopt is asked to fill out a "getting to know you" form. "It is intended to give us an idea of that person's lifestyle and how we can match a dog with them, make sure that animal is right for that lifestyle and home," she said. But she admitted the questions are not as extensive as a rescue would ask. The waiting time is not as long.

Each animal has a standard cage card that lists several characteristics (e.g., good with kids, likes to play), as well as breed characteristics, she says. All are given a behavior assessment and a prediction as to how that dog will make the transition to a new family. "Some do it very easily. Some may take a little more time," Robertson said. The Humane Society offers low-cost sterilization, vaccination, and a pet behavior help line for telephone questions, she said. Shelters often support new dog owners after they adopt a dog by employing a trainer who offers obedience classes and behavioral consultations.

Want to Know More?

For information about adopting a senior Yorkie, see Chapter 12: Finding Your Yorkshire Terrier Senior.

Life in a shelter can be very stressful for some dogs. Some may bark more than they usually do. Some may withdraw. A Yorkie in a shelter may be exhausted when he is finally adopted.

Wherever you decide to get newly adopted Yorkie, understand that he has lived with other animals and may have been exposed to disease, so one of the first things you should do is take your new dog to a vet for a check-up.

CHAPTER 6

YORKSHIRE TERRIER GROOMING NEEDS

On any scale, Yorkie grooming needs rank high. Whether short or long, all that beautiful, glorious Yorkie hair needs regular care. Long hair needs to be brushed nearly every day. Short hair needs to be trimmed regularly and brushed often. Short hair comes with regular appointments with a good pair of shears—yours or a professional groomer's. But grooming a Yorkie doesn't stop with hair. Add in all the other components of good grooming: Nails have to be trimmed. Eyes and ears have to be inspected and cleaned. Teeth have to be brushed quite often because Yorkies tend to have dental problems. And finally, it's time for a bath.

Good thing grooming your Yorkie can be a bonding experience! It is time the two of you spend alone and engaged in something that will make life better. And while you're at it, you can teach your Yorkie grooming manners. Since your Yorkie will spend so much time being groomed, he must learn to stand still, allow you to pick up his feet, and tolerate a hair dryer. Most importantly, he has to learn not to jump off the grooming table. Yorkies have broken legs by jumping only a few feet (m) to the floor.

Of course, he doesn't have to learn this all at once. At first, for example, you could brush him one day and cut his nails the next day. He will learn faster if you stay calm and happy. The reward for all this is that feel of luxurious silkiness when you touch your Yorkie. Seems like a fair reward for all that work, wouldn't you say?

BRUSHING

Grooming starts with a brush. Before you can give your Yorkie a bath or cut his hair, you have to brush it. Yorkie hair mats very easily if it has not been brushed, and mats are both unsightly and annoying to the dog. Big mats of knotted hair pull on the skin, creating an irritating pressure spot. Because dogs will scratch or bite at mats, these nasty hair balls are to be avoided at all costs. Many Yorkie owners brush their dogs every day. Others, whose dogs have shorter hair, still brush them two or three times a week.

How to Brush Your Yorkie

When he was a puppy, you could groom your Yorkie's hair with a soft brush in just a couple minutes. But now that he's an adult with more hair, a few more steps have to be added.

A Yorkie kept in a full coat (left) will need a lot of grooming; many pet owners prefer a shorter cut (right) to make grooming a bit easier.

- First, find somewhere that will become his grooming place. A table dedicated to grooming is a good idea because it is more comfortable for you, allowing you to see what you are doing without bending over. Your Yorkie will also know he has to be on his best grooming behavior when he is on the table. Fit the table with some kind of non-skid mat—a placemat, door-mat, or a piece of rubber cut to fit, so he doesn't slip. Good lighting is important for all the detail work involved in grooming.
- Be careful not to let your Yorkie jump off the grooming table. Stay with him, keeping one hand on him—especially at first. Yorkies are fearless, but jumps or falls from even a few feet (m) can break a leg. This is a good place to practice the "Stay" command.
- Assemble a brushing kit. You will need a pin brush, a large-tooth comb, a pair of small scissors (possibly blunt ended), and a grooming spray that detangles hair.
- Pick up your dog cheerfully, while saying a word that means you are going to pick him up, such as, "Up." Place him on the table and expect him to stand. Praise and reward him when he does.
- Take the large-tooth comb and the detangling spray and attack any tangles or snarls you see. Pull out any burrs he picked up in the yard. Pay special attention to behind the ears and where his legs meet his stomach. Out of sight, mats build faster there. If you brush often enough to remove even little things, like pieces of grass, you can

avoid most mats. Those knotted, solid, ugly mats of hair come eventually into the life of every Yorkie, but they seem to form more often in the cottony coat some pet Yorkies have. Be gentle when you try to untangle mats. They can be painful for a dog.

- If the mat won't budge after some effort, if it seems painful to the dog, and if you are not growing a coat for conformation, get out a small scissors and snip it out. Clip slowly and only as many hairs as necessary to make the mat budge. Try to anticipate when your dog has had enough and may squirm: Scissors can cut your dog's skin just as easily as they cut his coat. Praise and reward him often.
- Comb your dog gently from one end to the other. Some Yorkie owners use a detangling spray because they say it reduces broken hair; others prefer dry hair.
- Then use the pin brush and brush from one end to the other.
- Some Yorkies grow long hair that covers their anus and collects fecal matter. It is routinely clippered or scissored around the anus if this is a problem.
- Every time you brush your dog, do a health check. Look for lumps, cuts, or bald spots. Look for fleas or ticks. Look at the texture of the hair to see if appears strong and healthy. Hair reflects your dog's basic health, so pay attention to its feel and shine. It may tell you to change the dog's food or take his sweater off as soon as you get in the house. Clothes left on a dog all day can be bad for his coat. Look under his hair at his skin. Look for red spots that may be an allergy or dry skin. A change in shampoo may help, or he may need an antihistamine.

Want to Know More?

For steps on how to teach your Yorkie the "Stay" command, see Chapter 9: Yorkshire Terrier Training.

BATHING

Once you are sure there are no mats in his coat, you can move on to the bath. Small dogs like Yorkies can be bathed in a sink, another advantage of their size. Many people who let their dogs sleep on the bed or other furniture bathe their dogs every week. It doesn't hurt the dog, and he ends up smelling sweet, people are happier to see him, and they pay more attention to him. So, baths are good for dogs on many levels.

If you don't want to bathe your Yorkie every week, you don't have to, especially if you keep him in a short clip, which can go longer between baths. But this doesn't mean you shouldn't be prepared: Your little guy may roll in something in the yard or have an accident in his crate and need a bath, so always have shampoo and towels ready. If you decide to skip the weekly bath, try a grooming spray, which will help keep the dog's hair from matting and smelling "doggy" between baths. Many Yorkie owners devise a routine that includes a bath every week in the summer but every two to four weeks in the winter. A few manage to bathe their dogs every four to eight weeks or even less. How often you bathe your dog depends on the dog, on you, and on the terrain he plays in. The easiest, most convenient bathing system you can put together is what is most important; find a system that works for you so you won't be tempted to skip the bath.

How to Bathe Your Yorkie

- You will need dog shampoo, dog conditioner, and two towels. Start with a basic all-purpose shampoo and be prepared to switch to a specialty shampoo such as oatmeal or tea tree oil if your dog turns out to have sensitive skin.
- Wear a plastic apron or old clothes because you may get as wet as your dog.
- Choose a sink that has a spray hose, or find a large plastic cup or pitcher that you can use for rinsing. Some faucets stick out far enough so that a small Yorkie will fit underneath, and you can use this like a "mini-shower." Put a non-skid mat in the bottom of the sink.
- Take off your dog's collar and consider washing it later. Does it smell doggy? Does it have mud or food encrusted on it?
- Wet your Yorkie thoroughly. Check the temperature of the water often. It should be warm, not hot or cold. Use enough water pressure to get through the hair to the skin but not so much that it could hurt sensitive parts of the body.
- Shampoo carefully, avoiding the face and ears. Be careful not to get shampoo in your Yorkie's eyes and ears. If you have trouble keeping soap and water out of his ears, put cotton balls in just for the few minutes he is in the sink.
- Rinse thoroughly. Don't let your Yorkie stand in cold, soapy water. Pull the plug or open the drain once the rinse water gets soapy.
- Rub a little conditioner into his coat and rinse. Keep checking the temperature of the water. Be sure you rinse out conditioner thoroughly, including under his legs and tail.
- Dry your Yorkie with a towel, using a gentle squeeze rather than a rough rub. Rubbing wet hair is a good way to rub in mats. Use a wet corner of the towel and wipe off his face and around his ears.
- Put your Yorkie back on the grooming table and pat him dry with a second dry towel.
- Comb through his hair.
- Turn on a hair dryer specifically designed for dogs, or use your own hand-held dryer, so the hair will blow gently dry while you comb. Watch the temperature carefully—it should be lukewarm, never hot.
- Switch to the brush, and brush until his hair is dry or almost dry. Either hold the hairdryer in your free hand or use a hair dryer on a stand, so you have both hands for the dog.
- Put in a topknot if you want. Male and female Yorkies frequently wear bows in their hair to keep it out of their eyes.
    - Part in the hair on his head from the outer corner of one eye to a v-shaped wedge between the ears.
    - Pull the hair up and back, and put in a rubber band at the bottom.
    - Then loosen the hair under the rubber-band so it is not too tight.
    - Pouf it up a little in the front.
    - Cover the rubber-band with a ribbon. Ribbons and tiny rubber-bands specially made for Yorkies are available at pet stores and online.
    - Expect to cut the rubber-band out when it is time.

- Some Yorkie experts say the topknot should be taken down every day so the hair can be brushed and the skin can be massaged underneath.

EAR CARE

Regular ear care will keep your Yorkie's ears sweet-smelling and may help you spot an ear infection before it becomes serious. Ears must be cleaned separately, not with shampoo and water, because water that gets into an ear and stays there encourages bacterial growth. Some people put cotton balls inside their dog's ears when bathing them to help keep out water.

How to Clean Your Yorkie's Ears

- First hold one ear and look carefully inside. His ears should be pale pink with little or no odor. Redness, a strong odor, or heavy black deposits are signs he may have an ear infection. Call your vet if you notice these signs.
- If your dog's ears look healthy, use cotton balls to clean around inside your dog's ears. A little warm water—just enough to make the cotton ball damp—may help, or you can buy a commercial ear cleaner. Do not push anything down inside his ears: You are not cleaning down deep inside his ears, just around the outer parts.
- If his ears look wet when you are finished, dry them gently with a soft towel.
- Trim the hair off the top third of his ears and even inside his ears if it grows long. Yorkies should have ears with upright triangular tips that are free of long hair.

EYE CARE

The eyes require very little care. No specialized equipment or products are necessary here—your only job is to assess the health of your dog's eyes and keep him looking bright-eyed.

How to Clean Your Yorkie's Eyes

- Start by looking at your Yorkie's eyes—really looking at them. Look for food stuck in the eyelashes, eyelashes that are not properly aligned and may be bothering your dog's cornea, or discharge. If you see a serious discharge, especially one that is yellowish or green, call your vet.
- Use a damp washcloth or bath towel and wipe your Yorkie's face, especially around his eyes. Dry thoroughly.

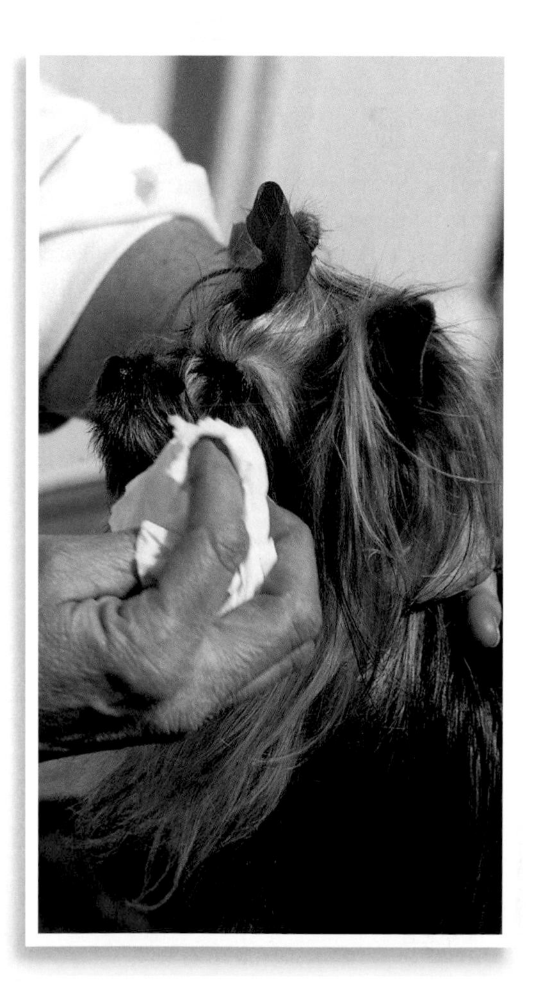

Use a damp cloth to wipe your Yorkie's face.

- The Yorkshire Terrier Club of America recommends keeping your dog's face clean and dry between baths, wiping away tears at least once a day if your dog tears. Tears can stain his coat.

NAIL TRIMMING

Cutting your Yorkie's toenails is a fact of life. Nails grow and need to be cut often. If you can hear your dog's nails clicking on the floor when he walks, it's time. Long nails can change the way he walks, collect dirt, and can be dangerous if he gets excited and starts scratching at the door, the pillow, or you. Besides, long nails on a small dog are just unsightly.

How to Trim Your Yorkie's Nails

- The first thing to do is get the right tool for the job. Shop for a pair of nail clippers you like and are comfortable using. Several varieties are available in pet stores. (Don't dismiss cat nail clippers just because it says "cat" on the package . . . these are great for toy dogs.) Avoid a large, heavy clipper that you might have trouble controlling with only one hand. Hold the clippers in your hand and work them several times. Imagine cutting a nail, the dog's foot in one hand, the clippers in the other.

Multi-Dog Tip

Have a spa day. Set up all the bathing equipment you need to bathe both dogs. Each dog has to be bathed alone, but the other dog can watch and you only have to clean up the sink once. Throw all the towels in the laundry at once and enjoy two clean dogs.

- Lay the groundwork for nail trimming with your dog before you ever pick up the clippers. Start by massaging your Yorkie's paws when he is sitting quietly on your lap. Talk to him and make him seem special because you are touching his feet. Massage each toe separately, holding it away from the others briefly. Be sure to massage all four feet.
- On nail clipping day, pick up your Yorkie and hold him in your lap or place him on the grooming table. Pick up one foot, using a word that you want to become a foot command, like "Foot."
- Push the hair back from one nail and look for the end of the quick. The quick is a collection of nerve ends and blood vessels in the nail that is very sensitive and bleeds heavily when cut. This is sometimes easier to see on the backside of the nail. Then look for where the nail curves. Keep your clippers above the curve and away from the quick.
- At first, clip just the tips off each nail.
- If you cut too far down, the quick will bleed. If that happens, get a cloth or paper towel and press it against the nail until the bleeding stops. Some home remedies, like packing the nail with cornstarch, will soak up the blood if it starts to accumulate. Or, you can buy commercial styptic powders that also work. Almost every dog owner clips a quick or two in the beginning. As you get more experienced, you should be able to cut all his toenails without any blood (most of the time).
- In the beginning, you may want to stop after one foot and start again the next day. Give your dog a treat and praise him. Make nail clipping seem like something fun and matter-of-fact that you do together. Try to have an air of confidence. He should see that this is something you are going to do no matter

Be careful not to cut the quick when you are cutting your Yorkie's nails.

what he does, but avoid confrontation. Resort to your skills as a positive dog trainer to convince him this is what he wants to do: Use lots of treats and praise.

- If he has long hair growing between his toes or shaggy looking feet, trim the hair before you cut his nails. Clip the bottoms and sides quite close to the skin with a scissors or, better yet, a hair trimmer.
- Many dogs will soon adjust to having their feet handled and nails clipped, and will cooperate on command. If yours isn't one of those, consider regular nail appointments at a groomer. Nails need to be cut more often than your Yorkie needs a haircut, so if you are using a groomer for a haircut every two or three months, you will need to make nail appointments in between.

DENTAL CARE

The Yorkshire Terrier—like all toy breeds—can have many more dental problems than bigger dogs. Small dogs have the same number of teeth a big dog has but in a much smaller mouth. Sometimes Yorkie baby teeth don't fall out and must be pulled under anesthesia. Some owners schedule that surgery for the same day they have their dog spayed or neutered to avoid a second anesthesia.

Yorkie teeth should be cleaned every day, according to the Yorkshire Terrier Club of America, but at the very least twice a week. A Yorkie's mouth is very small and the teeth are sometimes crowded. Plaque forms, then tartar, and then gum disease. According to Lowell Ackerman, a veterinarian and author of *Canine Nutrition*, about 85 percent of dogs older than

About 85 percent of dogs older than four years have peridontal disease.

four years have periodontal disease. This can lead to pain when chewing, infection, and tooth loss, he says. Many senior Yorkies have had more than one tooth pulled.

By the Numbers

By the time he is seven or eight months old, a Yorkie has his adult teeth. These are the same teeth he will have when he is 15 years old. Take care of them from the beginning so they will last.

The American Veterinary Dental College lists several signs of oral and dental diseases in dogs: bad breath, loose teeth or teeth that are discolored or covered in tartar, a dog who shies away from you when you touch his mouth, drooling or dropping food from the mouth, bleeding from the mouth, and loss of appetite or loss of weight.

Connie Kramer, director of RetroDoggy Rescue, says the Yorkie's reputation for dental problems is well-earned. "A lot of it is genetic," she says. She recommends eliminating soft food and scheduling a regular professional cleaning with your vet at least once a year, to avoid dental problems. Infected gums can spread bacteria throughout a Yorkie's body. "Dental disease impacts all of a dog's organs," says Kramer. "It can be fatal."

How to Brush Your Yorkie's Teeth

Buy dental equipment for your dog as soon as you get him. Choose from a soft toothbrush, a rubber finger toothbrush, or even sterile gauze wrapped around your finger.

Buy dog toothpaste. Do not use human toothpaste because it has ingredients that, when the dog swallows them, will upset his stomach. Dog toothpaste is frequently liver or chicken flavored and has enzymes that further help keep plaque and tartar at bay. Dogs generally like the taste of dog toothpaste, and may try to lick it off the brush.

Use a little toothpaste and rub the teeth and gums with your brush or finger. Try to get top and bottom, front and back. If your dog resists, skip the inside, since his tongue offers some tooth-brushing action.

No rinsing is required.

The occasional dental treat, which contains ingredients that fight plaque and tartar buildup, is a good idea, although these treats do not replace regular brushing. Some harder dental bones, such as Nylabones, have nubs that massage the gums, which helps to reduce the incidence of gum disease (gingivitis or periodontal disease), a very common problem in small dogs. Gum disease starts when tartar builds up at the base of the tooth and pushes the gum away. Bacteria grow in the gaps and cause infection. In severe cases, the teeth fall out or have to be pulled.

HOW TO FIND A PROFESSIONAL GROOMER

Most Yorkie owners are familiar with the inside of a grooming studio. It comes with the dog—Yorkies need a lot of grooming and not all owners are willing to do it. Finding a groomer is similar to finding a barber or stylist for yourself. And just like the hunt for your own hair dresser, the hunt for a groomer may not end with the first one. You may have to try two or three groomers before you find one you like.

When you take your dog in for grooming, you'll be leaving him there for several hours. During that time, the groomer is responsible for your dog's safety, so which groomer you hire is a very important choice. Spend a little time before you make that decision.

Ask other Yorkie owners. Ask about the groomer's cost, patience, and quality of work. Does the dog have cuts or scabs after visiting the groomer?

Visit some local places. A nearby grooming shop is a plus, but only if it passes all your tests. Does the groomer specialize in Yorkies or at least know how to handle and groom small dogs? Does it smell bad when you walk in?

Training Tidbit

Teach your dog to enjoy the grooming table before you even try to groom him. Offer him a treat as soon as he gets there and every few minutes after that, at least at first. Talk pleasantly to him and make it seem special that he is getting all your attention. Keep training sessions short at first.

Are dogs barking in a frenzied or panicky way? Are dogs growling? Are the groomers working happily, smiling at dogs and talking to them? Are there small dogs? Is the cost within your budget? Do the safety precautions meet your standards?

Ask groomers what coat clipping options they offer for Yorkies. Be sure the groomer understands exactly what you want. Yorkies can be cut in several styles (puppy, Schnauzer, simple trim), and the two of you should agree on what your dog will look like. Talk about what other services you need, such as nail clipping or tooth brushing. Some groomers will check and express the anal sacs if they are full, a good option to choose.

If you are on a tight budget, look for a canine barber school. Sometimes grooming students will cut your dog's hair at reduced rates.

Ask your breeder and your vet about grooming services. They may offer grooming or know someone who grooms Yorkies in their home.

Look online or in the phone book for mobile groomers who will come to your house. They have a van that is equipped as a grooming studio and can groom your dog in your driveway. You don't need to provide any tools or equipment or even water, although the van may plug into your electrical socket. This has the advantage of reducing the time your dog is out of the house. The groomer

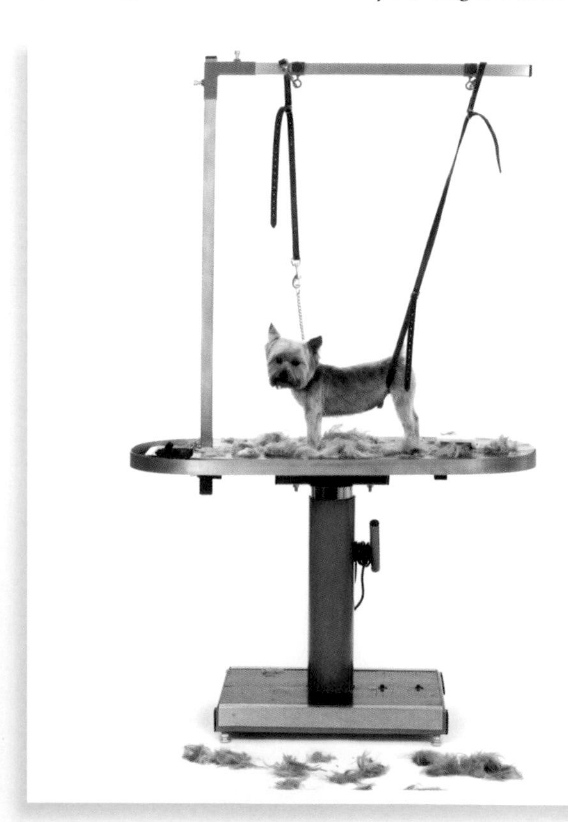

You may decide to let a professional groomer groom your Yorkie.

Anal Sacs

The anal sacs are two little pockets on either side of the dog's anus that fill gradually with oil. Dogs use this liquid to mark their territory. The vet can show you how to express the liquid out of the sacs at home but it is sometimes a smelly and messy task. The best time to do it is right before your dog gets a bath. Left untouched, some anal sacs get impacted, causing irritation and making the dog scoot on the ground. Other dogs are able to keep their anal sacs in perfect condition without any help from you or the groomer.

comes to the door, and picks him up, and returns him as soon as she finishes, unlike at a regular studio, where you drop the dog off and pick him up later. At a regular studio, your dog almost always has to wait for at least a short while, before and after his appointment. A mobile van usually has no other dogs and is quieter than a grooming studio. If your dog is nervous around other dogs, especially bigger dogs, or if you have more than one dog, this may be a good option.

Look for a groomer who belongs to a groomers' professional organization. These organizations require the groomer to learn basic facts about different breeds and sometimes have ethics codes. They also offer trade shows with seminars as continuing education.

Cleanliness should be obvious and a priority at any groomer's. Disease and parasites can be passed along in grooming equipment or from the cages the dogs wait in. Ask your groomer how she sanitizes equipment.

CHAPTER 7

YORKSHIRE TERRIER NUTRITIONAL NEEDS

Feeding your dog is one of the most important things you do for him every day. Good food helps him grow strong, keeps him healthy, and gives him strong teeth and coat. Yorkies may be small in size but their nutritional needs are just as big as any other dog's and should be carefully considered when you pick a food.

GOOD NUTRITION IS ESSENTIAL TO A YORKIE

Those tiny legs are powered by the energy in the food he eats. So is the shine on his coat, the look in his eye, and the number of days he is healthy. So, what goes into the food you feed him is very important. Yorkies eat tiny meals several times a day, but what is in those meals is of gigantic importance. Because their stomachs are so small, Yorkies have no room for doggie junk food. Each ingredient has to contribute something good. A poor-quality ingredient takes up space that should be filled by a top-quality one.

When to Move From Puppy to Adult Food

Here's what the veterinary nutritional experts at Michigan State University have to say about puppy foods: "Commercially prepared complete and balanced dog foods typically have an Association of American Feed Control Officials (AAFCO) claim for all life stages, adult maintenance or for growth. Fifteen to twenty years ago, there were distinct differences between puppy and adult foods, but the lines have blurred significantly in the past five to ten years. What is typically recommended is that puppies be fed a growth-type food until they reach 90 percent of their skeletal maturity. For toy and small-breed dogs, this might be when they are eight or nine months old. Another reasonable point in time to transition to adult food is around the time the dog is spayed/neutered (usually six months). If you study or evaluate a wide variety of adult and puppy foods in the U.S. today, you will see quite a bit of overlap in the range of energy, protein, and fat provided. What this means is that there are more similarities than differences, and pet owners should focus on *how* they are feeding (to avoid obesity) rather than *what* they are feeding."

Building Blocks of Nutrition

Dogs need about the same things in their diet that people need, because we evolved together and ate the same things—it's one of the reasons the partnership has lasted so long. Dogs are not carnivores, or true meat eaters. They are omnivores. They eat just about everything. Meat is usually an important part of the diet of a healthy dog but dogs cannot live on only meat. Research into the dog's nutritional needs continues, but sides have already formed in the dog community at large. Some dog owners won't feed their dog anything processed, and others won't feed certain ingredients (such as corn). Some breeders have entrenched ideas about how much protein or fat a dog should eat. Some veterinarians worry mostly that American pets get too much of both.

Regardless of the details, a dog's diet should contain a balanced mix of carbohydrates, fats, proteins, minerals, vitamins, and water.

Carbohydrates

Carbohydrates in dog food usually come from grains and sometimes from vegetables and fruits. The diet of pet dogs includes a much higher percentage of carbohydrates than their wild relatives', and this is cause for one debate in the canine nutrition world.

Dogs process most easily digested (soluble) carbohydrates into energy. Insoluble carbohydrates, or those that are not easily digested, act as fiber in your dog's digestive system—this fiber comes from the hulls of grain, beet pulp, or grains such as corn. Fiber works in dogs the same way it works in people—to improve colon performance.

The pro-carbohydrate camp, including most commercial dog food makers, say that carbohydrates are cheaper than meat, provide a bonding ability that allows dry kibble to stick together, give the dog energy, and can help prevent both diarrhea and constipation. The anti-carbohydrate side argues that dogs in the wild eat only a small percentage of carbohydrates and that some dogs are allergic to carbohydrates, such as corn or wheat.

Fats

It may surprise some dog owners to know that dogs need fat. Fat, by itself, is not an evil to avoid at all costs but the source of essential fatty acids and energy. Fat is good for a dog's skin, coat, and immune system. Fat also helps brains develop. But all fats are not created equal. Some are better for your dog than others, and some contain the almost magical *essential fatty acids*.

Fatty acids include omega-6 and omega-3, both of which play a big part in many of your dog's physical systems. A dog cannot make essential fatty acids but must get them from foods, such as fish oil. Fatty acids are beneficial to your dog in a long list of ways including possibly reducing allergies and arthritis. Research is ongoing in many areas that could connect fatty acids to health benefits.

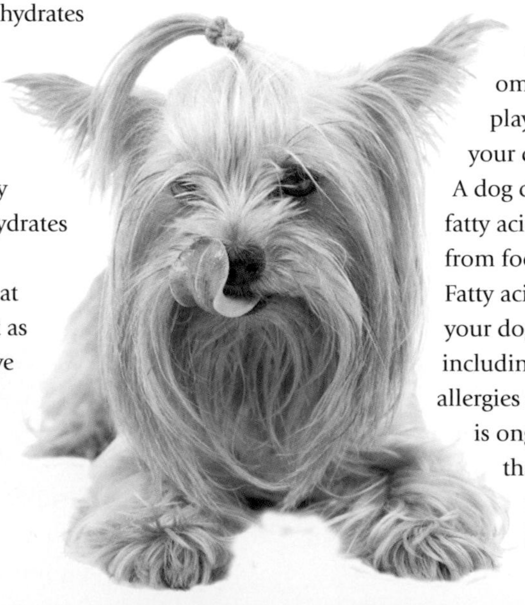

Good nutrition is essential for your Yorkie's health.

Minerals

Dogs need some very familiar minerals, such as calcium and phosphorous, and some lesser-known ones, such as manganese and selenium. In addition, they also need some you might not think they need: sodium, chloride, potassium, magnesium, iron, zinc, copper, and iodine.

These minerals are found in foods but often not in high enough quantities or in the right proportion. Dogs who eat a balanced commercial diet, which has added minerals, usually get enough minerals to meet average needs. Dogs who eat a homemade diet need a supplement. Minerals are tightly linked—one often helps the other work better—so your dog needs each one in specific amounts. It's a balance that must be maintained. If you add more of one, it affects the way another works (or doesn't work). This is where a background in chemistry would come in handy!

Minerals overlap in action, and help each other do the multitude of functions that go on every second that your dog breathes: Cells have to be made to replace dead ones; energy has to be created; the immune system has to fight off the bad guys; the heart keeps silently pumping. All thanks to a group of minerals that sound as if they belong in a soils science class, not dog food.

Calcium and phosphorous help your dog's heart and nerves work better and keep his bones and teeth healthy. Manganese is essential for the absorption of vitamins such as C, E, and B_1, as well as collagen production and bone and cartilage growth. Selenium works with vitamin E and keeps your Yorkie's immune system functioning. Sodium and chloride help your dog's body keep the right amount of fluids inside cells and outside them, and these minerals also help digestion. Potassium helps enzymes, muscles, and nerves work better. Magnesium is another mineral that helps with teeth and bones, heart, and enzymes. Iron is part of hemoglobin in red blood cells that continually need to be replaced. Zinc is also important in replacing cells, as well as in the action of enzymes, DNA, and immune systems. Copper helps metabolize energy and distribute oxygen in the blood. Iodine is required for the production of thyroid hormones.

By the Numbers

By the time your Yorkie is eight months old, he should be eating a high-quality adult maintenance food, but it is okay to switch from puppy foods to adult food earlier. The important thing is that any dry kibble you buy have an AAFCO label.

Proteins

Dogs break protein down into amino acids that they use for energy, as building blocks for growth, and in the immune system. Proteins are one of the most important things dogs eat, but proteins are not interchangeable. Different proteins have different levels of amino acids, and some are more digestible than others. So, picking a protein is important and combining two or more proteins also makes sense.

Proteins come from meat, of course, but also from fish, eggs, and some plants, such as corn. Without enough protein, dogs lose weight and have poor coats and reduced immune systems.

Vitamins

Dogs need small amounts of vitamins, and they need those vitamins to be balanced. Too much of one and not enough of another can be trouble. If you are feeding a commercially

Dogs need about the same things in their diets that people need.

prepared food that is complete and balanced, you should not need to add a vitamin supplement for a healthy dog. Adding just one vitamin can throw off the work of the rest.

Vitamins are either fat-soluble or water-soluble. Fat-soluble vitamins can be stored in the liver, but water-soluble ones are excreted if not immediately needed by the body.

Fat-soluble means the vitamins rely on body fat for absorption. These include vitamin A, D, E, and K.

Vitamin A plays a role in good vision and a healthy immune system. In dogs, it also helps maintain good skin and appetite. Vitamin D helps your Yorkie absorb and use calcium. If your Yorkie plays outside in the sunshine three times a week, he will produce the vitamin D that he needs. Vitamin E is an antioxidant that also helps make red blood cells and helps with vitamin K absorption. Vitamin K works to help blood clot.

Water-soluble vitamins are not stored in the body and need to be replaced often. These include the B-group of vitamins and vitamin C. The B-group has about 10 vitamins: thiamin, niacin, riboflavin, pantothenic acid, pyridoxine, biotin, B_{12}, choline, folic acid, and inositol. The B-group is essential in the way your dog metabolizes protein, carbohydrates, and fat. Dogs can make their own vitamin C, which the body uses to make the collagen in connective tissue.

Water

All dogs need cool, fresh water available most of the time. Water is an essential of their diet, even though you may not think of it that way. It helps the digestive process, moving food through the system, and it is a part of nearly every chemical reaction in a dog's body. Water is also involved in a whole host of other important jobs, such as regulating your dog's temperature and contributing to his blood and lymph systems. Dogs lose water every day just by breathing, urinating, defecating, and drooling. Dogs who eat mostly dry food will need to drink more water than dogs who eat mostly canned food. But whatever they eat, dogs need to have a clean bowl of clean water available all day, every day. If you drink the tap water in your house, your dog can, too. Just keep the bowl clean and the water fresh. A good rule of thumb is to refill the dish every time you feed your dog. Change the dish or wash it with soap and hot water every couple days.

WHAT TO FEED YOUR YORKIE

Choosing a dog food can be a complex and confusing task—it's not as easy as falling in love with a Yorkie. But many high-quality dog foods are available, and any of several options can give your Yorkie a highly satisfying and healthy diet. You and your breeder can feed your Yorkies different foods and both see satisfying results. You can pick one food this year and get successful results, and pick another food next year and get equally successful results.

But several poor-quality foods also exist, and that means you can choose the wrong food. The right answer begins with research. Read the labels of commercial dog food. Understand the ingredients. Research the nutritional needs of dogs before you serve a raw or homemade diet, and understand which needs can be met by food and which needs require supplements.

Commercial Food

Commercial food is any dog food that is made by a manufacturer. It is any food you didn't cook yourself—whether dry, semi-moist, or canned.

Commercial dog foods go back to the 1860s, according to the Pet Food Institute. An American salesman named James Spratt, from Ohio, watched London dogs eat leftover ship's biscuits. He set out to improve on that by mixing wheat meals, vegetables, beetroot, and meat. His business succeeded by selling dog food to English country gentlemen, who fed it to their sporting dogs.

Today's commercial dog foods are a little more scientific. Pick one that is certified by the AAFCO as complete and balanced, and has a label to prove it. The label means the food was tested and judged able to keep a dog alive and well all by itself—no supplements required. For many dog owners, this "complete and balanced" claim is the reason to serve commercial food. The food has been tested against basic nutritional standards and found to include all of them, at least on a minimal level.

"All adult dogs have the same basic nutritional

Always have fresh water available for your Yorkie.

needs, regardless of breed," veterinary nutritional experts at Michigan State University say. "Yorkshire terriers, like any other breed, have requirements for nutrients, not ingredients. Many commercial dog foods contain meat as the first ingredient; however, that is not a requirement. Protein and fat percentages on food labels are relative, not precise; percentages should not be used to compare different products because they don't reflect the actual amounts. Owners should be more concerned about the kilocalories (kcals) per cup or can of food, because this information can be used to determine daily portions to be fed. Unfortunately, the kcals/cup is not required to be on a label . . . it's optional . . . but owners can call manufacturers or look on their websites for this valuable information."

Dry/Kibble

Dry kibble is a popular choice, outselling every other kind of commercial food by billions of dollars. It stores well, is easily measured, and leaves almost no mess. It is reasonably priced, considering its completeness and convenience.

Things to remember about dry food: Manufacturers frequently overestimate how much dogs need. Start by feeding your dog less than the instructions on the bag recommend. Always check for an expiration date. Even though it seems like it will last forever, dry

Commercial food made specifically for toy breeds is available.

A home-cooked diet is not simply feeding your Yorkie table scraps—you must do your research to supply a balanced diet.

foods do go stale and lose nutritional value, especially once the bag has been opened. In extreme cases, they can become rancid. Buy only what you can use in a month or two, and store kibble in a dark dry place. Keep the kibble in the bag it came in, inside an airtight container.

Choosing a kibble is a matter of some research. Different companies promote different things in their food, such as probiotics or vitamins. Specific food is made for dogs by size, age, and weight control. Different companies have different protein and fat levels in their food.

Several companies make foods for toy breeds; these lines were created with an eye toward reducing dental problems and meeting the higher energy needs of small dogs. They have about 27 or 28 percent protein and 16 or 17 percent fat. Some claim ingredients that can improve a dog's coat or digestive system. "Dry dog foods made for toy dogs are acceptable because they are complete and balanced to meet the published minimal nutrient needs. From a nutritional standpoint, there is nothing unique or special about a toy breed food," Michigan State University veterinary nutritional experts say.

Read the ingredients on the label. The first ingredient should be chicken, beef, lamb, salmon, or some other type of meat or fish. This is better than by-products that include lungs, spleen, kidneys, brain, liver, blood, and bone. It is better than corn or other hard-to-digest foods. Avoid foods even if they have a meat listed first when the next three ingredients are some type of corn, such as ground yellow corn, corn gluten meal, or just corn meal. Together, those three corn products will outweigh the meat. Grain-based diets are not ideal for healthy dogs.

Semi-Moist

Semi-moist dog foods contain more moisture than dry foods and must be packaged in a sealed pouch to retain the moisture. Never high on the list of foods veterinarians or nutritionists recommend, semi-moist foods contain more sugar and salt than dry foods, as well as some dyes and chemicals used to preserve them. They are designed for the eye of the human shopper and not for the nutritional well-being of the dog. Most experts suggest you use semi-moist foods as an occasional treat, if at all.

Canned

Canned dog foods run the gamut from high to poor quality. Read the label carefully to determine which is which. It is possible to find a high-quality canned food you can feel good about giving your Yorkie. The same basic principles apply to canned food labels that apply to dry. A meat or fish should be listed first, and it should identified just by the type of meat (chicken, beef) and not as a by-product (chicken by-product). Whole grains and vegetables are good (rice is better than rice bran). Sugar is unnecessary and so is artificial color.

> *Nutritional Analysis*
>
> **Some veterinary colleges, such as the one at Michigan State (www.animalhealth.msu.edu/Sections/Nutrition/FAQ.php), offer a nutritional analysis of the homemade diet you are feeding your dog.**

The pros and cons of canned food depend on the needs of your dog and you. Canned food offers fewer preservatives because the canning process itself preserves the food. Canned foods have more moisture, and that can be a good or a bad thing depending on your dog. The moisture means the can may have less protein, but little dogs who need more liquid in their diet may find it in a can.

Many dogs prefer canned foods because of the smell and taste. But canned foods sometime smell unpleasant to people and leave dishes that have to be washed. Some cans hold two meals, and the leftovers have to be refrigerated—smell and all.

Some people stay away from canned foods because they believe they are not as good for a dog's teeth as dry food. "Canned foods (rather than kibble) are more likely to produce an environment in the oral cavity that promotes bacterial growth, and this increases the likelihood of dental disease," Michigan State University veterinary nutritional experts say. "Yorkshire Terriers, like most small breed dogs, are prone to dental disease." Some people mix a can of food into their Yorkie's dry kibble occasionally. Canned foods are very popular for older or sick dogs with weak appetites.

The most important thing about picking a canned food is to pick the highest quality you can afford. Yorkies eat a very small quantity of food, and this allows us to more easily offer them the highest quality made.

Noncommercial Food

Sometimes, even after you've read all the labels, no canned or dry food seems like the right choice. Maybe you want to be sure your Yorkie gets only the freshest ingredients that have had as little processing as possible. The solution may lie not in a commercially prepared dog food but in one you make at home. You have two choices: cooking a homemade food or offering him a raw diet.

Home-Cooked Diet

Cooking for your dog starts with research into exactly what nutrients he needs. It is more complicated than simply cooking him a steak every night and cutting it into little pieces. He might like that, but soon his health would show the ill effects of an unbalanced diet.

Exactly what your dog needs depends on his age, size, and activity level. If you are starting an agility program, he will need more food than a dog who never pants. A puppy needs more food than a senior.

At the basic level, dogs need carbohydrates, fats, proteins, minerals, vitamins, and water. A dish of chicken cooked in a little oil with brown rice, carrots and peas will satisfy a lot of his requirements, but he will need a vitamin and mineral supplement, too.

If you are embarking on a home-cooked diet, start by asking your veterinarian for advice. You need recipes that include different food groups, amounts to serve your particular dog, and hints on how to handle the food between feedings. Some foods may be cooked and then frozen in small portions. You also need advice on what kind and dose of vitamins and minerals to give him.

Cooking for your dog can be satisfying and rewarding, especially if your dog flourishes on his new diet. But double-checking your work is up to you. Keep an eye on his skin and coat. Look at his eyes. Smell his breath. Keep track of his stool. If something does not look right to you, examine what you are doing and try something else. Change a carbohydrate. Limit the proteins to one type. Or change the oil. Add a protein. The possibilities are almost endless.

The goal is to serve fresh food that has been only mildly processed in a balanced diet. Your dog will tell you soon if you are doing a good job.

Your children can help feed your Yorkie, but don't forget to supervise!

Raw

The raw diet is based on the idea that dogs will do better if they are fed a diet that closely resembles what they ate as wolves or as dogs before processed dog foods entered their lives. Dogs on a raw diet are fed mostly meat or fish and raw bones. They get little or no grain. They eat chicken carcasses, whole fish, eggs in the shell, pig's feet, and ox tails. This requires some rethinking for most dog owners, as well as a lot of research. First, teach yourself exactly what you can feed your dog and how much. Then find a place that sells chicken carcasses and pig's feet from organic sources. The food itself may be cheap —who else wants chicken necks?—but it must be of the highest quality and very fresh if your dog is going to eat it raw. Raw meat that has been sitting around has madly growing colonies of bacteria. Organic, grass-fed, natural—those are the avenues to go down. Avoid cooked bones.

Some raw food is available frozen. A popular raw food diet is the BARF (biologically appropriate raw food) diet, and several sources for frozen raw food are available that meet the BARF standards, so check with a major pet food store in your area.

Whether dogs on a raw diet need supplements is a matter of debate. Ask your veterinarian. Balance is always the goal.

The raw food diet requires extra care in preparing and cleaning up. Although the bacteria on fresh raw foods may not affect your dog, *E. coli* and *Salmonella* are not good for you. Wash your hands, the counters, and the dog's dishes with hot water and soap.

"Foods fed to our pets should be complete (all the required nutrients) and balanced (nutrients are in the right proportions)," veterinary nutritional experts at Michigan State University recommend. "Pet owners using a raw meat or cooked homemade diet should have the diet analyzed to confirm that it includes all the major nutrients, and those nutrients are in appropriate proportions. The primary concern of most veterinarians is that feeding raw meat diets poses an increased risk for *Salmonella* and *E. coli* bacterial infections to pets and people. No matter how aseptic one's technique in prepping and cleaning, the longer you work with raw meat, the more likely you are to increase your risk."

Special Diets

Occasionally, a dog requires special foods. Puppies, for example, need a special diet—a growth diet. Other special diets have been created for senior dogs, dogs with allergies, or those with very sensitive stomachs. Some dogs need a vegetarian diet or a single-protein diet.

Some major dog food manufacturers sell special diets, such as a dental care diet, and a few are available only through your veterinarian. These come in canned or dry form.

Occasionally, you can make your own special diet, especially if it is just for a short time. After certain kinds of surgery or illness, for example, some dogs require a bland diet; others might need one that is soft, or low in protein, or high in fat, and these you can manipulate at home, sometimes by simply reading dog food labels and choosing foods that meet your dog's temporary requirements (such as those with extremely high protein or fat levels).

Want to Know More?

For information about feeding a senior Yorkie, see Chapter 13: Care of Your Yorkshire Terrier Senior.

Supplements

Supplements for dogs are nutritional add-ons to your dog's diet that do not require a prescription, in most cases. They run the gamut from skin and coat supplements to joint supplements to multivitamins. Supplements are not an overnight fix for anything but, over the long run, you may notice a gradual improvement in some things.

Healthy dogs who are eating a complete and balanced commercial dog food do not need a supplement or vitamin for good health. Some dog owners and breeders want to add a supplement anyway, looking for any edge that might give them a better coat or help an arthritic dog stop limping.

Some commonly added supplements are fatty acids, and glucosamine and chondroitin. Probiotics are another common supplement, often given to help a dog's digestive system react to stress. Acidophilus, for example, is a "good" bacteria that can help stabilize the bacteria in your dog's system when stress causes diarrhea. It is handy to have on hand for occasional use, such as before car trips or boarding.

Dogs who do not eat a complete and balanced commercial diet will need a vitamin supplement to supply some of the missing vitamins and minerals. Ask your veterinarian for advice.

Treats

Dog treats are an important part of your dog's week. They come unexpectedly and taste delicious. They are another sign to him that you know just how to make him happy—and soon he comes to expect nothing less! Therein lies the rub. Too many treats or cheap treats made of sugar and salt can fill up your dog with empty calories.

The art of giving your dog a treat is one lesson that's fun to learn. Start with healthy food, perhaps another flavor of the high-quality kibble you already feed or biscuits made with the same standards your dog food is. Or, look for a treat made of something you never feed your dog, such as sweet potato. Try to cut every treat into small pieces. Use one treat at a time. If your dog comes when called, he gets one treat, not a handful. Buy fun treats for special occasions or training sessions. If you are in serious training or have come up against a wall in training, switch to something extra tempting, like baked chicken, again cut up in tiny pieces. Some dogs respond to treats depending on their smell—the worse it smells to humans, the better the dog reacts. (Some liver treats have a strong smell.) Those treats should be reserved for special occasions. And be sure to consider how many treats your dog has had when dishing up his next meal. Cut back if he has overdosed on treats at a party.

If you like to bake, look for mixes for homemade dog biscuits, especially popular in catalogs around the holidays. Cookbooks and websites have started to include dog treat recipes, also. Baking your own doggie treats is one way you can be sure exactly what your dog is getting.

Multi-Dog Tip

When you call your dogs in from the yard and they line up for a treat, tailor the size of the treat to their weight. Dogs cannot tell if one gets a bigger treat, as long as they all come out of the same bag or jar. If you have an obese or senior dog, give him a smaller piece.

A healthy adult dog should eat twice a day.

Bones

Dogs like to chew, and bones are a part of every dog's dream. But dogs should never get cooked bones of any kind. They are too brittle.

Raw bones are a different matter. Some raw bones can be good for your dog. Look for very fresh bones that have no rotten meat smell. You must closely supervise your dog when you give him any kind of bone and remove any raw bone at the end of a chewing session. Clean up any raw meat left on the floor.

If you don't want to deal with raw bones, substitute man-made ones. Companies such as Nylabone make bones that your dog will consume as he chews. The dog should be carefully supervised with this type of bone, too. Do not put him in a crate with an edible bone and leave for the day. Some dogs, especially those who eat too fast, can choke on the broken end of a bone. Rawhide also fit in this category. Some dogs can work a rawhide bone for a week, while others consume it in an evening. The faster eaters sometimes try to swallow a bigger piece than they should. Always wash your hands after handling raw bones or rawhide bones.

Another type of bone dogs like to chew is made of durable rubber or nylon, and again the most widely known is made by Nylabone. Buy one at a time until you determine which one your dog will chew. Some dogs like one kind and will have nothing to do with another. Buy a size that is at least big enough so that your dog can carry it around, with one end sticking out each side of his mouth. Too small a bone can be swallowed in a burst of chewing excitement. Supervise the chewing of these bones also, and discard them when the knobby ends have been chewed off.

WHEN TO FEED YOUR ADULT YORKIE

The great thing about a dog is that he will be happy to eat whenever you feed him.

But responsible dog owners know that dogs should be on a schedule. A healthy adult dog should eat twice a day, with meals spaced 10 or 12 hours apart. Some of the smallest Yorkies may need to eat more often, even as adults. Dog meals correspond to human breakfast and dinner, with the addition of lunch for the smallest in the pack. A dog's daily allotment of food should be divided into two or three meals. A dog who eats three times a day does not always eat more than a dog that eats twice a day—he just eats smaller meals more often.

OBESITY

A study published in the *Journal of Applied Research in Veterinary Medicine* in 2006 found that 34 percent of dogs older than 12 months were overweight or obese. Other studies have found obese dogs account for 25 percent of all dogs.

Dogs are overweight for the same reasons people are: They eat too much and exercise too little. "Improper feeding can lead to a variety of health conditions. The most common nutrition problem of pets in the U.S. is obesity, because animals are overfed and they don't get enough exercise. This sounds familiar, doesn't it?" say the nutritional experts at Michigan State University.

But the side effects of obesity are not as cut and dried.

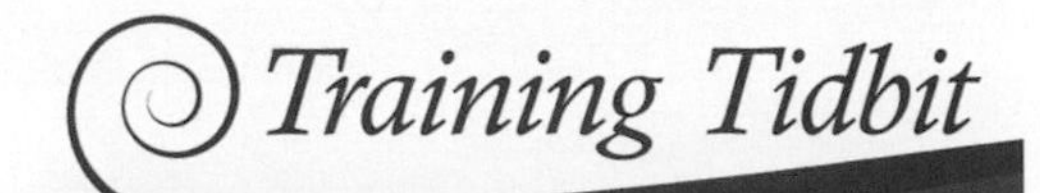

Dogs should have to work for food. Make them sit before you put down their dinner. Make them lie down or shake hands before you give them a treat.

Obesity can be a contributing factor to a long list of medical complaints including diabetes, arthritis, heart and liver disease, reduced stamina, and difficulty breathing.

The plain truth is that no dog has to be obese. Yorkies are not ordering dinner from a fast food menu loaded with calories. They eat what we give them. It takes a strong will to feed your Yorkie only what he needs but the stakes are high enough to strengthen your resolve.

Find other ways to show your Yorkie you love him—buy him a new toy instead of a treat and play with him so he runs more. Take him for a real walk. Cut all treats in half. Your Yorkie will be excited when you give him any treat, no matter how small. Offer him small pieces of raw carrot as a treat.

And, most importantly, measure the food you put in his dish. Do not estimate the amount of food that makes up his breakfast. Chances are you will think a half-cup of food is more than it actually is.

Feeding your dog the right amount of the right food is up to you. It is something you have to pay attention to as long as you have a dog because his nutritional needs may change from year to year.

CHAPTER 8

YORKSHIRE TERRIER HEALTH AND WELLNESS

Yorkshire Terriers are a long-lived breed, with a life expectancy of 12 to 15 years, and some Yorkies live even longer. Every Yorkie owner starts out hoping theirs will be the one to live 15 or even 17 years. The potential is there, since they are sturdy terriers who can thrive in almost any size home and adapt to a multitude of lifestyles. But several factors have to be met if your Yorkie is to live a long and happy life. The right genetic package helps. He has to have a certain amount of luck in avoiding accidents. Nutrition, of course, has to be excellent—and so does regular medical care. Someone—namely, you—has to be keeping track of his weight, his coat condition, his blood tests, his teeth, and his vaccinations. That means taking your Yorkie to the vet at least once a year for an annual exam.

ANNUAL VETERINARY EXAM

The annual physical is a chance for you and your vet to step back and really look at your Yorkie. This is one of those times when the sum of the parts can be more or less than the whole. You and your vet should look at your dog's physical exam, test results, weight, activity level, and general appearance to determine your course of action for the coming year. After an annual exam, you may decide to change his food, change how you feed him, increase his exercise, or hire a groomer.

A physical usually starts with a vet tech weighing your dog. She will ask you questions about what your Yorkie eats, how often he eats, what supplements he gets, how much water he drinks, how much exercise he gets. She will ask you if you are having any problems with your dog. She will note it and pass it along to the vet. Vet techs and vets are good resources, even for issues that are not medical. If you have a question, ask it.

Then your vet will examine your Yorkie from head to tail, listen to his heart and lungs, look in his ears and eyes, and check out his nose and mouth. She will pay close attention to his teeth, and may suggest he have his teeth cleaned at a follow-up appointment. She

Want to Know More?

For tips on how to find a veterinarian for your Yorkie, see Chapter 3: Care of Your Yorkshire Terrier Puppy.

The annual physical is a chance for you and your vet to step back and really look at your Yorkie.

will feel his abdomen and examine his coat and skin. She may have asked you to bring a fecal sample to check for parasites. She may do a heartworm test, and that means drawing blood. She may draw blood anyway to check for other things. She may play with your Yorkie for a bit, to see if he is alert and able to focus.

She may vaccinate your dog or give him a booster. (Be sure to ask what side effects to expect and what after-care your dog will need.) If your dog needs a rabies shot, she will give him the shot and give you a certificate and a rabies collar tag in case you have to prove he has had his shot. In order to license your dog or travel to some countries, you will have to produce the certificate.

Then she will suggest when to bring him back. Some years are uncomplicated, and she will expect you back the following year. Other years, she may schedule a follow-up appointment to recheck on allergies, weight, dental, or eating issues.

PARASITES

Seeing a flea crawl over your little Yorkie's face is a horrifying experience. But the fact is, Yorkies are animals, and animals attract parasites. The good news is we can successfully outsmart fleas and most other parasites with science and every day good dog care.

The enemy parasites include fleas, ticks, mites, fungi, and a variety of worms. They have a certain "yuck" factor, but it is less yucky to learn about preventing them than living with them.

By definition, a parasite is a living organism that lives off another living creature. Parasitic worms do not go out and find their own food. They rely on your dog. That thought should be enough to spur you to take preventive action.

In some cases, parasites can jump from your dog to you. In that case, they would live off you—yet another reason to take parasite prevention seriously.

Internal Parasites

Internal parasites include a host of worms that live inside your dog and affect him in different ways. It may seem to you that there is the threat of a worm for every physical function your dog has and that would be almost true, at least when it comes to heart, lungs, intestines, blood, skin, and hair. But science has stepped up to this challenge and for every worm we know about, there is a treatment. For many, there is even a way to prevent them from making your dog sick. The fast lesson is—avoid areas littered with feces and be faithful about giving your dog year-round heartworm preventive.

Heartworm

Heartworm is both one of the most serious parasites your dog can pick up and one of the easiest to keep at bay. Heartworm can be fatal—even the treatment is high risk—and it is always transmitted to your dog by mosquitoes. A mosquito bites an infected dog, picks up some baby heartworms (microfilariae), and deposits them in the next dog it bites. Six months later, that dog has fully grown heartworms, some 14 inches long. The worms cause serious heart and lung damage if they are allowed to grow.

Mosquitoes with heartworm contamination live in every state, and even dogs who only go out occasionally are at risk, according to the American Veterinary Medicine Association (AVMA). Its list of heartworm symptoms includes coughing, difficulty breathing, lethargy, and loss of appetite. But all these symptoms come months or even years after that dastardly mosquito bit your dog. It is often impossible to link the two. Your vet will have to test your dog for heartworm with blood work, ultrasound, and x-ray, according to the American Heartworm Society. Treatment is available, and is designed to kill worms in your dog's lungs. Until your dog can successfully eliminate the dead worms from his lungs, he is at risk of one of them blocking his arteries (and causing pulmonary thromboembolism).

The good news is you can almost eliminate the risk of heartworm by giving your dog a

By the Numbers

Heartworm infestation is a very serious disease that Yorkie owners should guard against. Even puppies as young as eight weeks old can start taking heartworm preventive at their first puppy exam. They should take it every month after that throughout their life.

preventive regularly—usually a pill given to your dog monthly. The heartworm preventive is prescription-only and only for dogs who test free of heartworm. So, to protect your dog from heartworm, take him to the vet every year and ask for the heartworm blood test and a prescription for the preventive. The cost of the preventive is based on the weight of the dog, so again, the Yorkie's size is an advantage here.

Then remember to give your dog the pill on schedule, even during the coldest season, when you expect no mosquitoes. The American Heartworm Society recommends year-round preventives, especially since many heartworm preventives also help control other worms.

Hookworm

Hookworms live in a dog's intestinal wall, "hooking" on tightly, and sucking his blood. Their eggs are excreted in an infected dog's feces and can live in the soil for a long time. The next dog is infected when he licks the larvae off his feet or they penetrate his skin.

The first thing you can do to protect against hookworm is to clean up any feces as soon as possible. Avoid dog parks that have not been kept clean of feces or even sidewalks where no one picks up after their dogs. Try not to let your dog eat the feces of other dogs (a habit known as *coprophagia*).

Next, talk to your veterinarian about a hookworm preventive. Many heartworm preventives also include an anti-hookworm ingredient. This is a good reason to continue heartworm prevention treatment year round, because the blood loss and weight loss from hookworm can be hard on a dog. Hookworm symptoms include lethargy, pale gums, and bloody diarrhea.

Hookworm is a parasite that people can get, so avoid walking barefoot in areas where you know your dog has defecated.

Roundworm

Roundworms are more common than hookworms, especially in puppies. Adult roundworms live in animal intestines and are excreted with feces. Puppies are sometimes inclined to eat the contaminated feces of wild animals or unfamiliar dogs, so clean up all feces and be careful not to take a young puppy to places littered with feces. Dogs can also get roundworm by eating wild animals that are infected, such as mice, or by licking their feet after walking through contaminated feces or soil.

Symptoms of roundworm include weight loss and a potbellied look. Sometimes you will see worms in the stool. If your puppy has roundworms, pick up all stools as quickly as you can and wash your hands. Roundworms can live in soil for a long time, and they can infect humans.

Your vet should check your puppy's stool at least twice in his first year. Adult dogs are often checked once a year. Many heartworm preventives kill roundworms very effectively.

Tapeworm

Tapeworms live in your dog's intestines. They are white flat worms that have bodies made of connected segments. The segments sometimes break off and are excreted by your dog. You may find small, white, rice-like debris on your dog's rear end or in his bed.

Dogs get tapeworms when they eat a flea or a mouse or squirrel that is infected, so this is another reason to protect your dog from fleas with a flea-control product.

Dogs with tapeworms often have no symptoms, other than shedding the worm segments. If you find worm segments in your dog's hair or in his feces, take him to the vet for treatment.

Whipworm

Whipworms look like little whips, thin on one end and thick on the other; they survive by eating your dog's blood. Your vet can check for them and treat if necessary.

Whipworms live in your dog's intestines and get there through his digestive tract. Dogs pick up whipworms by eating soil or anything else contaminated by another dog that already has them. Dogs excrete whipworm eggs in feces that contaminate soil or tennis balls that roll through them. Whipworm eggs can live in soil for long periods, so keep your dog away from areas littered with other dogs' feces, including mud puddles. A mild infestation may be hard to detect, but as the worms get more numerous they cause bloody diarrhea that can lead to death.

External Parasites

External parasites attack your dog on the outside, through his skin. They bite, sucking his blood and sometimes squirting a toxin inside. Dogs can be allergic to the toxin or, in really severe cases, become weakened from blood loss. Dogs are sometimes so annoyed by parasites on their skin that they scratch or lick incessantly, swallowing the bugs and causing sore spots that can cause additional problems.

Check your Yorkie for fleas and ticks after he's been outside.

Fleas

Fleas may be one of the few creatures on earth that nobody likes. Finding a flea on your dog can be overwhelming when you have done everything you can think of to prevent them. Fleas are persistent and can jump a surprising distance considering how small they are—from 7 to 13 inches (18 to 33 cm) depending on which study you believe—more than enough

If you have more than one dog, they should all be treated if one turns out to have mites.

to get them from dog to dog, from dog to dog bed, from dog to car seat, from dog to human. Fleas are pesky, hard to eradicate, can carry worms, and can drive your dog crazy with itching. Fleas have been known to torture dogs who don't go outside—in these cases, the best theory is that fleas came into the house on another animal such as a cat, on the clothes of people who have dogs with fleas, or on people who walked through a flea-infested area. Other theories include entry on a mouse or bat or even a squirrel. If you have moved into a place within the last few months and find fleas, the fleas may have been there before you.

You can spot the presence of fleas by the chaos they leave in their wake. Your dog may be scratching and chewing, as if to get something off his skin. You may even see a flea—a small dark dot jumping erratically toward a hiding place on your dog, or floating in his bath water. More likely, you may see flea dirt—dried blood excreted by the flea after it's eaten its fill. This looks like large grains of black pepper but squishes dark red when moistened. You can find this sometimes by combing through your dog's hair with a fine-toothed flea comb.

The best approach to flea control is prevention. Some monthly heartworm preventives and topical treatments—liquid applied on the dog's back between his shoulders—are very effective against fleas. Heartworm preventives sterilize the fleas, so you won't have eggs or larvae, which prevents the fleas from multiplying. Topical treatments will get rid of the adult fleas almost immediately but not affect the eggs that have already been laid. You may need both.

Fleas are so hard to eradicate because they lay so many eggs so fast. The eggs are amazingly resilient, fall off the dog into the grass, the carpet, and bedding and can lay dormant for long periods.

If your dog has not been on any preventive and shows up one day with fleas, you have a multiple-tiered task ahead.

First, take your dog to the vet to confirm that he has fleas. The vet will probably prescribe a topical treatment for immediate relief. Consider a monthly heartworm preventive that sterilizes future fleas and kills any tapeworm your dog could get from the fleas.

Then it's time to attack the larvae, wherever they are.

A flea's life has four stages: egg, larvae, pupa, and adult. Within two days of eating your Yorkie's blood, an adult flea begins laying eggs, almost 30 a day. The eggs develop into larvae in a few days and then into a pupa or cocoon. This is the tricky part. Almost unseen, fleas in the earlier stages can lie dormant for months.

At the same time you treat your dog, treat your house and yard. Start by washing your pet's bedding and vacuuming everything you can—furniture, drapes, car, baseboards, underneath the couch. Be careful to change the bag in the vacuum or empty the bin immediately, seal up the contents, and get them out of the house. The next day, vacuum again. It may take several days' vacuuming to remove all the flea eggs.

If you have a more serious infestation, you may need to use an insecticide or hire a professional exterminator. If you're doing it yourself, read the label carefully, be sure the product is effective against fleas and will not harm the dog, then follow the directions carefully. Use as little as you can. You may need to keep your dog off the sprayed area for a day or two, because dogs lick their feet and some insecticides can be harmful to dogs.

In the yard, fleas like warm moist places, not hot and dry. If you live in an area with deep frost, outdoor fleas may go dormant for the winter—but not the indoor ones. If you live in more temperate climates, outdoor fleas are active all year.

Mites

Several types of mites would like to set up housekeeping on your dog. Mites are tiny parasites that feed off your dog, causing irritation and itching. They require veterinary treatment and sometimes special shampoos. If you have more than one dog, they should all be treated if one turns out to have mites.

One of the most common is the ear mite, or *otodectic mange*. If your dog is shaking his head or scratching at his ears, or if his ears have a funny smell, he may have ear mites. A vet will have to clean his ears and treat them with a miticide.

The sarcoptic mite is another of these pesky arachnids, sometimes known as *scabies* or *scabies mange* because it makes your dog look mangy. (Mange is any uneven and damaged coat with irritated skin.) These mites jump on your dog from another dog, or from grooming

Multi-Dog Tip

If one of your dogs gets fleas, ticks, mites, or worms, take all your dogs in for a check-up. Your dogs may have picked up the parasites in the same place the first one did, or they may have migrated from one dog to the next.

Yorkies are susceptible to Legg-Calve-Perthes disease, a hip deformity.

equipment or a contaminated kennel; once they are on your dog, they tunnel into his skin. If your dog is diagnosed with this type of mite, clean your house as if he had fleas.

A less common mite creates *walking dandruff* (or *Cheyletiella mange*). Usually eliminated by flea preventives, this mite creates a rash that flakes off like dandruff. When the mite moves under the flakes, it looks as if your dog's skin is moving.

Chiggers are mites that live in decaying vegetation. Your dog may discover them on a hike. Chigger larvae are colorful—red, yellow, or orange—parasites, so small that they are hard to see.

Ringworm

Ringworm is a fungus that attacks your dog's skin and hair, causing round blotches of bald, scaly skin. Dogs get ringworm from other dogs and from some plants. The bad news is that they can just as easily pass it on to you.

Your vet can treat ringworm with antifungal shampoos, creams, and medicines. Some dogs will heal without medical help but, in the meantime, other dogs and people may become infected. Take your dog to the vet and follow her bathing instructions. It may take some time, but don't give up on the treatment. Wash your dog's bedding with bleach to eliminate the fungus and prevent reinfection. Scrub any other surfaces where your dog spends time, such as his crate, car blanket, patio, or furniture. Clean grooming equipment, leashes, and collars.

Ringworm is not common, and most dogs can be treated. No vaccine for ringworm is available.

Ticks

Ticks are six-legged as larvae and eight-legged as nymphs and adults. They hide in the grass near woods and leap onto a dog as he walks by. The tick is out for blood and will eventually bury his head in your dog and gorge itself until it swells up. Ticks are nasty carriers of several diseases including Rocky Mountain spotted fever, Lyme disease, canine ehrlichiosis, canine babesiosis, and canine hepatozoonosis. Some of these can spread to people. Plus, some dogs are allergic to tick saliva. So, avoiding or removing ticks before they can attach to your dog and reproduce is a good idea. Whenever your dog has been in a park or a wooded area, examine him for ticks. If you find one, avoid squeezing it, because tick blood is harmful to people as well as pets. Wearing a glove, use tweezers to pull the tick off smoothly, so its head does not stay in your dog. Drown the tick in rubbing alcohol and toss it in the trash, not into the sewer system.

If the head remains imbedded in your dog, or he has many ticks attached, call your veterinarian. If you are taking a vacation in the woods or an area known to have ticks, ask your veterinarian about tick preventives.

YORKSHIRE TERRIER HEALTH ISSUES

Although many Yorkies live a good long life, others are susceptible to several health conditions that the breed seems to be predisposed toward. The Yorkshire Terrier Club of America recommends that Yorkies be tested for the following conditions: eye disorders, patellar luxation, hip dysplasia, Legg-Calve-Perthes disease (at 12 months or older), and hypothyroidism. An additional test, for liver bile acid, can help identify a liver shunt.

Eyes

Yorkies in general have only a few eye problems, says Sharon Griffin, a member of the Yorkshire Terrier Club of America Health Committee. They sometimes get severe dry eye that can result in damage to the cornea, so take your Yorkie to the vet if he scratches at his eyes or squints. Older dogs can get cataracts that eventually blind them. Cataracts affect the dog's lens, and that can be removed, just as it is in people. The Canine Eye Registration Foundation (CERF) test by a canine ophthalmologist can determine if your Yorkie has any genetic eye diseases. Even young puppies can be tested. Breeding dogs should be tested every year.

Hip Dysplasia

In dysplastic hips, the bones don't fit together properly. The hip is a ball-and-socket joint, with the ball (the round head of the femur) fitting tightly into the socket (an indentation in the pelvis). Usually, in dysplastic dogs, the pelvis is too shallow for the femur, creating a lax fit. This, in turn, wears down the bones and cartilage faster than a normal fit, and the dog develops arthritis. Treatment may include weight loss, pain medication, supplements, crate rest, and surgery.

The Orthopedic Foundation for Animals (OFA) rates dog x-rays for hip dysplasia with passing grades of Fair, Good, and Excellent. Hip dysplasia is not a big problem in Yorkies, but if you want your dog's hips evaluated, take him to a local veterinarian for special OFA x-rays that will be sent off for evaluation. The

Advice From a Liver Shunt Expert

Olga Fireman runs a national web list for people who have small dogs with liver shunts (http://pets.groups.yahoo.com/group/DogLiverDisease/). "I started researching liver problems because we got a dog in rescue who had had liver shunt surgery in puppyhood," she said. Many Yorkies with liver shunts end up in rescue because the owners can't afford the surgery, she says, with liver shunt surgery costing between $3,500 and $7,000, partly because the diagnostic tests are so expensive. Some dogs with a mild version can be managed without surgery, according to Fireman, and other dogs are too sick for surgery. "At some point, the risks of surgery outweigh the benefits. It's a pretty risky procedure," Fireman says. She has adapted a medical management model developed at Cornell University that starts with a vegetarian diet because she says dogs with liver shunts cannot handle the protein in meat. She recommends a regimen of supplements.

Fireman has noticed a connection between severe or long-term shunts and Yorkie behavior. She remembers one five-pound (2 kg) male Yorkie. "He was very aggressive. He bit me every chance he got," Fireman says. "He was so sick. The toxins built up and crossed the blood-brain barrier. He was like a mean drunk."

The rescue dogs she is able to save and put up for adoption have to go to homes willing to put out some extra effort. The liver of a Yorkie who has had a liver shunt may be damaged and not able to handle what a normal liver can. "We've seen too many dogs put on regular protein after surgery, and then they begin to have problems," Fireman says. "I want this dog on four meals a day forever and use the supplements. Vegetarian protein. No store-bought treats. No rawhide. No flea and tick preventives. Heartworm preventive at a reduced dosage."

Yorkies can be tested for liver bile abnormalities very early, she says, between nine and eleven weeks. All Yorkies should be tested by six months, she says, but some breeders don't. Unfortunately, according to Fireman, dogs with no symptoms can be carriers of the gene and, when bred, this leads to litters with puppies who are carriers of the disorder and puppies with liver shunts.

dog must be two years old for OFA evaluation. In a small sample testing of 74 Yorkies, the OFA found that 5.5 percent had abnormal hips.

Legg-Calve-Perthes

A hip deformity that Yorkies do get is Legg-Calve-Perthes. In this disorder, some bone cells are starved of blood and die, causing lameness. This has a genetic link, but it can also be caused by trauma. Treatment includes pain medication, crate rest, and surgery. Sometimes the disorder requires a complete hip replacement. Toy dogs sometimes have symptoms as early as four months. The OFA also rates x-rays for Legg-Calve-Perthes.

Liver Shunts

In some puppies, the blood that is supposed to go through the liver for cleansing continues to bypass the liver, as it did before birth. As the dog grows up, toxins accumulate in the blood.

Some dogs have complete liver bypasses or shunts and some have only a partial shunt.

Liver shunts are a congenital problem in Yorkshire Terriers that every owner should know about and be on the alert for. Liver bile tests can show something is amiss, and x-rays can confirm shunts or portosystemic shunts. Surgery is the most common treatment, but some dogs who cannot tolerate surgery can be managed back to better health by strict adherence to a special diet.

Patellar Luxation

If your Yorkie suddenly lifts up a hind leg, yelps, and waits a minute before putting it back down, he may have patellar luxation, the American Kennel Club Health Foundation says. This is a common problem in Yorkies and all small breeds. OFA statistics show that about 24 percent of Yorkies have patellar luxations. The patella is the dog's kneecap, and it should fit in a groove between two ridges on the femur. In patellar luxation, the patella slips over the ridges, out of position. This is caused by genetic deformity—the bones just weren't formed correctly. Usually, the kneecap slides back into place, and the dog moves on. In severe cases, the patella can't get back to its normal position. Severe or even moderate cases require surgery. The groove can be deepened or the kneecap can be attached in place. The good news is, the surgery is highly successful. The American Kennel Club Health Foundation says dogs who have had the surgery generally live normal lives. Untreated, the condition gets worse and more painful. Patellar luxation can be diagnosed early in some cases, while dogs are still puppies.

Thyroid

The thyroid is just below a dog's larynx in his neck. Its hormones are responsible for

Lack of energy may be a sign of a thyroid problem.

regulating the dog's metabolism. Because it is involved in everything that goes on in your Yorkie, almost any kind of symptom may be a symptom of thyroid dysfunction. In other words, it can be hard to diagnose. Some symptoms that might trace back to thyroid dysfunction are lack of energy, poor coat, and weight gain. Fortunately, most Yorkies have few thyroid problems.

Autoimmune thyroiditis causes hypothyroidism. This is an inherited disease in which the dog's own body attacks its thyroid. It is treatable with thyroid hormone.

Tracheal Collapse

Tracheal collapse happens in toy breeds when the cartilage rings in the trachea fail to maintain their shape. The dog's windpipe (trachea) is held open by a series of firm cartilage rings. When this cartilage isn't as rigid as it should be, the rings can collapse, making it hard for the dog to breathe. The classic symptom of a collapsing trachea is a goose-honk cough.

Losing weight, using a harness instead of a collar, and taking glucosamine may help a mild case. A more severe case requires surgery to implant artificial support in the trachea.

CANINE HEALTH ISSUES

Yorkshire Terriers are dogs, and as such, are susceptible to those health issues that affect all dogs. These can be chronic, temporary, contagious, or life-ending. But the good news is that it is unlikely your Yorkie would get all of these—even if he lives to 15! On the other hand, knowing how to identify a problem quickly could reduce the amount of time your Yorkie is sick.

Allergies

Like all dogs, Yorkies can be allergic to a type of food, to grass, flea bites, pollen, and any other of a long list of things—which makes it hard to determine exactly what your dog is allergic to and eliminate it. With work, however, you can solve at least a few of these puzzles and ease his allergies. Start with a visit to your vet. Before you go, try to identify a pattern in your dog's symptoms. Does he sneeze after swimming? Does he throw up after a certain type of treat? Allergies can affect your dog's skin, or his respiratory or digestive systems. He can develop an itchy rash or itchy pads on his feet that he will lick until they bleed. He may sneeze and look at you out of watery eyes. Or, he may vomit, develop diarrhea, or lose his appetite.

Once you identify the cause of the allergy, you can take action. Food allergies go away if you find the specific culprit he is allergic to and eliminate it from his diet. Flea bites can be reduced by anti-flea products. Mild allergies to grass or pollen can be treated with an over-the-counter product, such as Benadryl. (Always consult your vet before giving your dog any medication; your vet will tell you how much to give your dog, how often he can have it, and whether or not it will interact

Like all dogs, Yorkies can be allergic to a big list of things.

with any other medications he is taking. Antihistamines like Benadryl can make some dogs sleepy and that might not be good if you are planning an active day. Ask about other side effects.)

Tracking down exactly what your dog is allergic to can take time and patience. Commercial dog foods have several common ingredients that some dogs are allergic to, such as corn or wheat. If you suspect a corn or wheat allergy, look for commercial foods that don't have one or the other or both and try that. Depending on how severe your dog's symptoms are, you may have to try a new diet, or a new type of protein he has never had before, such as venison or duck. Then, gradually add other things back into his diet until you discover what causes the symptoms. This can take weeks, but don't give up. Allergies can make your dog miserable and eliminating the symptoms is worth a herculean effort on your part.

Cancer

Dogs, in general, get cancer at about the same rate humans do, according to the American Veterinary Medical Association (AVMA). The AVMA has identified ten symptoms that could lead to a cancer diagnosis:

1. Abnormal swelling that persists
2. Sores that do not heal
3. Weight loss
4. Loss of appetite
5. Bleeding or discharge from any body opening
6. Offensive odor
7. Difficulty eating or swallowing

If your Yorkie's ears get wet during bathing, it increases the chance of ear infections.

8. Hesitation to exercise or loss of stamina
9. Persistent lameness or stiffness
10. Difficulty breathing, urinating, or defecating.

If you see any of these in your Yorkie, make an appointment with your vet.

Cancer is a collection of cells that grow out of control until they interfere with normal functions. Treatment consists of trying to kill cancer cells with drugs or radiation, or by removing them through surgery. Diagnosis and treatment of cancer at a major university veterinary school can be very expensive. The causes of cancer are, of course, a topic of major research, both for human cancer and canine, and so is its treatment. Many scientists now see similarities between human and canine cancer and hope that research in one will lead to improved treatment and increased survival rates in both.

Cancer is a very common cause of death in older dogs, including Yorkies. About six million dogs are diagnosed with cancer every year, according to the Animal Cancer Foundation. The foundation supports research that compares animal and human cancers, since we share the same environment and many of the same foods. We also share a genetic similarity in the way some cancers are inherited.

In 2009, the U.S. Food and Drug Administration (FDA) approved the first veterinary drug to treat cancer, Palladia, for skin-based mast cell tumors. Dr. Cheryl London, of the Ohio State University College of Veterinary Medicine, led the research, according to the American Kennel Club Health Foundation.

Ear Infections

Ear infections can start in many ways. Bacteria grow in wet ears, especially if there is a lack of air circulation because of thick hair. If water gets in the ears during bathing, or if you push it in by using a cotton-tipped swab, the chances for an ear infection increase. Sometimes, fungal infections get started while your dog is on an antibiotic.

If your Yorkie starts shaking his head or rubbing an ear, take him to your vet. Other symptoms could be a foul odor in the ear or waxy build-up. Early treatment of an ear infection is best. At the vet, his ears may have to be cleaned, examined, and a sample of the buildup taken for examination under the microscope; he'll then be treated with medication, and you will have to continue the medication at home.

Eye Infections

Symptoms of eye problems can be obvious, if your dog's eyes are watery and teary, or he has matter in them. Sometimes he will blink more than he usually does or squint. He may even rub his eyes with his paw. Eye problems may occur in his tear duct, his eye, or his eyelid. This is when you need your vet: She can diagnose exactly where the problem is and what to do about it. You can help her by noting what color any eye secretions are. Blepharitis, for example, is a bacterial infection of the eyelid with a mucous that looks like pus. It is treated with antibiotics. Sometimes if an eyelid swells, it could be an allergy to an insect bite and is short-lived and needs no treatment. Conjunctivitis (also known as *red eye* or *pink eye*) is an inflammation that can be caused by a virus, bacteria, or an allergy. Treatment varies depending on the cause, but usually includes flushing the eye and applying an ointment.

Sometimes dry eye is mistaken for conjunctivitis. Dogs with dry eye have a disorder of the tear gland. They produce fewer tears and more of a discharge that is like thick mucus. Dogs with dry eye have a dull appearing eye. Dry eye can be treated with drops or, in some cases, drugs.

ALTERNATIVE THERAPIES

Even traditional medicine has taken a second look at some ancient alternative therapies lately. A few, like acupuncture, have become part of mainstream medicine. Others are being studied in rigorous tests. Many alternative therapies have their base in the Chinese art

Acupuncture is an ancient chinese needle treatment.

of herbal medicine, with its long history of success in treating some maladies. Others are newer, such as homeopathy. If you are attracted to an alternative therapy, discuss this with your vet. Very often, the most successful treatments seem to involve a combination of traditional Western medicine and alternative therapy. Homeopathy, acupuncture, and herbal treatment are part of a broader category of medicine known as *holistic care*.

Acupuncture

This ancient Chinese needle treatment is gaining acceptance in the world of Western medicine because of success stories from animal owners. In acupuncture, needles are placed in the dog at strategic points for healing or relief of pain. The International Veterinary Acupuncture Society (IVAS) says acupuncture is used for paralysis, musculoskeletal problems such as arthritis, and skin, respiratory, reproductive and gastrointestinal problems. Acupuncture can stimulate nerves, increase blood circulation, reduce muscle spasm, and trigger the release of endorphins and cortisol, according to the IVAS. It is considered safe if done by a trained veterinarian practitioner. Acupuncture may take several treatments to achieve success. Each treatment can last up to 30 minutes. The American Academy of Veterinary Acupuncture (AAVA), an affiliate of the international group, has 800 members, according to Simon Flynn, executive director. If you are looking for an acupuncturist, Flynn recommends choosing one who is certified by a group that requires continuing education, such as his group (AAVA) or the Chi Institute. "If I am going to an acupuncturist to treat my animal, I'm going to want someone who is interested in continuing education and learning," Flynn says. "For that reason, I would go to one of those organizations. I would go to AAVA." Whether your regular vet will refer you to an acupuncturist depends on the vet, Flynn says, but the conversation should start with the veterinarian who has treated your Yorkie. If you say you would like to try acupuncture she might refer you, or she might suggest something else to try in her office. But give her a chance to respond to acupuncture. "There is increasing acceptance of it as alternative therapy," Flynn says.

Chiropractic

The American Veterinary Chiropractic Association (AVCA) certifies licensed doctors of chiropractic medicine and veterinarians who have completed programs in animal chiropractic and passed an exam. Chiropractic medicine specializes in the adjustment of vertebral joints, extremity joints, and cranial sutures, according to the AVCA, to improve a long list of physical issues, including pain in the neck, back, leg, or tail; muscle spasms; nerve problems; difficulty chewing; postsurgical care; bowel or bladder disorders; maintenance of joint and spinal health; and chronic internal medicine disorders. Chiropractic specialists focus on aligning the bones in the dog's spine and joints, and say dogs readily accept the treatment. Several sessions may be required. The session will

Flower Essence

One widespread use of alternative medicine is flower essences—tiny amounts of flowers suspended in a liquid given to people and dogs for behavior issues. Rescue Remedy may be the most famous—it is composed of five different essences and is used to calm dogs.

start with a case history, a gait analysis, and a physical exam of potential trouble spots. Chiropractic is not intended as a substitute for traditional veterinary care, but as complementary care.

Herbal Medicine

The increase in the popularity of herbal medicines corresponds to several trends in Western countries, including the rise of natural foods consumption in people. Herbs have been in use, of course, for thousands of years, but in Western countries, they declined in popularity as pharmaceuticals became more effective at treating illness. The side effects of some powerful modern drugs, however, have persuaded some to delay or avoid these medications, looking instead to herbal remedies as safer and less likely to have side effects. Others say that modern medicine is narrowly concerned with treating the symptom and not the cause, and the search for safe and effective treatments has led those people back to the herbs our ancestors used. Others turn to herbal treatments when nothing else seems to be helping their dog. Others want the goodness of the whole plant, not just one part, and they want it as unprocessed as possible.

Dog owners research several issues when they are considering a herbal treatment: Is there a study or any proof that the treatment works on what is wrong with your dog? Does the herb have any side effects or interaction with anything else your dog is taking? The idea that herbs have no side effects is mistaken. Some herbs are very powerful and, if used poorly or in excess, can cause harm. Garlic, for example, can be tolerated by dogs in small amounts but in huge quantities can cause anemia. Some experts in herbal medicine also sell the herbs they recommend to you, thus creating a conflict of interest. It is to their benefit if you buy multiple products. Finally, the American Animal Hospital Association (AAHA) reminds us that the FDA considers herbal medicines to be nutrition supplements or nutraceuticals and does not regulate them. Exactly what is in that bottle of healing herbs does not have to be proved. Many products have never been tested by rigorous studies.

That said, some herbs can be safely used as a complement to traditional medicine. Cranberry is used for urinary or kidney dysfunction in dogs, just as it is in people. The AAHA lists a few other alternative treatments that are in widespread use: glucosamine and chondroitin are nutraceuticals that are not technically herbal because they come from shellfish and animals, but they are supplements that are widely used for arthritis and joint issues; echinacea is used to boost the immune system; aloe is used as a soothing ointment; ginger is used to settle upset stomachs; vitamin C is an antioxidant that is believed to have many uses including anti-aging and anti-arthritis properties; milk thistle is used for liver problems; and gingko is used for aging animals with cognitive dysfunction or the canine senility.

Another use of nutrition to fight illness in

Experts have a few tricks to make it easier to give a dog a pill. Wrap the pill in a thin coating of food such peanut butter and bread or sink it in a small piece of hot dog. Ask your Yorkie to sit in front of you. Offer the pill as a reward for sitting.

dogs is yogurt for gastrointestinal distress. The good bacteria in yogurt help restore the intestine to health.

Ask your vet for help with Yorkie doses. In many cases, human-grade herbs can be bought and adapted for dog use.

Homeopathy

Samuel Hahnemann, a German doctor, created homeopathy in 1796, basing it on the law of similars: *Like cures Like*. If a substance created symptoms similar to those of a disease, Hahnemann taught, it could be used to treat the disease. But as a treatment, he diluted that substance down to infinitesimal levels.

Homeopathy looks at the symptom as evidence that the body is trying to heal itself, and it works to help the body, rather than eliminate the symptom. It is all about boosting the dog's own immune system into high gear.

Some herbs can be safely used as a complement to traditional medicine.

Homeopathy is used by professional clinicians to treat a wide variety of ailments. Seek advice before treating your dog yourself. Although most homeopathic remedies are safe, a novice may choose the wrong one or use it incorrectly, wasting treatment time. Homeopathic remedies can be used with conventional treatment in most cases.

Massage

Canine massage is a well-established way to restore the canine athlete, improve dog–owner relationships, and relax dogs with behavior problems. Deep massage therapy is different from petting your dog in his favorite place. It is a systematic stimulation of his skin and circulation system, and a stretching and soothing of his muscles by someone who knows dog anatomy. You can take a course in massage to learn the therapeutic way to massage your own dog, or you may choose to find a professional massage therapist. Different types of canine massage are available.

Linda Tellington-Jones is one of the most famous practitioners of a massage technique that can be used on dogs, as well as on people and other animals. She created the Tellington TTouch, a system of circular massage movements designed to wake up the body's own cells. The massage also relaxes the dog, allowing him to participate in training. Her type of massage can help with behavior problems, such as leash pulling, and with physical problems, such as carsickness and aging, she says. She offers training sessions throughout the country.

Other canine massage therapists use familiar massage techniques that were developed for people, such as Swedish therapeutic massage

A combination of traditional Western medicine and alternative therapy can be successful.

with aromatherapy. These are designed to improve blood circulation, relieve arthritis pain, and ease the pain of strained muscles.

You can do some doggy massage at home without any training, and participating in this soothing ritual may relax you both and help deepen the bond you have with your dog. Your Yorkie is tiny, so your first concern should be to do no harm. Be aware of his body with your touch and do not press too hard. Start with your Yorkie on your lap. Stroke him gently from head to tail. Rub behind his ears, between his eyes, down his nose, and under his chin. Use a soft yet firm touch. Rub each shoulder in a circular motion, then stroke down each leg. Rub his feet. Stroke his back, and rub his hips in a circular motion. Stroke down each back leg and rub his back feet.

He may not want to stay still the first time. Do not force him: Massage should be relaxing, something you should both enjoy. He may learn to like it. Try for short sessions, extending the massage each time you do it.

EMERGENCY CARE

All dogs have emergencies, and Yorkies are no exception. In fact, Yorkies may need more emergency care than most because of their size. They may be stepped on or even sat on, and end up with a broken bone. Emergencies run the gamut from life-threatening to annoying (to the dog), but it is up to you to get your Yorkie through. Stay calm and keep the number of a 24-hour emergency vet clinic nearby.

First Aid

Accidents happen: Your dog eats something he shouldn't, or he takes on a bigger dog and gets bitten. Suddenly, your Yorkie is looking to you for help. Experienced dog owners have a first-aid kit or shelf with the things they need to grab in an emergency. Some things to consider adding to your dog first-aid shelf:

- tweezers to pull thorns out of pads
- scissors to cut collars that get stuck on something with the dog in them
- thermometer to take a dog's temperature
- clean rags to stop bleeding
- antibiotic ointment
- syringe to give liquid medicine
- flashlight

Bites

Close to the ground, out and about, your dog will come across lots of things that bite or sting. Your first job is to determine what bit him. Next is to stop the bleeding.

First on the list of bites is a dog bite. Each dog bite is unique and requires a different reaction. If, for example, you have two Yorkies and one nips the other while they are playing, little medical care is required. You know both dogs are healthy and have had all their shots. Stop any bleeding with pressure from a clean cloth and clean up the blood.

If however, your Yorkie is attacked by a strange dog, your reaction will be much different. The first goal is to stop the bleeding. Apply pressure to the wound. Use a clean cloth or sterile gauze squares. Try to get any information you can on the other dog. After a few minutes, wrap the wound tightly and go to your vet or a veterinary emergency room.

If an insect bites your Yorkie, figure out what bit him. Some spiders are poisonous to dogs. Other spiders, as well as ants and bees, cause local reactions, such as swelling. Get out the flashlight and look for a stinger or anything else that may be in the insect bite. Get the stinger out without squeezing it. Apply a paste of baking soda and water to the sting. If the swelling is severe, you may need to apply an ice pack. Calamine lotion may also be used. If the dog continues to react, take him to your vet. Antihistamines such as Benadryl may be useful in cases of severe swelling.

If a snake bites your dog, it is important to take a second to identify the snake. Your vet's diagnosis and treatment will depend on what you saw. Watch your dog for swelling, pain, panting, drooling, vomiting, diarrhea, or uncoordinated walking that might indicate he was bitten by a venomous (poison) snake. In that case, keep your dog calm to slow the spread of venom and get to your vet immediately.

Wild animal bites should always be seen by a vet; feral cats and other wild animals carry disease and parasites.

Bleeding

It is sometimes hard to find a wound underneath a full Yorkie coat. If you spot blood on your Yorkie, your first job is to find the wound and stop the bleeding. You may be able to do that by applying pressure, or you may need a tourniquet. Apply pressure with a clean cloth or sterile gauze pads. Tourniquets are used as a last resort on the legs and tail if direct pressure has failed to stop the bleeding. Place a leash, cord, or a strip of fabric between the wound and the dog's heart. Tighten the tourniquet until the bleeding stops. Loosen the tourniquet every 10 minutes to check for rebleeding.

An ordinary wound, such a scrape, can be cleaned and bandaged at home but a deep wound should be seen by a veterinarian. They are easily infected and may need stitches.

Broken Bones

Unfortunately, Yorkies get more than their share of broken bones. They are little dogs who think they are big enough to jump off the back of a couch or out of your arms. And frequently, such a jump ends in a broken leg.

How will you know if your Yorkie has a broken bone? Broken bones are painful. Your Yorkie may not be able to walk. Broken bones swell and, in the worst cases, they poke through the skin and are visible.

Dogs in pain are not as sweet and willing as they usually are, so handle your dog with care. You may have to keep a hand around his muzzle so he can't bite. Find a way to support his broken limb so it doesn't move. This may require tying a rigid protective casing around his leg. Take him immediately to the vet or emergency veterinary hospital.

Hypothermia is a concern for all toy breeds—put a coat on your Yorkie and don't let him stay in the cold for too long.

It's a good idea for dog owners to have a disaster preparedness plan.

Frostbite

Hypothermia is a concern for all toy breeds. Even Yorkies with very long hair have only a thin, single outer coat. They lack the thick undercoat that sled and sporting dogs have to keep them warm out in the cold. Yorkies need to wear a sweater when you do. A dog with hypothermia starts shivering then becomes lethargic. If you took his temperature, you would find it has dropped several degrees below normal. (Normal temperatures can vary from dog to dog but usually hover slightly above 101 °F [38 °C]). When the dog has been very cold, he may get frostbite. Part of his body actually freezes—most likely his tail, footpads, ear tips, or scrotum in a male. You can tell by looking carefully at those extremities: Frostbitten skin is pale white or has a bluish tint. Soak it in warm water—not hot—for 20 minutes without rubbing. Take your dog to a vet. Frostbitten skin can be painful while healing and irritating to the dog.

Heatstroke

Dogs sweat only a little through their footpads and rely on panting to cool themselves. When the air is warm or hot, they have a more difficult time staying cool. Hot cars, extended exercise on a hot day, even being muzzled under a hot hair dryer have been known to cause heatstroke.

Dogs in heatstroke pant heavily. The inside of the mouth appears bright red, and the dog may vomit or have bloody diarrhea. The dog may collapse. Speed is important in treating heatstroke. Take your Yorkie into air-conditioning as quickly as you can. You may have to spray him with a cool mist or even place him in some cool water, depending on how severe his symptoms are. A cool washcloth placed on his belly or footpads may help mild cases. When the crisis has eased, call your vet.

On hot days, provide your dog with cool water and a cool place to sleep. This is not the time for deep fuzzy blankets or mattresses. Skip the heavy exercise.

Poisoning

Dogs will eat almost everything, but everything is not good for dogs. Sometimes you will get to the scene just as he picks up something and swallows it. Other times, you will not know what he ate that made him sick.

A long list of things that are poisonous to dogs includes prescription drugs, chocolate, rat poison, yard pesticides, and over-the-counter painkillers such as ibuprofen and acetaminophen.

If you know what your Yorkie ate, call your vet or the ASPCA Animal Poison Control Center at (888) 426-4435, where vets are available 24 hours a day (there is a charge). The poison control center suggests that you pick up whatever is left of the poison your dog ate and bag it, in case you have to go to your vet (and bring the container as well). You can also call the National Animal Poison Control Center, 1-900-680-0000 (a fee is charged).

Follow your vet's instructions about inducing vomiting; induced vomiting is not a good idea if the poison is a cleaning solution or acid, a sharp object, or if the product label specifically states "do not induce vomiting." Hydrogen peroxide will induce vomiting but Yorkies require very little, a half-teaspoon to a teaspoon.

If you didn't see him eat anything dangerous, you may suspect poison if he starts drooling, vomiting or has diarrhea. Call your vet.

Poison Control

Keep these phone numbers handy:

- **ASPCA Animal Poison Control Center: 1-888-426-4435**
- **National Animal Poison Control Center: 1-900-680-0000**

Disaster Preparedness

The idea of dog owners being prepared for a major disaster gained popularity after 2005 Hurricane Katrina left thousands of abandoned pets in its wake. Pet owners were told to leave their animals behind because no plan existed for their care.

Your hometown may not be subject to hurricanes, but every dog owner should have a plan for disaster, no matter what the type. What would happen to your dog if you had to leave your house because of a fire, flood, landslide, or tornado? What if you had to leave in a hurry? Or, in an opposite scenario, what if you were trapped in your home for days or a week?

The American Kennel Club urges dog owners to plan and prepare for emergencies before they happen. Dogs should be permanently marked with tattoos or microchips in case they get separated in a crisis. Dog tags should have cell phone numbers or e-mail addresses, in case you are on the move when your dog gets lost. Research more than one escape route from your home, and collect evacuation materials such as maps for the house and the car. Make sure you find a place where you can go that will take dogs. This could be a safe haven that will take you and your dog, or it could be a boarding kennel that guarantees it will look after the dog if you have to go to a shelter that does not accept animals. Relatives in close-by cities can serve as safe havens.

Your dog needs his own emergency kit, including food and water in airtight containers, medicine, bowls, a crate with a blanket, poop pick-up bags, a sweater, a grooming brush, a chew toy and a fetch toy, and leashes. Paper towels and a flashlight are nice to have. (You may want to pack a spare crate with emergency equipment and leave it in the car.) Remember to change the food and water every few weeks. The American Society for the Prevention of Cruelty to Animals (ASPCA) suggests adding a recent photo of your dog in case he gets lost.

Finally, always keep at least a week's supply of food and dog medicine on hand in the house, in case you are unable to leave your home.

CHAPTER 9

YORKSHIRE TERRIER TRAINING

One of the advantages of living with a Yorkie is his quick-wittedness. Yorkies are smart little dogs who can learn faster than many other types of dogs. They are terriers, though, and that means they can be stubborn, too. The trick to teaching them is to find a way that makes it fun for your particular dog to do what you want. This usually means lots of short training sessions, rewards that hit your dog's glee spot, and a tone of voice that means you are happy, too. It means breaking complicated commands down into easy-to-learn segments, and practicing each segment many times before moving on to the next.

Sue Walters, who has trained several Yorkies to agility and rally championships, said training a Yorkie is all about baby steps. "If you try to push them, they will shut down on you," Walter said. She is training her Yorkie, Jazzy, for competitive Open obedience. "She was retrieving the dumbbell at home just beautifully. I got to obedience class, we all lined up, and we threw the dumbbell. She went out there, and she was sniffing and sniffing and totally ignored the dumbbell. I got so frustrated. I was disappointed because she had been doing it so well at home." Walters, who is as patient a trainer as there is, raised her voice. "I kind of yelled at her. She shut right down on me," Walters said. Worse, Walters knew it would be a long slow road before Jazzy would be retrieving the dumbbell again. Walters started retraining the very next day. "The next day at home we played with it. I got excited about it. She did really well," Walters said. "The next week in class she did it really well. It was all in how I handled it. You can't push them. People expect overnight improvement. It's not going to happen."

INTERMEDIATE OBEDIENCE COMMANDS

Because Yorkies are so little, it is tempting to pick them up to avoid trouble and just remove them from the scene. Some Yorkie owners see less incentive to teach them to heel and down-stay as they would if they had a big dog. But that attitude short-changes Yorkshire Terriers. They are dogs, just as much as Golden Retrievers are dogs, and they can learn to follow obedience commands. They deserve to experience that sense of accomplishment that comes from working hard and making you happy. Plus, dogs of any size who obey are more likely to get out and about, stay in shape,

Training Tidbit

Change rewards weekly or twice weekly. Use soft food treats and vary them to add variety to your training routine. If your dog is having trouble with one command, increase the desirability of the treat. Switch from chicken to liver, for example.

and be well-socialized. After your dog has learned the "sit" and the "down" commands and to walk on a loose leash, he is ready for some new, slightly tougher challenges, like "heel," and for some fun tricks.

Release Word

Intermediate obedience exercises should all end with a release word. This is a word that tells your dog you are done and he can relax. Pick a word and use it to end all the exercises. Some people use "Release" or "Okay" or "All done."

Tiny Treats Are Best

It is easiest to teach obedience commands with a food lure, but the size of the individual treat should be very tiny. The idea is to tell your dog he is doing the right thing by giving him something he likes. He will get the message with just a small treat. In training, you can go through quite a few treats, so make sure that the total amount of the treats does not equal an extra meal for your dog. Make small training treats by cutting up meat such as a hot dog or cooked chicken into very tiny pieces. Some people successfully use baby carrots cut crosswise into small pieces. You can buy special highly flavored training treats at large pet stores, or you can try cutting up semi-moist treats, such as bacon-flavored strips, into small pieces.

A few dogs work better for a toy, like a tennis ball or a squeaky toy, than they do for food, so determine what motivates your dog and use that as the reward. Playing with a toy, however, can add time to a training session.

How Long?

Success comes more reliably if you work in regular training sessions, but that doesn't mean scheduling gym time. It means any five minutes you can spare to focus on your dog. Regular does, however, mean every day for the best results—four or five times a week at least. Don't expect your dog to learn a new challenge the first three times you practice it. Be happy with little bits of success, and soon you'll find them adding up to a complete victory.

WATCH ME

Teaching "Watch me" is a good basis for more advanced obedience commands. It is especially effective for the "heel," because when a dog is heeling, he pays careful attention to his person, watching that person almost all the time. If your dog is not accustomed to paying close attention to you, teach your Yorkie the "Watch me" command.

"Watch me" is a good basis for more advanced obedience commands.

How to Teach Watch Me

- Stand in front of your dog with a treat and call his name.
- If he looks at you immediately, give him a treat.
- Eventually start saying his name and "Watch me!"
- Hold the treat up near your face so he can see it.
- Give him the treat if he continues to watch you.
- Gradually lengthen the time he is required to watch before he gets the treat.
- Eventually hold the treat behind your back or in your pocket so he can't see it—he only gets the treat if he looks in your eyes.
- If he is looking for the treat, you can stand in front of him with a treat in each hand.
- Hold your arms out straight and watch him try to figure out which treat he should look at.
- Suddenly, he will look at you for help.
- Say, "Yes. Watch me." Give him a treat.
- When you repeat this exercise, give him the treat from the other hand, so he cannot predict which hand will deliver the treat.

HEEL

Dogs who can heel are true companions. They

walk along next to us like the adventurers they are. These dogs are the reliable ones, the ones we can take anywhere because we know, in a commotion, they will be right there, at our side, heeling. Dogs who can heel get exercise, mental stimulation, and a change of scenery. They also get to go places on their own four feet and experience the world from their own perspective.

In the "Heel," your dog is paying attention to you. You can put your dog in the "Heel" when you are out walking and come across a distraction such as another dog, a frail person who might trip on your dog, or something that takes up a lot of sidewalk space, such as a baby stroller.

"Heel" means your dog has to walk next to your left leg, not in front of it or behind it. It is a very specific behavior, almost military in its precision. He has to pay attention to you, because if you slow down or speed up, he has to, too. When you stop, he stops and sits.

Heel Versus Let's Go

"Heel" is not the same as "Let's Go." They both start with a buckle collar or harness and a six-foot leash but "Let's Go" means "It's time for a walk." The "Heel" is a much more formal command that requires your Yorkie to pay much more attention to what he is doing. "Let's Go" is the command you would give for a relaxed stroll after dinner. "Heel" is what you would say on a crowded city sidewalk when the light turns green and you have to cross the street. Your Yorkie should be able understand and follow the "Let's Go" command before you start on "Heel."

How to Teach Heel

- Start teaching the "Heel" with your Yorkie sitting on your left side.
- Hold the leash in your right hand and a treat in your left.
- Move forward, saying, "Heel." Be enthusiastic.
- Hold the treat down as low as you can on your left leg.
- Take only a few steps, stop, say "Sit," and give your dog the treat if he stayed with you.

This is an example of starting slow and keeping your expectations realistic. Break a complicated exercise like "Heel"—walking on the left side, paying attention to the owner, keeping pace, and sitting straight when your stop—into little pieces. Even if you are used to taking long walks with your Yorkie, you have to start over with a new command like "Heel." Break the command sequence into tiny parts, and don't expect too much when you introduce it.

- Repeat this exercise—a couple extra steps each time—until you can walk quite a distance with your Yorkie staying next to your left leg before you give him the treat.
- He should sit when you stop. He should sit squarely next to you, not at an angle or sideways. If he is not sitting properly, maneuver him into the correct position by

> ***Multi-Dog Tip***
>
> Teaching more than one dog to "Stay" can take much longer, but must eventually be done. Teach each dog the command individually first. Then, practice as a group. Line up the dogs, back up, saying "Stay," and return to reward all of them as fast as you can. Start the group training as soon as the dogs know the meaning of "Stay."

"Let's Go" is for informal walks.

walking a few more steps and holding the food exactly where you want him to sit. Only reward a dog who is sitting in the correct position.

- He should also keep his eyes on you while he is heeling. If he does not, say, "Watch me!" and reward him if he does.
- Eventually stop holding the treat down low when you are heeling. Keep the treat in your pocket and give it to him at the end.
- When you stop walking, say, "Sit."
- Gradually walk faster and slower, praising the dog for staying with you. Walk in circles, a figure-8, and a square route that has right and left turns.
- Then try heeling somewhere that has distractions, such as a playground or parking lot. This is a challenge for most dogs, who will take their eyes off you and either lag behind or speed up ahead of you. Start training the "Heel" from the beginning. Hold the treat down low and attempt only a few steps at a time. Say "Watch me!"

This command is best learned when practiced every day, just a few minutes at a time, but it can take a substantial amount of time to learn.

Don't expect quick success. This is not an exercise for very young puppies. Be sure to use your release word when the exercise is finished or when you want to take a short break.

Teaching the heel takes time and progresses up different levels. Once your dog heels on the sidewalk at home, then you can teach him to heel on a crowded city block. You can teach him to heel at different speeds and past very tempting distractions.

STAY

The "Stay" command is useful in many circumstances, whether your dog is standing, sitting, or in a down position. It tells him to stand still on the scale at the vet's office or on the grooming table. It tells him to "Stay" at street corners if a car is coming, or to remain quietly in his crate or in the house while you open the door. This command can be a lifesaver.

Stay is really about self-restraint. Your dog can control his impulses, but it's harder for some dogs to learn to stay than for others, and it can take a while. Think about how hard it is for a healthy energetic young dog to control his desire to run and jump and explore. Then you can appreciate his monumental accomplishment when he learns to "Stay."

How to Teach Stay

- Start with tiny treats in one hand, behind your back, and face your dog.
- Bend low, hold up one hand in front of your dog, and say, "Stay."
- If he stays, offer him a treat.

The down-stay is useful if you want your dog to lie down quietly for a short period of time.

- Keep your hand open in front of him and repeat the "Stay" command.
- Gradually decrease the number of times you say "Stay" as you lengthen the time he can remain in one spot.
- When you are finished with the stay, say your release word, so the dog knows he can move again.

DOWN-STAY

The "Down-Stay" is useful if you are at an outdoor café and want your dog to stay quietly under your chair. It is also useful for the same reason during a meal at home or when you are doing something such as moving a large pot of hot pasta to the sink to drain. You can put your dog in a "Down-Stay" so you don't trip on him.

How to Teach Down-Stay

- Start with a handful of tiny treats.
- Put your dog in a down position and stand opposite him. (For a refresher on how to teach down, see Chapter 4.)
- Bend low, hold your flat hand up straight in front of him, and say, "Stay."
- Reward him with a treat after a few seconds.
- Repeat until he can hold the stay for a full minute and say your release word.

Then make it a little more challenging.

- Put your dog in a down-stay and walk backward a few steps and return to reward him.
- Repeat this several times until you can walk to the far side of the room and he remains in his down-stay.
- At first, repeat the down-stay command when you start to return to him but eventually drop that extra cue.
- Then put him in a down-stay and, with your back to him, walk away a few steps, stop, turn back, and walk to him to reward him. Repeat, again until you can walk to the end of the room and remains down.
- Eventually, you can walk around a corner, pause, and return to reward him for staying in a down position.
- Be sure to say the release word so he knows when he can get up. Dogs should be able to stay in a down-stay about three minutes.
- Then try adding distractions. Ask someone else to walk by your dog while he is in a down-stay. Take him outside and practice on a leash near a street with cars going by. Practice when you are at the vet or the groomer's, on a walk, or getting into the car for an outing.
- His reward can be getting in the car, chasing a squeaky toy, or getting a belly rub if you are out and about without treats.

> ### *By the Numbers*
>
> **The sit-stay may be the easiest for a young puppy (under eight months old) to learn. Older dogs (older than five years) may find the down-stay easier. Less dominant dogs may also find the down-stay easier.**

SIT-STAY

The sit-stay is similar to the down-stay in every way except your dog's position. Instead of lying down, your dog must sit in one place until you release him. Some dogs will find the sit-stay easier. It is useful if you are on a walk and stop to look in a shop window or talk to a friend. In a sit-stay, your Yorkie will wait patiently until you say the release word and move on.

Ask for the "Watch Me" command before putting down the food bowl.

How to Teach Sit-Stay

- Start with a handful of tiny treats.
- Tell your dog to sit, and stand opposite him.
- Bend low, hold your flat hand up straight in front of him, and say, "Stay."
- Reward him with a treat after a few seconds and say your release word.
- Let him jump around a little, then practice again.
- Repeat until he can hold the stay for a full minute, always remembering to say your release word.
- You can vary the stay by walking backward a few steps and then forward to reward him. Then, turn around and walk away a few steps, stop, turn back, and walk to him to reward him.
- Eventually, you can walk around a corner, pause, and return to reward him for staying in a sit position.
- Be sure to say the release word so he knows when he can get up.
- If your dog gets up too soon, say, "No" or "Oops" quietly but firmly, go back to him, and start over.
- This time, do not move as far away or stay away so long.
- Reward him more often for a couple times.
- Repeat the command. Make success his habit.

A more advanced challenge for the sit-stay:

- When he has learned to sit-stay, try circling him while he is in his position, going completely around behind him and out in front again.
- Some dogs will want to jump up and keep you in front of them.

- Say "Stay" repeatedly while you are circling at first, hold out a treat where he can see it, and move as quickly as you can.
- Gradually reduce the number of times you say "Stay," then practice with the treat hidden.
- Be sure to say the release word at the end.

STAND

The "stand" is useful in grooming and at the vet's office. In the "stand," the dog is really in a stand-stay, standing without moving until you release him. This means all four feet are planted solidly and are not moving. You can train for this on the floor but also on a grooming table, so you do not have to bend.

How to Teach Stand

- Start with a "sit" command.
- Hold a treat in front of your dog's nose and say, "Stand" as you move the treat straight away from the dog's nose.
- Keep your hand right at nose level and only move it a little way.
- Most dogs will stand but not move forward. That is what you want.
- If your dog does that, reward him.
- If he does not, ignore him for a few seconds then start over.
- Dogs who are used to sitting for a treat may take a little while before they understand they can earn a treat by standing. Encourage them by making the treat an especially desirable one, such as cooked chicken or liver bits.

Like all obedience commands, "stand" should be practiced several times a day at first. Find odd moments to practice—while you are waiting for the microwave or during a commercial on television. Practice once or twice and stop. Or, make your dog earn his dinner. Practice "Stand" or any of the stays for a few seconds before you put the food down. When you are done, be sure to say the release word and praise your dog. He is really working to make you happy. Show him he has done so.

SHAKE

Tricks are easy to teach, and they can give both you and your dog a fast sense of accomplishment when more traditional training is going slow.

Teach your dog to shake:

- Ask him to sit, say, "Shake," pick up a paw and shake it.
- Do this two or three times in a row.
- Practice once or twice a day, and soon your dog will offer you his paw when you say, "Shake."
- It's a guaranteed way to impress the neighbors when you are out for a walk.

USING THE COMMANDS

Now that your Yorkie knows a few obedience commands, it's time to make him earn his food. Eliminate free treats. To get his dinner or a treat, your Yorkie must successfully complete one of the new commands. "Watch me" is perfect for use when you are holding food, but any of the "Stay" commands will also work. If your dog fails to complete the command, say "Oops" and turn around with the food in your hand. Wait a few seconds, then turn back and give the same command.

Want to Know More?

For a refresher on basic obedience commands, see Chapter 4: Training Your Yorkshire Terrier Puppy.

CHAPTER 10

YORKSHIRE TERRIER PROBLEM BEHAVIORS

Yorkshire Terriers, like dogs of many breeds, can be your best friend. But, also like other dogs, a Yorkie with behavior problems can be your worst nightmare. Most Yorkies end up in the buddy category, but if yours is making you pull your hair out—at least temporarily—help is available. You are not the first to have a Yorkie who barks or chews your socks or nips at people. Professional dog trainers and behaviorists are well-versed in stopping these problem behaviors.

Most problems stem from conflicts between what Yorkies were designed to do and what they do now: Rat-catching independent hunters sometimes have a hard time adjusting to a pampered life in an apartment. Hard-wired to find, challenge, and eliminate any threat to their territory, Yorkies must adjust to security and the expectation that they will be gentle, accepting hosts for your guests. Sometimes it just isn't going to happen without a little expert help.

BEHAVIOR HELP

What is an animal behaviorist? The National Association of Animal Behaviorists (NAAB) says that it is someone who specializes in resolving behavior problems in companion animals, emphasizing positive training techniques and behavior modification. Typical problems they can help with include aggression, separation anxiety, house soiling, destructive behavior, fears, barking, jumping, poor recall (the come command), phobias and obsessive-compulsive behaviors. That's a mouthful to think about in a five-pound (2 kg) dog, but frequently the very size of a Yorkie can be part of the problem. Yorkies inspire some people to treat them like a human baby. Yorkies who are not treated like dogs frequently do not act like well-trained companion animals. If they are babied, carried everywhere, and not made to follow any rules, they may become spoiled dogs. They need structured discipline, just like people do. If they get a job to do, even better.

Animal behaviorists and even some dog trainers may offer personal consultations in your home. They will come and observe what your dog is doing and how you respond, then create a plan to resolve the problem. They will start the process, showing you how to handle your dog. With some problems, they might even be able to end the problem behavior in the first or second visit. Behaviorists and trainers can be helpful with dogs who steal food or bark when the doorbell rings or attack guests.

You can find animal behaviorists by asking your veterinarian, dog groomer, or obedience class teacher for referrals. You can find dog trainers by asking other Yorkie owners (be sure to ask if the dog trainer is good with small dogs). Then ask if the trainer will work with you one-on-one to solve your problem. Frequently, finding a solution to one problem will involve creating an entirely new way of managing your dog. You may have to adopt an attitude of calm authority all the time, for example, in order to get your dog to listen to you.

AGGRESSION

Aggression can be anything from curling a lip to growling to charging or biting. It can be focused at another dog or at a person. Aggressive dogs frequently raise the hair on the back of their neck so they look bigger, trying to win the argument by scaring off the enemy. If that doesn't work, at some point aggressive dogs lose control and start biting.

The terrier group is one of the more aggressive dog groups by nature. Their feisty willingness to take on vermin of substantial size, relatively speaking, has been encouraged from the start. They have been rewarded throughout history for guarding their territory from invaders, hunting and killing vermin, and raising the alarm by barking noisily when they think something is out of order. But these characteristics can get dangerously twisted in a typical city or suburban home when such a dog tries to guard his food or toys, or when he is faced with a stranger coming into his house through the front door. The growling and biting instinct that served him well in catching rats can often lead to trouble in a family.

If your dog is from a shelter or rescue group, call and tell them the type of problem you are having. They have people and resources that may be able to solve your problem. If your dog is from a breeder, call and ask her what you can do to reduce aggression. Yorkie breeders have a wealth of experience that they are usually happy to share.

By the Numbers

Some Yorkies go through a fear period at 12 to 14 months of age. This could account for some new problem behaviors at that age. Don't make a big deal out of it, and wait for it to pass.

Management Techniques

- Start from the beginning to reduce your Yorkie's aggressive instincts by socializing your dog. Allow your puppy to go places, meet new people, and play with friendly dogs his own size. Be sure he meets all kinds of people—men, women, babies, children, old people, and people who wear hats or carry things that might scare a dog.
- While he is eating, put your hands close to his dish and drop additional food in. Teach him that hands near his food can lead to a good thing—more food.
- When he has something inappropriate in his mouth—a dangerous item or a piece of clothing—always give him something else when you take the first item away. Substitute a proper toy. Trade.
- Do not play any game that allows your

Yorkies can become aggressive toward other dogs for a variety of reasons.

Yorkie to control your bed or chair while you are left out. It is easy for some more territorial Yorkies to believe the bed and the chair are theirs and to try to keep people off—even you.

- If your Yorkie starts to show aggressive tendencies, respond by exhibiting steady leadership. Your goal is to show your dog that you are in charge.
- Ignore any attempt to guard furniture or food.
- Continue to schedule things such as walks or off-leash backyard exercise, where you are clearly in charge.
- Try to tire your dog out before he has a chance to get aggressive. Consider taking an obedience class, even if your dog is two or three years old. Many trainers offer refresher courses or courses in achieving an American Kennel Club (AKC) Canine Good Citizen Award that will give your dog something to do and make him tired.
- Try to reduce any new stress that has come into the house.

If your dog starts biting, it is time to find professional help. Ask your veterinarian to refer you to a behaviorist or trainer who will work with you one-on-one. The behaviorist will work with your dog but, you will have to continue the new regimen to make it truly successful.

Dog–Dog Aggression

Some Yorkies become aggressive toward other dogs for a variety of reasons, some entirely innocent. Sue Walters, groomer and owner of several champion performance Yorkies, has no toys cluttering her floors. Toys come out for play time and then are put away. If she leaves toys lying around, fights break out: "They all want the same toy," Walters says.

Other dogs are willing to take on another for social rank. Dogs have status in a group, and a new dog trying to join the group will have to establish his rank. If this happens when your dog is off leash away from home, you may have to rely on obedience commands to distract him. Sometimes a firm "Sit" will be enough to stop the preliminary action long enough for you to get close enough to pick him up. Or, a very well-trained dog may even respond to the "Come" command. If he does, reward him generously.

But if two dogs actually attack each other, do not put your hand between them to stop the fight. Shout, roll a ball past them, whistle, wave your arms, make any other type of noise you can to distract them but do not try to grab your dog until the fighting dogs have separated.

Afterward, analyze what happened and how much blame you can assign to your dog. If this happens repeatedly, find a professional who can help.

BARKING

Yorkies have a reputation in some quarters as being yappy little dogs. The flip side of that, though, is that barking can be a good thing at times. Yorkies have a reputation for being outstanding alert dogs, barking when they see or hear something threatening. Many people who have Yorkies in the house say they appreciate that warning before someone rings the doorbell.

Barking is a totally understandable behavior if you consider where Yorkies came from. Yorkies have three or four kinds of terrier breeds in their background. Terriers in general bark more than some breeds because of the nature of their job—it was their way of keeping their owners informed as to their whereabouts and their progress in chasing rodents. (In the unenlightened past, terriers were used in the "sport" of rat baiting. Imagine the show a terrier could put on in a pub if he was placed in a ring full of rats, with people shouting and urging him on. The more he barked, the more his aggressive nature worked itself up, and the more rats he could kill.)

Yorkies are never going to be quiet dogs. How uninteresting that would be! Ordinary, garden-variety barking that stops after a short time is what any Yorkie owner should be prepared to live with. Excessive barking is the problem. Yorkies have a high-pitched bark that can quickly annoy neighbors and some family members. In excessive barking, a Yorkie just won't quit, and the level of irritation quickly escalates.

Management Techniques

The first thing to establish is why your Yorkie is barking excessively.

Some Yorkie breeders say barking runs in lines. The dog either inherits an instinct for barking or learns from

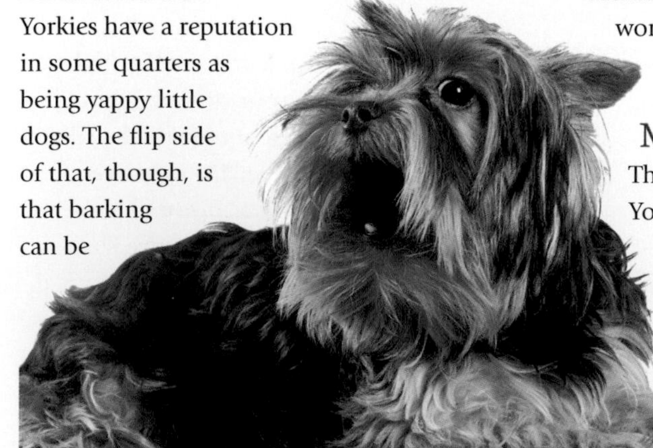

Yorkies have a reputation for being outstanding alert dogs.

his mother and other adult Yorkies to bark all the time. Other lines produce relatively quiet dogs. Vicki Meadows, Illinois breeder, says, "A lot of people call Yorkies yappers. My dogs are not that way. They will bark when something is wrong."

So ask your breeder if her dogs are barkers.

Some dog trainers say barking gets out of control when a dog is left alone too much and becomes bored or anxious. The solution here is to plan more activities for your Yorkie. Arrange for more exercise. Talk to him when you make the bed, wash the dishes, fold the laundry. Make him feel he is part of your team.

Others say dogs bark because their barking is never acknowledged and called off. This one is easy to test. If your dog barks at something he sees out the window, look out the window, say, "Oh, I see it's the snowplow. Good dog. That's all, now," and go away from the window. The dog should see that there is nothing to fear, no reason to bark, and you are on the job. He can stand down.

Dog trainers agree that yelling at your dog to stop barking is ineffective. The more noise you make, the more noise he will make to be heard. But you can train your dog to stop barking. Here are three ways—try each one until you find the one that works for you and your Yorkie.

Quiet Command

When your dog is barking excessively, distract him so that he stops. Throw something nearby, spray him with a little mist from a squirt bottle, or bang on something. When he stops barking, offer him a treat. If he remains quiet a few seconds, offer him another. Keep feeding him treats as long as he is quiet, spreading the treats out over longer intervals. Introduce the "Shh" or "Shush" or "Quiet" command. If he still barks, find a more attractive, smellier treat. Start over by distracting him when he is barking and offering him a treat when he is quiet. Stand very close to him and hold the treat very close to his nose so he can sniff it. He should be willing to stop barking when faced with such a prized treat so close to his nose. Offer the treats in shorter intervals than you did the first time, while saying "Quiet."

Watch Me Command

Another way to reduce the length of time your dog barks is to use the attention-getting command of Watch Me. When your dog starts barking at the doorbell, say, "Watch me." When he looks at you and stops barking, offer him a treat and say, "Good Dog. Quiet." Give him another treat if he watches you and stays quiet. You can make this go faster if a friend will stand outside and ring the doorbell every few minutes. Every time the bell rings and the dog barks, say, "Watch me!" then praise and reward your dog, adding "Quiet." Eventually, the theory goes, your Yorkie will become conditioned to the bell ringing and lose interest. He is quiet when you say "Quiet," and so he will learn what that means. This is a slow process, however, and when the doorbell rings the next day, he'll probably bark again. Don't give up.

> *Want to Know More?*
>
> **For a refresher on how to teach the "Watch me" command, see Chapter 9: Training Your Yorkshire Terrier.**

Speak Command

Other trainers suggest that teaching your dog

to bark can effectively help reduce barking. Here's how it works: Manage to create a sound that makes your dog bark, like opening the door. Praise your dog and give him a treat. Then do it again, but before you do, say, "Speak." If you have a dog who likes to bark, this should be easy to teach quickly. Soon he will bark when you say "Speak." Then you can teach him "Quiet" by rewarding him for the quiet times between "Speak" commands. Say "Quiet" when it is quiet and reward him, and eventually he will know the difference between "Speak" and "Quiet."

The goal of all three methods is to teach your dog the "Quiet" command so you can stop excessive barking before it gets out of control. If you can't, professional dog trainers and behaviorists can help with barking.

CHEWING

All dogs chew when they are young. They chew to ease teething pain, to recreate the comfort they remember from nursing their mother, to satisfy their curiosity about different things, and to ease boredom. But it is hard to rationalize when you are faced with wallpaper torn off a wall, a pillow with its stuffing all over a room, or the back of a shoe completely chewed off. It is easy to think the dog is getting back at you for something you did, but dogs aren't like that. Dogs live in the moment. They see something that looks interesting or their mouth hurts or they are anxious at being alone—and they start chewing.

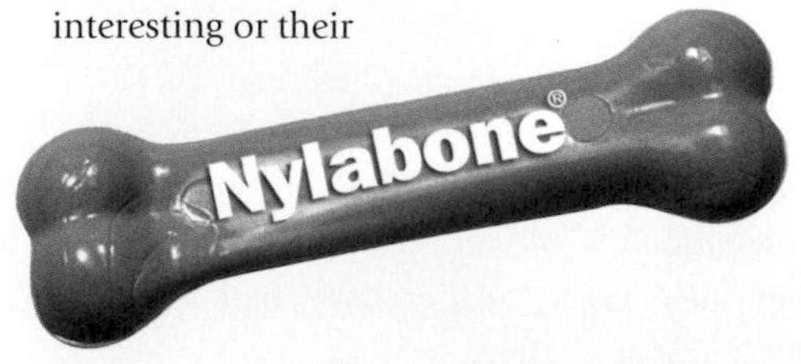

Give your Yorkie plenty of appropriate items to chew on.

Management Techniques

Prevention is the solution to destructive chewing. A puppy or an adult Yorkie with a chewing problem should stay in a crate or ex-pen when no one is available to watch him. He should have safe chew toys to satisfy his chewing urges. He should be allowed to play in rooms after most chewing targets have been removed.

Pick up your shoes, dirty clothes, mail, magazines, loose change, TV remotes, calculators, iPods, cell phones, and laptop computers. Buy a baby gate to keep your Yorkie in a puppy-proofed room. Stay with him and play with him. Offer a puppy who is actively teething a wet washcloth that has been knotted, wrung out, and frozen.

Spray strictly off-limit items with liquids that taste bitter to discourage your dog from chewing on them. Most dogs can be distracted by offering them a suitable chew toy, like those Nylabone makes, when they are starting to chew on something they shouldn't.

Dogs sometimes chew because they are bored, so take your dog places. Exercise him so he is tired when he gets home. Teach him new commands or tricks. Dogs who have learned to roll over, for example, will frequently start rolling over on their own to attract attention when they are bored. It almost always works!

Give Command

Eventually, teach your dog to "Drop it" or "Give" when he picks up something he shouldn't. Choose a command, "drop it" or "give." Give your dog a toy. Stand in front of him with a tasty treat close to his nose and say your command. Most dogs will drop the toy to get the treat. Give him the treat and praise him.

Repeat a few times a day with different things in his mouth until he understands what "Drop it!" means. Now, if he picks up something he's not supposed to chew on, you can get it back more quickly.

Leave It Command

Teach your Yorkie to "Leave it" when he starts toward something he shouldn't have. "Leave it" requires two treats, one for the floor and one in your hand. Put your dog in a sit-stay and toss a treat just out of his reach, saying "Leave it." Offer him the treat in your hand almost immediately. If his sit-stay is not strong enough to keep him in his place, put a leash on him and stand on the leash while you toss the treat and offer him another treat. Do not let him pick up the treat off the floor. Pick it up and feed it to him.

Practice both of these new commands several times in a row for several days a week. Invest in some durable chewing toys and offer them to your dog every times he "Drops it!" or "Leaves it!"

Some misbehaviors are best ignored. A Yorkie will try anything once to get attention, even attention that includes scolding. Foil his plan by turning your back and folding your arms.

DIGGING

Yorkies are terriers, and terriers dig. All dogs dig sometimes, actually, but terriers were designed to dig underground into burrows while chasing rodents. Digging makes a mess, both in the garden and on the dog. It is one of the prices we pay for keeping a dog, because the only way to guarantee your dog will never dig is to pave the whole yard or keep him locked in the house. Neither is good for your Yorkie.

Management Techniques

The next best way to reduce or eliminate digging is to spend more time in the yard with your little guy. Sometimes dogs dig because they are bored. They see something curious, and they start digging and—when they have nothing else to do—they just keep digging.

If you play with your dog, it will tire him out before he has a chance to dig. If you catch him digging, it's easy to discourage him if you are out there with him: Use a "Leave it" or "Off" command and offer him a special outside toy instead.

The biggest concern about digging is that your Yorkie could dig a hole under a fence big enough for escape. Patrol the fence line if you spot dirt under your Yorkie's nails and check for big holes. Dogs sometimes work on a hole for two or three days before it is big enough to allow escape. If he has started a hole, cover it with a patio block, big stones, or some other solid substance until he loses interest in that site.

If he is digging in your garden, put up a snow fence or chicken wire or some other fence to keep him out. Consider container gardening.

Some dog owners provide a digging pit for their dogs. Mark off a small site in the yard with a visible barrier so the dog knows where the pit begins and ends (or buy a small plastic wading pool). Either way, pile it with sand or topsoil and then bury dog treats close to the surface. When you catch your dog digging someplace else, say, "Dig in your pit" or some other command. Take your dog to the pit and show him one of the treats. This should convince him that digging in this place is more worthwhile.

JUMPING UP

People who love Yorkies sometimes let them jump on them. The dog is glad to see them when they come home, and the Yorkie owner is glad to see her dog. He's so cute and so small, after all—it seems harmless.

But a Yorkie sitting politely, waiting for your attention, is also cute—and less annoying. Yorkies who jump on people could scratch legs, damage clothes, trip a frail or elderly person, scare children, or drive off guests. But the worst thing is that a Yorkie jumping on people indicates that the Yorkie is in charge. This can lead to other types of Yorkie-in-charge behaviors that are much less cute: furniture guarding, people guarding, biting, begging and obesity.

A Yorkie who jumps on people may seem cute to you, but may annoy other people.

Management Techniques

To stop a Yorkie from jumping up on people, be consistent. Never pick him up or feed him or even talk to him when he is jumping. Even one slip on your part can send the whole training process back to the beginning.

Ignore him until he has stopped jumping. Then say, "Sit." Once he is sitting, shower him with all the attention he wants, as long as he is not jumping up. This goes faster if you have already convinced your dog that sitting is the best way for him to get a treat or your attention at other times of the day. It requires consistency, both in ignoring a jumping dog and in noticing a sitting dog and rewarding him as soon as you can.

When guests come, give them a dog treat to give only to your sitting dog and ask them to follow the new jumping up rules. And stand on your Yorkie's leash to enforce them.

LEASH PULLING

It is much more fun to walk a dog who is walking with you and not pulling away from you—even a toy dog. This type of walking is the "Let's Go" command—let's go for a walk together and not worry about heeling. The dog can walk next to you or slightly in front or behind you. He should be relaxed and so should the leash. He should keep track of you but not keep his eyes on you all the time. This allows him to explore and sniff the ground occasionally.

Management Techniques

Start with a simple band collar or harness and a 6-foot (2 m) nylon or leather leash. Stand with the dog on your left and the leash in your right hand. Put a few treats in your left hand. Say, "Let's go" and start walking. If your dog starts right off and walks near you without pulling on the leash, praise and reward him with a treat. Keep going, praising and rewarding as long as the leash is slack. If he walks too fast and gets ahead of you and pulls the leash taut, turn completely around and walk in the opposite direction. Only treat when he is walking near you and the leash is slack, or when he makes a point of turning to look at you and "check in."

This technique works for many dogs if you practice it regularly and do not move forward when the dog is pulling. If it does not work for your dog, change the technique slightly by stopping instead of turning around.

When your dog pulls the leash taut, just stop. Wait for him to either come back to you or at least stop and turn around to look at you and let up on the leash. As soon as the leash goes slack, start walking again.

You are teaching your Yorkie that a slack leash means he can go forward and a taut leash means he can't. The hardest thing is to teach yourself to be consistent. For this technique to work, you have to be very consistent and never move forward when the dog is pulling.

NIPPING

All puppies nip at people. But if you have an adult dog who nips, it is a more serious matter.

All dogs can bite: They have teeth, and they know how to use them. But as puppies, they learned bite inhibition from their littermates—

It is much more fun to walk a dog who is walking with you and not pulling away from you.

don't bite too hard or nobody will play with you. Usually that lesson stands them in good stead, and they remember not to bite too hard.

But dogs also have a bite threshold. In the right situation, when the amount of stress has built up to the breaking point, any dog will bite. Stress can come from physical pain, hunger, the presence of something that makes them uncomfortable (like a new baby), or an outright threat (like a bigger dog). It can also come from things you might not even imagine, like loud noises or visitors. Some dogs have a very high bite threshold. They can be pushed a long way before they bite. Others have a very

If your Yorkie's nipping is out of control, seek professional help.

low bite threshold. Almost their first reaction is to bite.

Carl Yochum, president of the Yorkshire Terrier Club of America, suggests that a dog's bite threshold is based not on what breed the dog is but how he has been socialized. Yochum says that Yorkies are not known as biting dogs. "If a dog of any breed bites, it is because they are not well-socialized," he says. Sometimes a Yorkie who nips first and asks questions later has an owner who forgot her Yorkie is a dog and needs a routine with discipline and boundaries, Yochum says. Like a big dog, a Yorkie must be taught the rules of all good dogs—don't bite people. But, as Illinois Yorkie breeder Vicki Meadows points out, because Yorkies are so little and their bites are not fatal in all but the most unusual cases, owners make excuses for them and never teach them not to bite. People have to insist their dogs don't bite. "My Yorkies just don't bite," says Meadows, "My dogs have never been biters. That's a defense mechanism dogs have."

Management Techniques

One way to reduce biting is to spot the things that stress your dog and remove them when possible. Keep your dog on a schedule. Keep visiting children under close supervision, and know when to call an end to play time and put your dog in his crate for a nap. Take away opportunities for your Yorkie to bite you. Eliminate confrontational and aggressive games that only spur your Yorkie's terrier instincts. Don't waggle your finger in front of your Yorkie's mouth. Stop wild running games before he gets overly excited and loses control. Try not to get angry. Yorkies can sense your anger, get riled up, and respond in kind.

Work positively to teach your dog not to bite people. Like all other training, training your dog not to bite involves training him to do something else.

If you see your Yorkie is about to bite you, just say, "No" and move away. Don't scream or shout or chase him. If you see he is about to bite someone else, try an obedience command he usually obeys, such as "Sit" or "Down" or even "Leave it." Give him something else to do, then remove him from the opportunity.

If your Yorkie nips at you, say, "Ouch! No!" and stop anything your Yorkie might consider fun, like petting, or treating, or even attention. But don't stop anything that is required, such as grooming. If he bites you, and you stop grooming, he will learn that he can stop something he doesn't like by biting. Simply hold his mouth shut with one hand while you continue with the other. Ask another person to help if you need a third hand.

Here comes the substitution: If he looks like he wants to or is trying to bite you, and especially if he is a puppy and is really just playing, offer him a toy. Try a knotted rope dog toy. It is soft enough so he can sink his teeth in, but durable enough not to fall apart. With this in his mouth, he can't bite.

You can extend this idea by praising your Yorkie whenever he picks up a toy and plays with it by telling him to go get a toy and rewarding him when he comes back with one. You can teach him the names of different toys and even hide them so he has to search for them. The idea is to make him feel that having a toy in his mouth is a good thing.

But if all this fails and your dog is still inclined to bite first and ask questions later, seek professional help. Ask your veterinarian for the name of a dog behaviorist who can help with biting Yorkies. Do it sooner rather than later. Biting dogs sometimes have to be put down.

Multi-Dog Tip

Bad behaviors spread like a disease from dog to dog. It is important to stop bad behavior as soon as you can. If need be, separate dogs for a while until they forget what mischief they were in.

CHAPTER 11

YORKSHIRE TERRIER SPORTS AND ACTIVITIES

Some Yorkies are overachievers when it comes to sports and activities. They win ribbon after ribbon in organized obedience, agility, and rally. The same determination they once put into chasing a rat, they now put into following an agility course. They have focus, intelligence, and athleticism. Finding a Yorkie like that and then teaching him is a quest for many people who are into competitive canine sports. But even if you are not into competition, you can find an activity your Yorkie will shine at and one that will be fun for you, too.

ACTIVITIES WITH YOUR YORKIE

Before a Yorkie can run an agility course or work at obedience, he has to walk. Literally. The greatest number of Yorkies and their owners never see an agility course or a competitive obedience ring. But they have a good time together walking down the sidewalk, hiking a trail to a campsite, or even participating in therapy work. Wherever you are, whatever you are doing is what your Yorkie wants to do. His favorite activity is being with you.

Camping

Yorkies are made for camping because of their size and their natural watchdog instincts. They fit in your tent and will let you know if someone or something is approaching. They eat little, so carrying their meals is easy.

Still, you will have to pack a bag for him. Pack a sweater, even in the summer, because evenings can be cool. Take water from home so he doesn't have to adjust to a new drink. Put in some toys, especially a chew toy. Consider taking an antihistamine like Benadryl in case he gets an insect bite.

If you are camping in a recreational vehicle, take his crate so he can relax (and sleep) in familiar surroundings. If you are hiking and putting up a tent, be sure to take his blanket. Consider how many miles a day you are hiking and whether your dog can walk that far. If not, you might need a backpack for him to ride in when he tires.

Be prepared to keep him on a leash or to put up an exercise pen, especially in wilderness areas where the chance of a coyote or a snake exists. He should stay with someone at all times and sleep in the tent with you. Check for ticks every night.

Yorkies are made for camping because of their portable nature and watchdog tendencies.

Canine Good Citizen Test

The Canine Good Citizen® (CGC) program from the American Kennel Club (AKC) rewards dogs and owners who work together to pass ten tests of canine good behavior. It is a fun goal for your obedience class, and the prize is a distinctive blue and yellow collar tag for your Yorkie that will tell one and all that your dog has good manners.

Some dogs will have to take beginning and intermediate obedience sessions to be able to pass the test; others will pass the test based on what you teach them at home. Each dog is different: Some dogs may have to take the test twice to pass, others will breeze through on the first try. Talk to your obedience instructor about your goal, and ask her if she offers the test or if you will have to take the test at a different site.

If you want your dog to be a therapy dog or do agility or competitive obedience, the CGC is a good place to start. The ten exercises test basic behaviors that your dog will need before he can do anything else.

Your dog must be able to allow a stranger to get close enough to converse with you; sit quietly while a stranger pets him; allow a stranger such, as a vet or a groomer, to groom or examine him; walk on a loose lead; walk by three strangers politely; sit, down, and stay on command; come when called; walk by another dog with no adverse reaction; accept a distraction, such as loud noise or a crate cart rumbling by; and stay with a stranger while you are out of sight for three minutes.

The CGC program is open to all dogs, including purebred Yorkies and Yorkie mixes.

Dogs must be old enough to have had the rabies vaccine. Lists of upcoming tests and training tips are posted on the AKC's website.

Therapy Work

Therapy dogs are working dogs who visit people in need of comfort. A Yorkshire Terrier may have been the first-ever therapy dog. Smoky, a Yorkie found by soldiers fighting World War II in the Pacific, visited soldiers recuperating in hospitals. Her work was so successful that she continued to work as a therapy dog for twelve years.

Today, dogs who do therapy work are trained, tested, and licensed for the work. Therapy Dogs International (TDI) says the first requirement is that therapy dogs have outstanding temperaments. These dogs get along with other animals they may come across on their rounds, they like people, they take strange sights and noises in stride. Therapy dogs can be any size, because their work involves getting close to people, letting people touch them, and listening if a person starts to cry or vent. Therapy dogs visit hospitals, schools, nursing homes, retirement centers, and libraries.

Delta Society says good things can happen when a dog visits: improved fine motor skills, wheelchair skills, and standing balance; better conversation and attention skills; the development of recreation skills; an increase in self-esteem; and reduced anxiety and loneliness.

If that sounds good to you, the first thing to do is to get your Yorkie ready to pass a therapy dog test. It includes all the CGC behaviors plus a few more. Only specially trained obedience instructors can give the therapy dog test, so check first to find out who offers it and when it is scheduled.

Find out more at www.tdi.org or www.deltasociety.org.

Walking/Jogging

Yorkies are sturdy little walkers who love an afternoon stroll. How far they can walk depends on the dog and on you. Some dogs are more athletic and can walk a long way (a mile or two or more) at a brisk pace. Others will be happy to go around the block once at a more leisurely pace. Some of it depends on how much walking you have done with your Yorkie and what physical condition he is in.

The same is true for jogging. If you start out slowly and jog a little bit at first and a little bit more the next time, your Yorkie can

A well-trained Yorkie can excel at therapy work.

Yorkies are sturdy walkers who love afternoon strolls.

learn to jog with you. If you are training for a marathon, though, you might consider a jogging stroller for your pal.

Be careful not to walk or jog too far with your Yorkie in severe heat or cold. Be sure to start with short distances in walking and jogging and build up stamina. Take water if you are going a long distance.

Consider treadmill training for serious jogging. Canine treadmills are excellent endurance builders. The dog runs once or twice a day on the treadmill, starting slow and building up stamina and muscle tone. Energetic Yorkies can burn off some of that endless energy and develop the physical ability to jog with you.

If your dog is not an enthusiastic walker, try to make walking more fun. Take treats, stop for a picnic, talk enthusiastically to him, or walk somewhere where your dog might have fun, like a doggie bakery or a beach. If you are having fun, he will, too.

SPORTS WITH YOUR YORKIE

Some Yorkies are natural athletes. With consistent training and conditioning, they can compete in canine sports such as agility and rally. In some sports, hurdles are adjusted for the size of the dog, but the canine athlete does all the exercises, no matter his size. They also can earn the same titles as big dogs, such as obedience or agility champion. Yorkies started out in one-on-one competitions with rats, and that competitive spirit lives today in many. They enjoy a challenge, and the crowds at ringside don't bother them. When they finish a run through obstacles, they look happy and satisfied and ready to go again.

Agility

The AKC says that agility is "the ultimate game for you and your dog and is one of the most

> ***By the Numbers***
>
> **Both the North American Dog Agility Council and the United States Dog Agility Association require that dogs be 18 months old before they start competition.**

exciting canine sports for spectators." Those who have agility Yorkies would agree. Agility is where that Yorkie attitude meets its natural outlet.

In agility, dogs run a course of obstacles off leash with a handler running near them to guide them through the obstacles in a prescribed order. Dogs are rated on time and how well they completed the course. Dogs who do well can run fast, can follow directions off leash, and are athletic and agile enough to climb an A-frame, jump through a hoop, race through weave poles, and skinny through two types of tunnels. Dogs run the course one at a time, and are scored based on how fast they ran and how many faults they had, such as hesitating before jumping or knocking a rail off a jump.

In agility, the courses gradually get more difficult, starting with 13 to 15 obstacles and ending with about 20 obstacles. In AKC agility, obstacles have six heights starting at 8 inches (20 cm) for dogs up to 11 inches (28 cm) at the shoulder. In United Kennel Club (UKC) agility, hurdles also start at 8 inches (20 cm) but they are for dogs up to 14 inches (36 cm).

Your dog can earn agility titles that can be put after his name, working up to the MACH (Master Agility Champion).

Why Participate?

- In agility, no professional handlers are used. It is a sport for dogs and their owners, so some people do agility to forge a deeper bond with their dog.
- Training for agility is something only the two

Racing through weave poles is just one of the fun obstacles in agility.

Agility Tale

Sue Walters, who trains several agility champions, got into it because it looked fun. "With my first dog, I made huge mistakes," she says. Now she has agility equipment in her yard in the summer. They practice sporadically. With a Yorkie, there is no right or wrong way to train, or only one right way. "It depends on the dog," she says.

She has a wall decorated with a white fence, and hanging from the fence are dozens and dozens of ribbons her dogs have won, mostly in agility. This takes time, and patience, and money.

Why does she do it?

"It's fun. That's the only reason I do it. It's fun to be successful."

One time she did ten trials with the same dog without a single qualifying run. That's a challenge she meets head on. "What can I do to fix this?" she asks herself.

People have asked her why she doesn't get a "real" agility dog, like a Border Collie, but Yorkies remain her first choice. "I love the breed—the size, the personality, the coat, the look. The people I have met who have been breed-related are really nice," Walters says.

of you will do, and if your dog enjoys it, he will come to enjoy those sessions with you.

- Agility is sometimes recommended for shy or uncertain dogs. Learning to accomplish new physical tasks can boost a dog's confidence.
- Agility is good exercise for dogs who have high energy, and great mental stimulation for dogs who get bored easily.
- Agility can also become a social activity for you. People who do agility sometimes train and travel together to competitions.

Getting Started

Agility requires equipment that you can buy, make yourself, or use at a dog club. An agility course typically has several types of jumps, a teeter, a pause box, two tunnels, an A-frame, weave poles, and an elevated plank called a dog walk. More advanced courses may have a moving bridge.

Most of these can be built from plastic plumbing tubes and lumber, but you may have to buy the tunnels. One is a flexible open tunnel about 15 to 20 feet (5 to 6 m) long that can be bent into different shapes. The other is called a *closed chute,* but it is open on one end. It connects to a long chute of nylon fabric that the dog has to push through. Many dogs like agility tunnels after the first time through, and some obedience classes and dog daycare centers have added them.

Obedience teachers often teach an introduction to agility class that will allow your dog to try it out before you make any commitment. You may also find a dog or obedience club that has equipment set up indoors for classes and practice year round. Other agility classes and meets are only available in good weather, when the obstacles can be set up outside.

Before you start agility, take one or two obedience classes to see how your dog performs away from home. Be sure he is reliable off leash for at least a few commands. Agility rings are frequently fenced, but this is an off leash sport. The fun is in watching your dog achieve success because he wants to, not because you are on the other end of the leash, pushing him to do it.

Canine Freestyle

Canine freestyle is dancing with your dog. It's a celebration of the relationship between owner and dog in a choreographed performance set to music. Both move to the beat of the music and perform precision steps. The dog dances between your legs, opposite you, next to you, and bows to you. Imagine your Yorkie doing that, and you can see why it's a crowd pleaser.

Competitive freestyle has four levels of difficulty. All except the very beginning are off leash. The dog has to heel on your right and your left side, turn, pivot, back up, and circle. He has to work at a distance from you sometimes, and pay attention to you at all times. Sometimes he has to jump over your leg or your arm or a cane. The performance is judged and scored.

Yorkies have had success in canine freestyle. Their natural agility and attitude helps them perform, but freestyle requires a dog who is good in competitive obedience. Just heeling on the right and the left is a trick that may take some time to master. Yorkies who are candidates for freestyle can perform in front of a crowd and a room full of distractions. They learn tricks quickly and are in great physical condition. They are very connected to their dance partner and can understand body signals.

Look for freestyle classes at obedience clubs.

Conformation (Showing)

Yorkies are flamboyant showmen, making them naturals for conformation shows. The show Yorkie in full coat is a phenomenal sight. Going to a dog show and watching the Yorkie judging is a treat for the Yorkie lover. They strut their stuff on elegant feet, and each one looks like he expects to win.

At conformation shows, Yorkies are judged individually against the breed standard. The dog who most represents the ideals in the standard wins. Some call it a beauty show but dogs who win are usually healthy dogs in good condition, well-trained at public performances, with good physical movement. All of that requires more than just a pretty face.

A Show Yorkie

Getting into conformation and succeeding at it may be difficult. Not all Yorkies are cut out to be show dogs, and getting a breeder to part with a top-quality show puppy is tough. Then, the puppy may not live up to his potential or he may develop a major medical condition that disqualifies him, and you will have to start over.

If you want to compete successfully, be sure to tell your breeder you are looking for a show puppy. Wait to take the puppy home until he is at least six months old; nine months is better. The breeder can tell what kind of coat and look the puppy will have by that time.

Show dogs are intact (not neutered or spayed), have long

Participants in canine freestyle often wear costumes.

straight silky hair parted down the middle, and match the Yorkshire Terrier standard closely. No dog is perfect, but a show Yorkie will meet more of the standard's requirements than not.

How Dog Shows Work

Conformation as competition is a fun social world for the owner/handler. To compete successfully, your dog will have to travel with you and/or your professional handler to shows quite often, sometimes on back-to-back weekends. A champion Yorkie has been the best Yorkie dog or bitch in enough shows to win 15 points, including at least two shows worth at least three points each (a major).

Points don't come from being best in show or even best of breed. The only way your Yorkie can get champion points is by beating all the other Yorkies of his gender. On the way to doing that, you will meet many people like yourself, who love dogs and love seeing them look their best and perform in front of a crowd.

Dog shows are a competition, and you may find yourself up against your friends in the ring sometimes. Dog people usually learn to leave the ring disappointments in the ring and start preparing for the next show. Keeping a Yorkie in show condition is hard work, and there's little time to waste bad mouthing the competition or the judge.

The purpose of a dog show is to find the best dogs for breeding. So, if you are successful and your dog becomes a champion, others may want to breed to him or her. Breeding Yorkies without genetic defects is everyone's goal, but

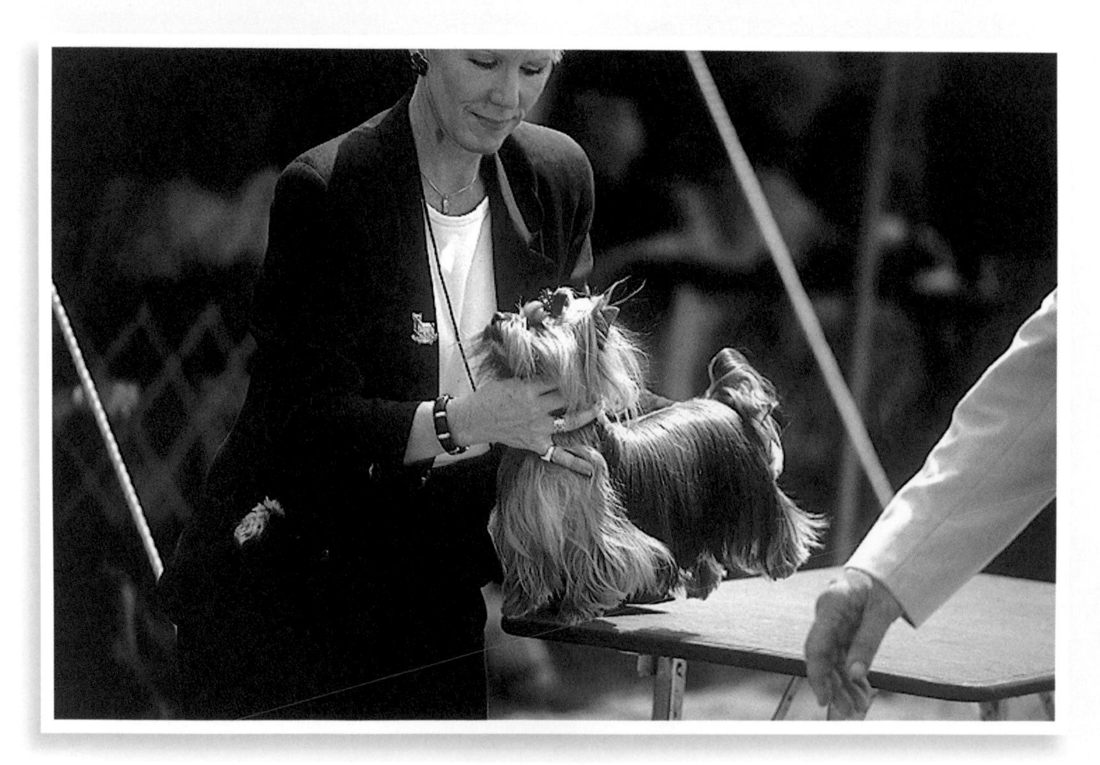

Yorkies are flamboyant showmen, making them naturals for conformation shows.

responsible breeding takes a lot of time and research.

Both the AKC and the United Kennel Club (UKC) have conformation classes for Yorkshire Terriers. The Yorkie is considered a Toy Dog in the AKC and a Companion Dog in the UKC.

Obedience

Competitive obedience requires your Yorkie to put aside his stubbornness and follow the rules exactly. He can do it if his relationship with you inspires him to cooperate.

Obedience requires precision heeling, jumping, fetching, and other obedience behaviors in exact conformance with the rules. When he sits, he has to be sitting straight next to you, not at an angle. When an exercise is finished, he has to go around your back and sit at your left.

It is a thinking dog's sport. The dog has to remember what he has to do next and carry it out despite distractions. Focus and concentration on you are required. You have to be the center of his attention the whole time the two of you are in the ring, or practicing for the ring.

Obedience is a sport for people and dogs who like to win, like to achieve, are detail-oriented, and have the time and patience to make it happen. It requires almost no equipment. A basic leash and collar at the beginning and a bucket of tiny treats are all you need. Soon you won't even need the leash.

Beginners start out as Novices in the AKC, heeling fast and slow and through a figure-8, exhibiting a down-stay, a sit-stay and a recall. If you succeed in Novice, you move on to Open and then Utility classes. The Open includes the Drop on Recall, the Retrieve on Flat, and the Retrieve over High Jump. Utility includes hand signals and scent discrimination.

Obedience training is something you can do at home, practicing in short sessions every day. But if you are serious about competing, you will have to practice in a public place with other dogs nearby, as well. Your dog must learn to sit for a full minute and stay down for three minutes in the same room with other dogs, with you nearby but not right next to him. It's a challenge!

Some people who do competitive obedience start with a successful CGC test. Others keep their dog in obedience classes year round, working every day on something, and still others join dog clubs to have a place and people to practice with. Successful obedience champions practice, practice, practice.

Rally

Rally is a combination of agility and obedience at a more relaxed level. An AKC Rally course has 10 to 20 stations with instructions for dog and handler at each one. A perfect "Heel" position is not required, and you are allowed to talk to and encourage your dog. The AKC sees Rally as the first step up from the CGC program. So, if you have passed the CGC test, you are ready for Rally.

Rally has different levels of difficulty, such as Novice, Advanced, and Excellent. In the

Multi-Dog Tip

When it comes to organized canine sports, it's every dog for himself. Just because one of your dogs is good at agility does not mean the other one will even like it. Try to find something that matches each dog's temperament.

If you are participating in a sport or just playing outside with your Yorkie, make sure he doesn't get overheated on hot days.

Novice trials, the dog is on leash, but he's not in the others. You lose points for a tight leash, a poor sit, resistance, and touching a jump, among others. In Novice, some of the stations require the dog to halt-sit or halt-down, make a 90-degree right or left turn, an about face turn or a U-turn, and a front finish, where the dog moves around to sit in front of you.

Some Yorkies love this kind of attention and interaction. They move quickly up the levels of difficulty, earning Rally Novice (RN) and Rally Advanced (RA) titles that go after their name.

You can start in Rally by finding an obedience class that specializes in it. The AKC's website has more information.

TRAVELING WITH YOUR YORKIE

The Yorkie's size makes him a perfect travel companion. He can travel on planes in the passenger cabin, he takes up little room in a car, and he fits happily in an over-the- shoulder soft carrying bag. The more you travel with your Yorkie, the more accustomed he will be to it and enjoy it. This is when the fun begins.

When traveling together, pack a bag for your Yorkie that includes a spare sweater or two, a spare leash, a brush, his blanket, and some favorite toys.

By Car

Car trips can be the high point in your Yorkie's day when you are only going on errands. Imagine how happy he would be on an overnight car trip. He gets to be with his people all the time!

Like any other adventure with your Yorkie, safety should come first.

- Before you leave home, be sure he has a collar tag with your travel identification, such as a cell phone number.
- A Yorkie (or any other dog) should never ride loose in the front seat. A dog can too easily be thrown through the windshield, into your line of vision, or killed by an inflatable seat bag. The safest way for your Yorkie to travel is in a hard-sided crate or in a special dog car seat, seat-belted into in the back seat. This allows him to see out the window.
- Regulate the temperature of the car with your Yorkie in mind. It should never be too hot or too cold. Never leave your dog alone in the car, no matter what the outdoor temperature is.

- Traveling by car should allow you to take enough food and water for however long you will be gone, as well as his dishes, treats to reward good travel behavior, and poop bags or pee pads.
- Take care when you stop at rest stops to securely fasten his leash before you unhook his seat belt. Excited dogs may not hear you call if they bolt out of the car and take off.

A few dogs get car sick. Some grow out of this, but others don't. If yours does, avoid feeding your dog the morning before a car trip. Some people find herbal remedies such as Rescue Remedy or feeding your dog a few ginger snaps help. Extra towels in the car are always a good idea when traveling with dogs.

By Plane

Yorkies fit in small travel crates/carriers under airplane seats, which means they can go when you go.

- Check with your airline to learn their animal passenger requirements, such as size of crate, health certificates, and fees.
- You may think your Yorkie is in a carry-on bag like any other and can just walk on, but your airline wants to know in advance when you are bringing a live dog. Make a reservation for him as soon as you know your schedule.
- Be sure your dog is wearing a collar tag with your cell phone number.
- Take enough food with you for a few meals

Check with individual airlines to see what type of carrier they accept in the cabin.

Training Tidbit

Before you head out on a long car trip with your Yorkie, try several shorter ones. Get your dog used to the car by gradually building up endurance and making it fun. Drive through a hamburger fast food restaurant and share a hamburger with your Yorkie . . . just be sure to skip the onions!

until you can find a store that sells your brand of pet food.

- Avoid feeding your dog or offering him a big dish of water immediately before getting on the plane. Take enough water for travel day and maybe the next day.
- Take a sweater with you, and pack another one in the luggage.
- Put a chew toy in the carry-on crate.
- Exercise your dog as much as you can before the flight and find a spot in the airport to put down a pee pad. Carry extra ones with you.
- Dogs must stay in the crate while they are on the plane.

Lodging

Many hotels and motels allow guests to have pets in their rooms. Sometimes there is a pet fee and you may have to put down a deposit. Some may ask that you not leave the dog alone in the room in case he starts barking.

If you are heading out on a long road trip with your Yorkie, plan ahead. Some motels only have a few rooms designated for dogs, and they may be filled if you get there without a reservation. Find motels that accept dogs for each night of the trip before you leave home. Travel sources, such as the AAA, publish lists of motels that accept dogs by state.

Staying in a hotel or motel with a dog requires a high level of diligence on your part. You represent the dog-owning public to this business and to non–dog owners also staying at your motel. Be a model dog owner by picking up after your dog every time and making sure your collection of filled poop bags gets in the right trash can. Clean up accidents in your room as quickly and thoroughly as possible. Reduce barking by making sure someone stays with your dog at all times. Don't allow your Yorkie to approach people in the lobby unless they have shown an interest in him. Check to see if dogs are permitted in all parts of the hotel, such as the pool, breakfast room, or exercise areas. Leave a generous tip for the housekeeper.

IF YOUR YORKIE CAN'T TRAVEL

Sometimes your Yorkie just has to stay home when you travel. The best option for each dog depends on the dog. Some may need to stay with familiar friends; others may need to stay in their own home with friends or professional pet sitters looking in on them several times a day. Those dogs may benefit from a day at doggie daycare if a friend can be persuaded to drop them off and pick them up. Professional pet sitters will need a key to your house and detailed instructions. Look for someone who loves dogs and who your dog is at least interested in. Local colleges and vet schools frequently have pet sitters, and local businesses that have national franchises can be found online.

If your Yorkie must be boarded, consider the size and safety of your dog first. Be sure to ask about toy dogs and what provisions the kennel makes for them. Avoid scheduled play times with dogs of all sizes. Ask your vet or dog trainer for recommendations on boarding sites. Look for one that allows small dogs time in the kennel owner's house. If that isn't possible, find one that provides individual playtime for your dog with people at the kennel. Find a kennel that is agreeable to your dog's feeding schedule, his diet, and whatever supplements your dog takes. Some kennels will bathe your dog just before you get back for an extra fee.

Want to Know More?

To keep your trip safe and pleasurable, your Yorkie should understand basic obedience commands. For a refresher, see Chapter 4: Training Your Yorkshire Terrier Puppy.

It is not easy to find the ideal boarding kennel, so try several before you find the perfect fit. Expand your geographic limits if the closest kennels don't work. Look for a kennel near the airport you fly out of. Consider one in a different city if someone you know lives there, recommends it, and would like you to visit when you pick your dog up.

Make sure your kennel knows how to reach you, when you are returning, and what your dog's basic schedule is. Expect your dog to be exhausted when you pick him up.

One additional word: some dogs get stressed by boarding, even at the best places. The upset in their routine and your absence may give them diarrhea while you are gone. Probiotics started the week before you leave may help reduce the severity of such an attack.

There are times when your Yorkie may not be able to travel with you—hiring a pet sitter or kenneling your dog are both options.

PART III

SENIOR YEARS

CHAPTER 12

FINDING YOUR YORKSHIRE TERRIER SENIOR

For some people, a senior Yorkie is the perfect pet. They are mellower, more inclined to match their schedule to yours, and have a temperament you can rely on. They are who they are.

Some people, especially senior citizens, have discovered that senior dogs go through life at a slower pace that may match their own. And because the dog can be screened, a more perfect match is possible. Have a boat and want a Yorkie who has sea legs? A senior with nautical experience may be right for you. Have a cat? A dog with cat experience would be perfect.

WHEN IS A YORKIE A SENIOR?

Since many Yorkies live to be 15 years old, they become seniors a little bit later than bigger dogs. Some giant dogs become seniors as early as five or six years old, but many Yorkies are seniors only when they hit 10 or 11. Others may need senior care at eight years. It depends on the dog. It is a very individual thing that is affected by a dog's genes, health, nutritional history, and temperament.

Yorkies slow down as they age but that, too, is in an individual thing. A senior Yorkie still has a lot of pep. Some eleven-year-olds can charge around like puppies—at least some of the time. As they get older, some Yorkies mellow and develop a wise look that appeals to a lot of people. Their eyes tell you they understand. Whatever you tell them, whatever happens, they take it in stride. Some of their reduced pace can be attributed to a touch of arthritis, but some of it is just the experience of knowing you will be there whenever they get there.

"They really do slow down," says Sue Walters, owner of four Yorkies in performance activities. "When they get to be about eleven or twelve, they definitely slow down. As they get older

By the Numbers

Yorkies sometimes live to be 17 or 18 years old. A Yorkshire Terrier in England named Sammy was in the news not too long ago when he was 23 years old. He had half his teeth left.

Yorkie rescue groups frequently have older dogs available.

they do start to tame down. They just feel, what's the bother, life goes on."

ADOPTING A SENIOR YORKIE CAN BE GREAT

If you don't have a homegrown senior Yorkie, adopt one. Yorkie rescue groups frequently have older dogs available that are sometimes more difficult to place because so many people are looking for a puppy.

Senior dogs are perfect for people who don't like to housetrain a puppy and who want to skip the chewing stage and the "zoomies" stage of endless energy. Senior dogs are usually past the reproductive age and have been spayed or neutered. People who adopt senior dogs know what they are getting. The dog already has the coat, the health issues, the temperament, and the look. You can tell right away if that appeals to you, if the health issues are too much, or if the temperament is a poor match. That makes it possible to eventually find a good match for your lifestyle.

Why a Senior May Need a Home

Why do good dogs end up in rescue, especially older ones? The reasons are many and varied. Senior Yorkies end up in rescue when their

Multi-Dog Tip

Getting a puppy may be a good idea if you have a senior Yorkie, or it may not be. Some younger seniors perk up when a puppy moves in. But older seniors may be irritated by puppy antics. Consider your own dog carefully before committing to a new one.

owner dies or can't afford major medical or dental expenses. Sometimes they are surrendered because of a divorce or a job move. Some are given up by couples that found them incompatible with a new baby or a baby that just started crawling.

Some senior Yorkies have had a good life until recently and ended up in rescue through no fault of their own. They are well-mannered and easy to live with.

Temperament

But the truth is, not all dogs in rescue are like that. Some have not been well-socialized and others have been coddled and treated like a human baby. They were surrendered because they were out of control and aggressive. Others have had serious health issues that overshadow everything else. These Yorkies will need a period of adjustment to learn what you expect and how to behave in your house. This can take time and patience.

Well-run rescues will start the process before a dog is released for adoption. They temperament-test new dogs and work with them on some behavior issues. They attack obesity. Some dogs have never had any structure and, once they are exposed to a regular schedule and rules, their difficulties melt away.

Whether your dog has been well-socialized or not, housetraining frequently lapses during transitions from rescue to new home. New owners may have to start the process over.

Health

And then, there's the obvious health issue. Some senior Yorkies end up in rescue because they have major health and dental issues that will require steady maintenance on your part. They have had broken legs, liver shunts, or decayed teeth. Sooner, rather than later, most

Well-run rescues temperament test new dogs before adoption.

Peope who adopt senior Yorkies give them a second chance at a good life.

will have senior issues such as reduced hearing or vision, sensitivity to hot and cold, and arthritis. And sooner, rather than later, they will come to the end of their lives.

Second Chances

In spite of all this, people who adopt senior Yorkies usually get satisfaction in providing a second chance to a dog who didn't get a lucky break the first time. They are excited to watch the dog unfold and develop new sides to his personality—even at an advanced age. They want the challenge of tackling a major health issue and improving the life of a dog. They feel content watching an old dog retire, sleeping the sleep of the secure and the well-loved. Sometimes, they say, a dog can even seem grateful. Adopters talk about adopting a senior dog as an opportunity to make a big difference in one dog's life.

Building a relationship with a dog like this can be very rewarding. Dogs can bloom under the right care. In some cases, senior dogs can even be given a new life as therapy dogs, visiting people in hospitals or nursing homes who identify with a dog up in years or who has a physical handicap.

WHERE TO FIND YOUR SENIOR YORKIE

Senior Yorkies are sometimes available at local shelters but generally you have a better chance of finding an older Yorkie by calling breeders and rescue groups. People who buy purebred puppies are frequently required to sign a contract promising to surrender the puppy to the breeder rather than take it to a shelter if they are not able to care for it—no matter how old the dog is. Breeders may also have an adult dog who has finished a breeding or a show career and is ready to be adopted.

Rescue groups across the nation also take Yorkies that shelters can't manage because of time, money, or space constraints. Shelters call a rescue group when a Yorkie is surrendered who has health or maintenance issues that are too complicated for that facility to handle. Dedicated volunteers in rescue groups pour time into rehabilitating homeless Yorkies, and even raise money to pay for it. They assess a surrendered Yorkie's physical needs and temperament and start improving both. Some pay for dental work or other medical needs, which might include surgery. They work with the dog to decrease bad habits. They won't release a dog for adoption unless they think he is well on the road to recovery and can make an adjustment to living with a new family. Some dogs spend months with a rescue group, living in a foster home.

If you approach a Yorkie rescue group about adopting one of their dogs, be prepared to answer enough questions to prove to the volunteers you are worthy of one of their dogs. They'll want to know if you've ever had a Yorkie or a small dog, if you have any children younger than 6, if you have a fenced exercise area, if you are prepared to have your Yorkie's teeth cleaned regularly, and if you have references they can check. Then, be prepared to pay for a rescue dog. Senior dogs have lower adoption fees than healthy puppies, but they are not free.

Select training rewards for senior dogs with care. Many older dogs may need fewer calories than younger dogs. Others may be on special diets that require less fat or no meat.

AT HOME

At home after a transition period, an older dog may settle into a routine and make very few demands. He may be easier to walk on a leash because he is past the headstrong stage. Regular short walks are a good idea for senior dogs, even ones with beginning arthritis. A walk loosens stiff joints and stimulates mental abilities. A chance to sniff new territory and take his time may be just the thing a senior Yorkie needs. Plus, it is a chance for the two of you to get to know each other and share an experience.

Want to Know More?

For what to look for in a rescue, see Chapter 5: Finding Your Yorkshire Terrier Adult.

CHAPTER 13

CARE OF YOUR YORKSHIRE TERRIER SENIOR

An old dog is the reward you get for years of care and attention to a young dog. An old dog is a prize indeed. You and your Yorkie can read each other's minds, anticipating the other's next move. The two of you have comfortable routines that just feel right. Even more than that, his personality is so well developed it has taken on a life of its own. Dogs who are loved for a decade or more seem to rise above the pack and exist on a different plane. He is a cerebral fellow. He is who he is, still not human but far more than the puppy you took in.

The good news is, today's dogs live longer. More of us will get to experience the joy of a senior dog. When does a Yorkie become a senior? The rule of thumb is that a senior dog is in his last third of life. If a Yorkie lives 12 to 15 years, his senior years will begin at age 8 or 10. As dogs live longer—16 years of age, 17 years—their senior years will also begin later. But the age at which each dog acts like a senior is different—depending on things such as genes, nutrition, and general health—and it is up to you and your vet to call it.

Whenever it happens, a senior Yorkie starts to slow down. He may not see or hear as well. He may show stiffness when he gets up or walks. His appetite or his weight may change. His mental abilities may also slow down, and he may seem confused. Your dog won't get all these symptoms, and he won't get them all at once. They may take years to develop to the point of hindering his activity. Good care can keep them at bay as long as physically possible.

The plus side of old age is that your dog's understanding of you and your conversations together have never been better.

FEEDING YOUR SENIOR YORKIE

Feeding an old dog is both an art and a science. Nutritional needs change as dogs age, and so does their appetite. Your Yorkie's meals may need constant adjustments—a little less fat, a little more fat, an appetite stimulant such as gravy, soft food if he has more than a couple of teeth missing. He may need a rotation of foods every day—one thing for breakfast, another for lunch, and a third thing for dinner. It's trial and error.

What to Feed Your Senior Yorkie

Assess your Yorkie's general weight and profile as you start the senior years. Is he overweight? Is this new? Some dogs need less food at the

Multi-Dog Tip

Seniors may need our protection from other dogs in the house, especially a boisterous puppy. A senior Yorkie should have his own place that he can retreat when other dogs in the house annoy him. Support him in his quest for tranquility and peace.

end of middle age, when they first start to slow down. They just don't burn off the calories like they used to. But then, the next time you turn around, your dog may have lost his appetite and not want to eat anything. He may lose weight. Flexibility is the key to successfully feeding an older dog. It takes a willingness to try new things.

Senior Formulas

Senior-formula commercial dog food usually has fewer calories and more fiber. If that is what your Yorkie needs, switch him gradually. This type of food may work during his early senior years but reassess his needs frequently, especially when he becomes a very old dog. He may need extra fat and protein then. Match the food you feed to the dog as he stands before you. No one diet works for all dogs all the time. Just because he has loved a dog food all his life doesn't guarantee he will eat it now.

Other Yorkies may continue to do well on the diet they have always eaten. Some may need just a little bit less to maintain a perfect weight.

Supplements

Talk to your veterinarian about your dog's weight and any supplements you are thinking of adding. Older dogs frequently take supplements for arthritis, heart, or coat but many herbs and vitamins are available. Some promise to restore the "bloom" to older dogs. Talk to your veterinarian about whether any supplements would interact with prescription medicines and how much to give your dog. Buy a small bottle to try before making a large investment.

Appetite

Appetite can be a frustrating thing in older dogs. Some days, they look at the food that so pleased them yesterday and just walk away. Other days, you can shop and cook a meal just for them and watch them walk away. Old dogs should be allowed to skip a meal but repeated loss of appetite should trigger a vet visit. It can be a symptom of serious disease.

At about 10 years, your Yorkie could be considered a senior.

If your dog passes the vet exam, and you know you are dealing with typical senior finickiness, then it's time to start experimenting.

- Try a new kind of dog food—soft food, smaller pieces of food, canned food, dog gravy
- Soak kibble in chicken broth and microwave it until it is just warm
- Try human food—baked or sautéed chicken and boiled rice is a good place to start. Use the chicken fat, but no salt or sugar; use chicken broth to make the rice. Make a batch, divide it into meal-size portions, and freeze what you can't use today and tomorrow.
- Try feeding your dog out of your hand.
- Try tasty items like bananas, bologna, canned pumpkin (not pumpkin pie filling), yogurt, or cooked sweet potatoes.
- Frozen fish, such as tilapia, can be sautéed and offered to dogs.

Check to see if another dog or cat is intimidating your senior at mealtime. Old dogs who competed eagerly for food when they were younger may just decide it's not worth the trouble now. Eliminate all treats that don't have exceptional nutritional value. Read labels studiously.

Make sure water is fresh and available.

Feeding Schedule

Active healthy seniors can continue to eat on the same schedule they always have. An ideal schedule is to feed your dog twice a day, about 12 hours apart. Seniors who are losing weight may need a third meal to entice them to eat more. Feed small, fresh meals and remove uneaten food after 30 minutes if the dog isn't interested. At the next meal, feed a different, fresh food.

Try new types of food to tempt a picky senior.

GROOMING YOUR SENIOR YORKIE

A few changes can make grooming your senior Yorkie a more comfortable experience.

- Now may be the time to trim your Yorkie's hair even shorter. Short hair is easier to take care of and requires less fussing. Some seniors will be relieved not to have grooming time; others will enjoy grooming as much as they always have because it is time with you.
- Incorporate a body massage into your grooming session to relax a senior dog. Rub his shoulders and hips slowly and gently. Gently massage his forehead and the top of his head.

- Consider grooming on a heated pad.
- Keep grooming sessions short.
- Accommodate your dog as much as you can by allowing him to lie down when possible.
- If you drop your dog off at a professional groomer's, try to reduce the time he is away from home. Ask if she will groom your dog while you wait, so he doesn't have to stay all day in a kennel.
- Be sure that, wherever your Yorkie is groomed, he stays warm. Older dogs are sometimes more sensitive to the cold. He should be dried as fast as possible after a bath.

SENIOR HEALTH CARE

Health care for your senior Yorkie is more like puppy heath care than adult dog care. It is much more regular and frequent. If your Yorkie is strong and active, then preventive care must be maintained at high levels. If he has developed a medical issue, such as arthritis or hypothyroidism, he will have to take supplements daily.

If your dog is diagnosed with a major ailment, your first impulse may be to look it up online. Be careful to check the source of the information: Stick to websites that are produced by major veterinary colleges or government agencies, because information on many other websites is not reliable. And stick to looking up straightforward definitions of diseases and how they progress. Avoid trying to find a treatment. One trap that many people fall into is to assume dogs can be treated the same way as humans with the same diagnosis. Treatment for people and dogs with the same disease frequently varies, as does the prognosis. Only your vet can tell you exactly what is best for your dog. Don't delay professional treatment while you self-doctor your dog based on advice

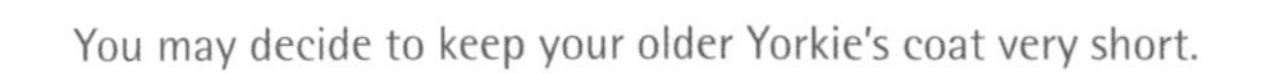

You may decide to keep your older Yorkie's coat very short.

you get from the web or well-meaning friends. Your Yorkie deserves professional care.

Preventive Care

At some point, your Yorkie will need to see the vet at least twice a year for checkups. A lot can happen in six months, and your vet should keep tabs on his blood, weight, and overall appearance. Expect her to do complete blood count and chemistries tests, urinalysis, and parasite tests.

An outside expert sometimes notices things people who live with a dog just don't see. A look in the eye, dullness of coat, a stiffness that is just developing—those things are sometimes hard to see for people too close to the dog. Trust your vet's immediate reaction to your dog.

Ask Your Vet

When your Yorkie is eight, talk to your vet about how your dog is aging. She may suggest you start coming twice a year instead of once a year, that he has a senior blood test, and that he switch to senior dog food. Or, she may suggest delaying this senior care for a year or three.

This is the time to ask if your Yorkie needs as many vaccination boosters as usual, especially if he doesn't go out much. Each case is different, and vaccination schedules depend on your Yorkie's immune system and whether you have other dogs in the house who go places where there are lots of dogs.

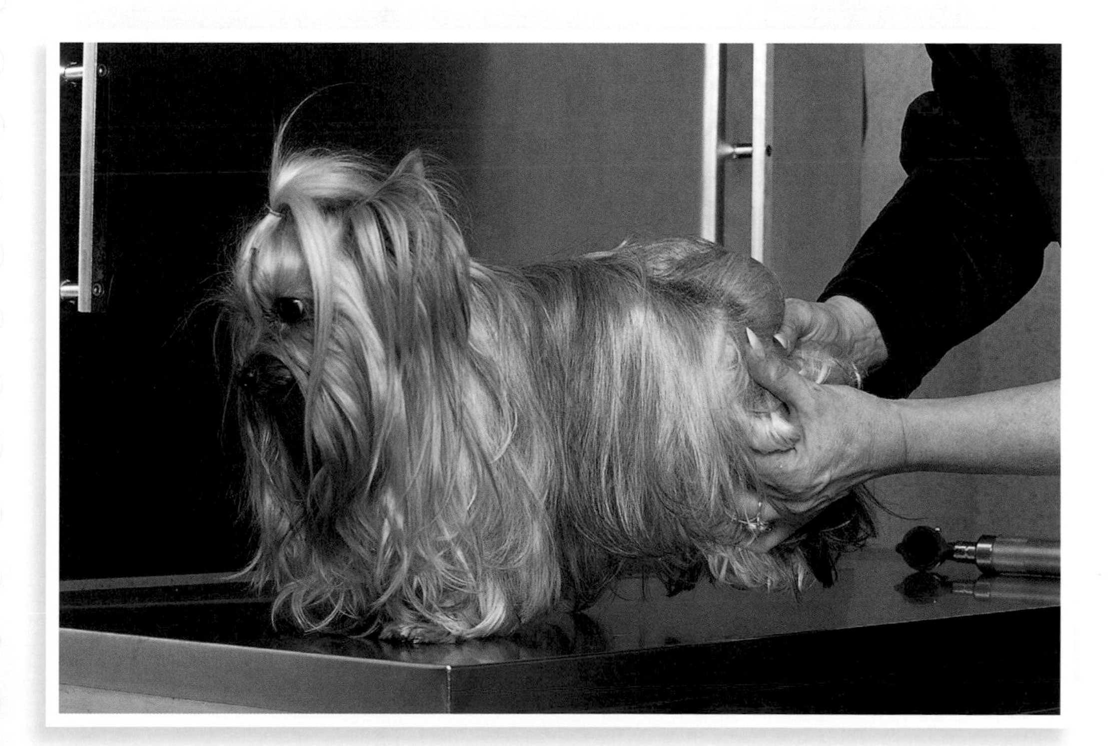

Senior Yorkies should visit the vet twice a year for a checkup.

Some illnesses cause depression, aggression, or lethargy.

Your Yorkie's diet should be another topic of conversation at these vet visits. Whether you make your own dog food or buy it, your vet should analyze the proteins, fats, carbohydrates, and fiber it contains to make sure it is a balanced diet and appropriate for your dog at this age.

Be sure to mention any change in your dog's temperament. Some illnesses cause depression, aggression, or lethargy.

Senior Illnesses

Like people, older dogs sometimes develop illnesses they never had as puppies. These are specific to their age, and you may not be familiar with them. It is often difficult to tell which symptoms are typical of an older dog and which indicate a serious illness. This is one of the reasons why your dog should see a vet at least twice a year. Chances are, your dog will develop at least one chronic illness associated with old age but with any luck, it will be slow moving and not affect his quality of life too much.

Arthritis

Dogs with arthritis have stiff or painful joints. They may walk slowly when they first get up, favoring one leg. Steps up or down may be a new problem. Your heart may want to make life easy for your Yorkie with arthritis and carry him everywhere, but giving up on all exercise is a mistake. Dogs with arthritis should walk to exercise stiff joints and keep them moving. Short leash walks every day are a good idea, but try to eliminate wild racing or jumping.

Your vet will x-ray your Yorkie to make sure arthritis is the cause of lameness. She may recommend a weight-loss diet, and she may recommend supplements and pain killers.

Supplements such as glucosamine and chondroitin may help in the long term; they are available over the counter, at both human and canine pharmacies. Ask your vet how much to give your Yorkie. This is not a quick cure or a permanent, fix but it does seem to help some dogs, at least for a while. Glucosamine and chondroitin, as well as a few other supplements, such as green-lipped mussels and sea jerky, work to protect and repair your dog's cartilage, which is frequently destroyed in arthritis.

Pain-relief medications may also help (but not Tylenol, which is toxic to dogs). Canine aspirin is available and is much safer for your dog than regular aspirin, as are prescription painkillers. Ask your vet which medication is best for your dog and what dose to give him.

Yorkies with arthritis may be irritable sometimes. They may enjoy a heated dog bed, designed with your dog's safety in mind and available in dog catalogs or large pet stores. A set of doggie steps up to—and down from—his favorite nesting place may also be a good idea. Discourage jumping down. Swimming is an excellent exercise for dogs with arthritis, as long as it is supervised. Acupuncture and massage also may help dogs with arthritis. You can find canine specialists for both online or by asking your vet.

Canine Cognitive Disorder

Known as the doggy version of Alzheimer's disease, canine cognitive disorder (CCD) affects your dog's thinking, memory, and even learned behavior. One of the first symptoms is disorientation. Your dog may seem lost or forget where the door to a room is. He may not recognize people he has known for a long time. He may sleep more but not at night. He may pace, circle, or tremble. He may forget to go outside when he has to go to the bathroom. Sadly, he may no longer seem to interact with people as he once did.

Diagnosing CCD starts with eliminating everything else such as blindness, deafness, and cancer that could be causing the symptoms. Then it includes listing all your dog's symptoms and assessing whether he is affected enough to have CCD.

Some medications are available to treat dogs with CCD, but it is a progressive disease. Managing it at home may include extra care to ensure that your dog does not get lost outside the yard, because he may not be able to find his way home. He may have to be confined to one room or one floor of the house if he consistently gets confused or stuck in one place in the house.

By the Numbers

Senior dogs may have senile deafness, a gradual hearing loss that starts at age 10. Usually, these dogs will still be able to hear some sounds, usually high-pitched ones.

Want to Know More?

For more information on eye problems in Yorkies, see Chapter 8: Yorkshire Terrier Health and Wellness.

Dogs with congestive heart failure are often put on a low-salt diet.

Cataracts

A cataract is a cloudy film in the lens of the eye. It spreads until the entire lens is cloudy. It can occur in both eyes, eliminating the transparency of the lens and severely reducing a dog's ability to see. The cloudiness from a cataract sometimes looks like a crystal.

Senior dogs who have a bluish filminess in their eyes probably have nuclear sclerosis. In that condition, age causes the lens to harden and may affect your dog's close-range vision but does not lead to blindness. Cataracts can be much more serious, because they are actually opaque, preventing your dog from seeing.

The lens can be surgically replaced if the dog's quality of life is affected, but the surgery requires general anesthesia.

Dogs can be blinded by cataracts. But in familiar surroundings, with owners who don't move furniture around and help when they can, blind dogs can lead happy lives.

Congestive Heart Failure

When toy breeds get congestive heart failure, frequently the cause is chronic valvular disease. In congestive heart failure, the failure refers to the heart's failure to pump enough blood that has been oxygenated to meet the dog's needs. In chronic valvular disease, the valves in the heart degenerate over time, especially, in toy breeds, the mitral valve. That can cause the heart to fail in its pumping job. Chronic valvular disease has no known cause.

Without enough blood pumping through the dog's body, his major organs, such as the liver, kidneys, and lungs, may be affected.

The first symptom of congestive heart failure is fatigue. The dog tires easily. He may cough, especially at night. Eventually, his body may swell, he may breathe rapidly, and lose his appetite. His lungs fill with fluid.

Your vet can treat congestive heart failure with the same drugs used in people who have it. She will probably suggest your dog be put on a low-salt diet and get reduced exercise. Some dogs with valve failure can be managed successfully for a long time. Coenzyme Q (Co-Q-10) is a supplement that is frequently used for heart health. Ask your vet if it would be appropriate for your dog.

Cushing's Disease

Hyperadrenocorticism, or Cushing's disease, is one of the late-in-life disease that can affect some senior Yorkies. The adrenal glands, just above the dog's kidneys, produce corticosteroids that regulate electrolytes, suppress the immune system, and reduce

Cushing's disease is one of the late-in-life disease that can affect some senior Yorkies.

Don't forget to shower your senior Yorkie with love and affection!

inflammation. In Cushing's disease, they produce great quantities of adrenal hormones—too great. In small dogs like Yorkies, the cause is frequently found in the pituitary gland. It produces a hormone called ACTH that pushes the adrenal glands into overproduction. Symptoms include hair loss, dull and dry hair, pot belly, lethargy, loss of muscle mass, and weakness. Dogs with Cushing's disease will frequently drink more water than usual and urinate more often—which may also be symptoms of just general aging. If you notice your Yorkie spending more time at his water dish, consult your vet immediately. Complications of Cushing's disease include diabetes and blood clots.

Cushing's disease is treated with medication under close veterinary monitoring but the outlook for a long life with Cushing's disease is not good. Diagnosis and treatment can be very expensive.

TRAINING AND EXERCISE

Training your senior Yorkie may seem like an oxymoron until you consider what training looks like from the dog's point of view: attention and treats.

Yorkies, who have a well-earned reputation for being headstrong, like attention and treats as much as any dog. The combination can work wonders, even with older, slightly set-in-their-ways dogs. So, don't give up on training just because your dog is 10 or 12 or 14. Sneaking out of the house with just your senior Yorkie for some one-on-one attention may be just the thing he needs to perk up. Look for tricks classes offered by your favorite dog trainer. Or, opt for teaching your senior a few commands or tricks by yourself.

- Pick a time when your dog is usually not asleep. Some dogs sleep all morning and are more active in the afternoon. For others, it is just the opposite.
- Leave any other dogs behind. This is a time for just the two of you.
- Consider switching to a harness. Older Yorkies, especially the overweight ones or those who have chronic bronchitis, sometimes get tracheal collapse. Their windpipe collapses, making it hard for them to breathe. If your dog is overweight or is coughing, use a harness for teaching things like heeling.
- Use treats he really likes.
- Employ the most positive training you can muster. Use lots of praise when he does something right and just ignore him when he flubs up.
- Look for things to teach him that he can master. Avoid really athletic feats if your dog has started to slow down or develop arthritis.
- Look for softer areas such as grass, sand, or outdoor carpet to work on.
- Keep sessions short.

Teach House Rules

If the new dog in your house happens to be a senior, train him to follow the house rules. Yes, you can. How long this will take or how easy it will be depends on what kind of life he had before. Use a crate just the way you would use it with a puppy. Take him to a regular obedience class. Use treats or toys or clickers.

Your older dog has a history with people. He has probably learned that people are interesting and worth watching. He will be watching you. Be consistent. Be firm. If you don't want him jumping on you when you get home, ignore him when he is jumping. Do not make any exceptions. If you don't want him begging at the table, don't give him a piece of food when you are at the table. Ever. Not one.

Always use the same vocabulary. Pick a word for each command (sit, stay, down) and always use that word. Say "Stay" every time, not "wait" sometimes or "stop" other times or even "just a minute." Make it as easy as you can for your dog.

Avoid yelling when you can. A dog biting an electric cord might stop if you yelled. A dog crossing the street might stop if you yelled. But otherwise, it is better to talk to dogs in a

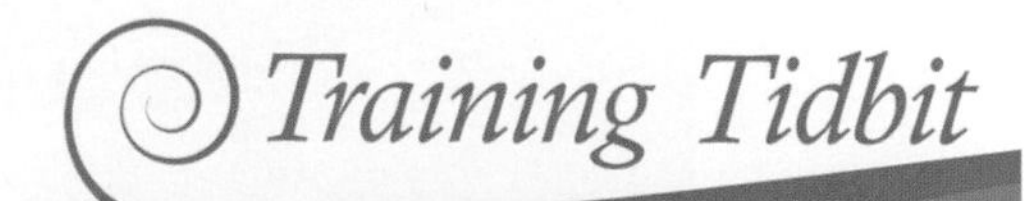

Old dogs move a little slower and have less endurance. Adjust training expectations accordingly. Don't expect your 12- or 14-year-old Yorkie to start agility. But keep trying to teach new tricks. It's good for both of you.

conversational tone. Old dogs have learned to "read" humans. They understand inflections and tone. Take advantage of that when training an older dog. Make training seem exciting, and make your dog seem like a genius when he accomplishes something. He will get it. And he will appreciate it.

Games for Older Dogs

Games are a great way to keep your senior Yorkie mentally stimulated.

Hide and Seek

You can play Hide and Seek with a person or an object. If you have had your senior dog long enough for him to learn the names of all the people in the house, start by asking him, "Where's So-and-So?" Then go with your dog, room by room, until you find that So-and-So is in the shower. Make a big deal out of finding So-and-So. The next day, try it again. The third day, wait to see if your dog will go off on a search by himself. Eventually, he should be able to search the house for someone he knows, even if that person is hiding in a closet.

You can also play Hide and Seek with a toy. Pick up a dog bone or stuffed animal and show it to your dog. Give it a name or call it by a name your dog already knows. "Here is squeaky man." Tell your dog to "Stay" and take

A fun indoor game can help keep your senior occupied.

the toy to the other side of the room and put it down where the dog can see it. Go back to your dog and tell him to "Find the squeaky man." If he goes to get the toy, reward him with a treat. If he doesn't, start a search with your dog. "Let's find the squeaky man. Oh, here it is. I found it." Then take the toy and put it in another room, near the door, so the dog may see it or can see it with just a little effort. Tell your dog to "Find the squeaky man." Repeat all the steps, each time hiding the toy in more difficult places. If he is having trouble, stay at one level of difficulty before moving to the next.

Tunneling

You can buy a tunnel for your yard at canine agility sites, but sometimes it's more fun to make a small one that's just the right size for your Yorkie and set it up in the house. You can make a tunnel out of several cardboard boxes of about the same size. Tape them shut and cut out both ends, then tape the boxes together to form a tunnel. Or, build a temporary tunnel by pushing chairs together and draping them with a bed sheet. Make sure the tunnel is big enough to allow your dog to pass through without touching the sides or the roof. Put your dog in a down-stay at one end of the tunnel and go to the other end. Lay on your stomach and look into the tunnel. Call your dog. Use a treat to lure him into the tunnel. If your senior has never seen a tunnel, you may have to throw a treat into his end of the tunnel and tell him to get it. Or throw a ball. Figure out what would encourage your dog to venture into the tunnel. Most Yorkies like tunnels after they have had a good experience with one.

Wave

Ask your dog to sit. Pick up a paw with your hand and gently wave it. Offer him a treat. Do this several times, saying "Wave" each time, until he offers his paw himself.

Then watch your old dog shine. He will know he has learned something new and will strut in front of you.

Just for Fun

Just for Fun Agility is a movement away from the organized sports nature of agility and more toward agility as fun you can have with any dog. It's for people who want to use the idea of an obstacle course with dogs who are not professional athletes. Find a JFFA group online.

CHAPTER 14

END-OF-LIFE ISSUES

All good things end—most too soon. So it is with the lives of our Yorkies. Even the long-lived ones who make it to 17 or 18 must go sometime. It is our lot in life to outlive our canine friends and feel that loss keenly. Several people can help you get through this difficult time, such as a vet, a friend who has lost a pet, and family members who knew your Yorkie and can share happy memories. Reach out for whatever help you need for as long as you need it.

WHEN IS IT TIME?

Dogs die for many reasons. The death we may wish for our dogs, quick and painless in their sleep in their own home, may not be in the cards for your dog. One day, you realize your dog hasn't seemed happy in a long time. He doesn't wag his tail or look interested in anything. His health has deteriorated. He eats very little. He never goes out. Sometimes he is in pain. Maybe he has an illness or a condition that has no cure. His quality of life has declined to a very low point and nothing you can do will bring it back.

It is time to think about euthanasia.

Nobody likes the thought of being the one to decide when a dog dies. But many dog owners come to the conclusion that it is better to be that person than the one who keeps her dog alive in suffering and misery. Most dog people would say it is the better and necessary of two bad choices.

Dogs live much longer now than they used to but that is little consolation to a dog owner faced with a very sick 15-year-old Yorkie. It is, however, one reason why euthanasia is a decision you may have to make. Modern medical treatment can postpone death for months or even years. We have conquered and routinely treat disease that would have killed a dog 50 years ago when they were two or six or eight years old. But even such a positive thing has a negative side. Medical treatment is not

Training Tidbit

When your dog is seriously ill, you can ease up on the rules. A dog with cancer who has lost his appetite may be coaxed with the human food he most craves, even bacon.

Talking about your Yorkie may be the best way to deal with grief.

yet a guarantee of immortality. Finally, sadly, someone has to say, "enough."

Some people say they just knew when it was time for their dog to go. Some people will even say the dog seemed to tell them by a look in his eye or an action.

But the rest of us have to make the decision based on facts.

Veterinary sources suggest asking: Is the dog having more good days than bad? Can he still do things he loves? Is he in pain that cannot be relieved? Is he eating and drinking?

If not, especially if he is in pain that cannot be relieved, it is time to call your vet and talk about euthanasia.

Euthanasia

Euthanasia is usually an injection that causes the heart to stop. It just stops. If you are with your dog, you may see some muscle spasms or even a deep breath but your dog will just appear to go to sleep. The vet will check to make sure the heart has stopped. It is quiet, peaceful, and you can take comfort in that.

People who have a good relationship with their vet may opt for a familiar and kind face at a time like this. The dog also knows his regular vet. But some people prefer that a visiting or mobile vet come to their home, so that their dog can die at home.

In most cases, the dog is too sick to care

deeply, so you should choose the option that is most comfortable for you.

Hospice

Hospice for dogs is a relatively new idea that you should discuss with your vet. It is for the pet owner whose dog has a terminal disease. The owner has decided not to seek medical treatment, but wants to help her dog live comfortably and without pain for as long as possible. In hospice care, owner and veterinarian work as a team. The vet comes up with a plan that will allow the dog to live comfortably and the owner carries it out, administering medications and nursing the dog. Sometimes a vet tech may make a house call.

Hospice has some advantages. It spares the dog any further aggressive treatment and allows him to remain at home. The pet owner has professional help assisting her in prescribing pain medications. It allows other dogs in the family to see what is happening to their friend.

Home hospice care may require training for the pet owner in giving injections or other medications. A pet owner who lives alone may have to shoulder a sad burden that can feel very heavy on some days.

GRIEF

For some pet owners, the relief of not watching their dog suffer every day helps alleviate the deep sense of loss they feel. But for others, even a very sick dog was a presence they relied on, a bigger-than-life memory of happier days.

Those differences are only the beginning of the very real, very personal grief you will feel when your dog dies. Things may remind you of him when you least expect it. People offering sympathy may provoke a flood of tears.

But, generally speaking, talking about your Yorkie and how you feel may be the best way for you to heal. Find someone who is willing to listen without judging and talk about the happy days with your dog. Collect pictures of him in a photo album. Accept the fact that you will go through at least some of the five stages of grief: Shock and denial, bargaining, anger, depression, and acceptance. Many telephone hotlines have pet loss specialists, especially those run by veterinary colleges.

By the Numbers

Euthanasia is usually associated with old age but sometimes we have to make a decision to euthanize younger dogs. Dogs get terminal diseases at different times in their lives, and this can affect their quality of life. Sometimes a small dog is attacked by a larger dog and must be euthanized when the injuries are so severe they, too, would affect his quality of life.

Consider holding a memorial service for your dog. You may want to bury your dog or his ashes and hold a service at that time. Or, you may just want to invite some friends over and remember your dog's life and how many people he affected.

EXPLAINING PET LOSS TO CHILDREN

The death of a dog who has been part of a family with children should be shared with children. Children should go to some vet appointments when the dog is sick. This way, they can listen and learn just what is wrong with their dog and prepare for the end. They can see that the dog is sick and that medical help will not cure him. This should help calm their imaginations. Whether you take them to the euthanasia appointment is a personal call. But children should definitely be included

Many telephone hotlines have pet loss specialists.

in any kind of a memorial ceremony, such as spreading the ashes. They can be involved in making a photo album or writing a poem or a story about their dog. They should get a vote on how to memorialize him: a stone, a bush or tree, a large framed photo, a donation to a canine health foundation.

Children may deal with feelings of anger or guilt, especially older children who have gone away to college.

Several good children's books deal with loss of a pet, including classics such as *Charlotte's Webb* by E. B. White, *The Tenth Good Thing about Barney* by Judith Viorst, and *Dog Heaven* by Cynthia Rylant.

HELPING OTHER PETS DEAL WITH LOSS

If your sick dog lingers at home for a time, your other dogs will get an idea something is wrong. If your dog dies at home, the other dogs may be invited to sniff their old friend's body before he disappears.

But if your dog dies elsewhere, your dogs at home may not know what has happened. Talk to them. Tell them what happened. They may not understand all the words but if you use the dog's name and simple phrases, they may begin to catch on, especially if you are crying and seem at a loss. After all, they knew he was sick.

A dog who relied on the dog who is now gone may feel the loss heavily. Spend extra time with that dog. Offer him extra privileges, such as more lap time or car time or whatever he really likes. Use this opportunity to bond with that dog. If he is the only dog left at home, you can have a one-on-one relationship now.

The fact that dogs grieve other dogs is now accepted in veterinary circles. Signs include listlessness, change in appetite, and different sleep patterns. Some recommend leaving your house the way it was for awhile. Do not remove any pet beds or toys, including those that belonged to the dog who is gone. Allow the dog you still have to gradually accept the fact that his friend is not coming back.

If he continues to be lethargic, make a vet appointment. He may not be grieving but be sick.

Getting a new dog after a short time may perk everybody up or it may add strain to an already-stressed household. Only you can decide which it would be.

Multi-Dog Tip

Dogs grieving another dog may change their sleep patterns. They may choose new places to sleep now that one dog has gone. But still, none may choose to sleep in the place of the dog who is gone.

50 FUN FACTS EVERY YORKSHIRE TERRIER OWNER SHOULD KNOW

1. Yorkies curl their tongues when panting.
2. Yorkies can be taught to swim.
3. Eating some human pills that fall on the floor can kill a Yorkie.
4. Yorkies hunt rats, mice, voles, squirrels, rabbits, and frogs.
5. Huddersfield Ben, the first Yorkie, died in 1871, and was stuffed by a taxidermist.
6. A Yorkie in England recently celebrated his 23rd birthday.
7. Many Yorkies wear red ribbons because it sets off the tan hair color so well.
8. Bananas and banana bread make good training treats for Yorkies.
9. Yorkies, like most small dogs, have more dental problems than most bigger breeds.
10. Yorkies may be small, but they are descended from wolves just as all dogs are.
11. Only one Yorkie has won the Westminster Dog Show.
12. Many Yorkies can be hard to housetrain, but not all.
13. Even Yorkies who don't go outside can get heartworm.
14. The window for puppy socialization closes at four or five months.
15. Small dogs evolved from Middle Eastern wolves about 12,000 years ago.
16. A Yorkie, Smoky, may have been the first therapy dog, visiting World War II soldiers.
17. Yorkie puppies are born black and tan. The blue shows up later.
18. Yorkies are a single-coated dog and don't shed very much.
19. Yorkies, like a handful of toy breeds, are more likely to have potentially fatal liver problems than many bigger breeds.
20. Onions are not good for Yorkies (or any dogs).
21. Always measure your Yorkie's meals with a measuring cup.
22. If your Yorkie's ears are folded over, it may be from the weight of hair. Trim the hair off the tips.
23. Yorkie hair is more like human hair than most dog breeds' hair.
24. Yorkies wear sweaters for two reasons: They are cute and to keep these thin-haired dogs warm.
25. Baby teeth do not always fall out in Yorkies and sometimes have to be pulled.
26. Yorkies need to learn grooming manners because they spend so much time being groomed.
27. Buy dog toothpaste for your Yorkie, liver

or chicken flavored. Don't use human toothpaste.

28. Yorkies have the same number of teeth a large dog has—just smaller.

29. Both male and female Yorkies wear ribbons in their hair.

30. Yorkies may be difficult to housetrain but a Yorkie who urinates in the house may have a urinary tract infection.

31. Yorkie males who mark in the house may have to wear a bellyband, a type of skinny diaper.

32. Yorkies have small litters, two to four puppies.

33. Single-color Yorkies do not meet the standard—it calls for blue and tan coloring.

34. One Yorkie made the list of Lifetime Top 20 dogs overall in American Kennel Club agility competition, Desmond Aloysius Shelby.

35. Travel with a recent photo of your Yorkie in case he gets lost.

36. Yorkies should weigh between 4 and 7 pounds (2 and 3 kg).

37. Most breeders remove a Yorkie's dewclaws, an extra toe on the front feet and sometime on the rear feet.

38. Yorkies usually come with docked tails in this country, but European law forbids it.

39. Yorkies get more than their share of broken bones from falls and being sat or stepped on.

40. Harnesses are good for Yorkies because they sometimes get collapsed tracheas.

41. Toys for Yorkies should have no small parts, such as doll eyes that a dog could choke on.

42. Plain or vanilla yogurt can ease a Yorkie's upset tummy.

43. Audrey Hepburn starred with her own Yorkie in the movie Funny Face.

44. Dog associations do not recognize or approve the teacup Yorkie classification. There is no such thing as a teacup—it is a marketing ploy.

45. Exercise pens can be used inside and out to keep a Yorkie safe.

46. Yorkies are small but enjoy walks on their own four feet.

47. Rub corn syrup on a Yorkie's gums if he is having a hypoglycemic attack.

48. Yorkie puppies may need to eat four times a day at first.

49. Pack water from home if you go away overnight with your Yorkie.

50. Raw carrots make a great treat for Yorkies.

ASSOCIATIONS AND ORGANIZATIONS

Breed Clubs

American Kennel Club (AKC)
5580 Centerview Drive
Raleigh, NC 27606
Telephone: (919) 233-9767
Fax: (919) 233-3627
E-Mail: info@akc.org
www.akc.org

Canadian Kennel Club (CKC)
89 Skyway Avenue, Suite 100
Etobicoke, Ontario M9W 6R4
Telephone: (416) 675-5511
Fax: (416) 675-6506
E-Mail: information@ckc.ca
www.ckc.ca

Federation Cynologique Internationale (FCI)
Secretariat General de la FCI
Place Albert 1er, 13
B – 6530 Thuin
Belgique
www.fci.be

United Kennel Club (UKC)
100 E. Kilgore Road
Kalamazoo, MI 49002-5584
Telephone: (269) 343-9020
Fax: (269) 343-7037
E-Mail: pbickell@ukcdogs.com
www.ukcdogs.com

Pet Sitters

National Association of Professional Pet Sitters
15000 Commerce Parkway, Suite C
Mt. Laurel, New Jersey 08054
Telephone: (856) 439-0324
Fax: (856) 439-0525
E-Mail: napps@ahint.com
www.petsitters.org

Pet Sitters International
201 East King Street
King, NC 27021-9161
Telephone: (336) 983-9222
Fax: (336) 983-5266
E-Mail: info@petsit.com
www.petsit.com

Rescue Organizations and Animal Welfare Groups

American Humane Association (AHA)
63 Inverness Drive East
Englewood, CO 80112
Telephone: (303) 792-9900
Fax: (303) 792-5333
www.americanhumane.org

American Society for the Prevention of Cruelty to Animals (ASPCA)
424 E. 92nd Street
New York, NY 10128-6804
Telephone: (212) 876-7700
www.aspca.org

The Humane Society of the United States (HSUS)
2100 L Street, NW
Washington DC 20037
Telephone: (202) 452-1100
www.hsus.org

Royal Society for the Prevention of Cruelty to Animals (RSPCA)
RSPCA Enquiries Service
Wilberforce Way, Southwater, Horsham, West Sussex
RH13 9RS
United Kingdom
Telephone: 0870 3335 999
Fax: 0870 7530 284
www.rspca.org.uk

Sports

International Agility Link (IAL)
Global Administrator: Steve Drinkwater
E-Mail: yunde@powerup.au
www.agilityclick.com/~ial

The World Canine Freestyle Organization, Inc.

P.O. Box 350122
Brooklyn, NY 11235
Telephone: (718) 332-8336
Fax: (718) 646-2686
E-Mail: WCFODOGS@aol.com
www.worldcaninefreestyle.org

Therapy

Delta Society
875 124th Ave, NE, Suite 101
Bellevue, WA 98005
Telephone: (425) 679-5500
Fax: (425) 679-5539
E-Mail: info@DeltaSociety.org
www.deltasociety.org

Therapy Dogs Inc.
P.O. Box 20227
Cheyenne WY 82003
Telephone: (877) 843-7364
Fax: (307) 638-2079
E-Mail: therapydogsinc@qwestoffice.net
www.therapydogs.com

Therapy Dogs International (TDI)
88 Bartley Road
Flanders, NJ 07836
Telephone: (973) 252-9800
Fax: (973) 252-7171
E-Mail: tdi@gti.net
www.tdi-dog.org

Training

Association of Pet Dog Trainers (APDT)
150 Executive Center Drive
Box 35
Greenville, SC 29615
Telephone: (800) PET-DOGS
Fax: (864) 331-0767
E-Mail: information@apdt.com
www.apdt.com

International Association of Animal Behavior Consultants (IAABC)
565 Callery Road
Cranberry Township, PA 16066
E-Mail: info@iaabc.org
www.iaabc.org

National Association of Dog Obedience Instructors (NADOI)
PMB 369
729 Grapevine Hwy.
Hurst, TX 76054-2085
www.nadoi.org

Veterinary and Health Resources

Academy of Veterinary Homeopathy (AVH)
P.O. Box 9280
Wilmington, DE 19809
Telephone: (866) 652-1590
Fax: (866) 652-1590
www.theavh.org

American Academy of Veterinary Acupuncture (AAVA)
P.O. Box 1058
Glastonbury, CT 06033
Telephone: (860) 632-9911
Fax: (860) 659-8772
www.aava.org

American Animal Hospital Association (AAHA)
12575 W. Bayaud Ave.
Lakewood, CO 80228
Telephone: (303) 986-2800
Fax: (303) 986-1700
E-Mail: info@aahanet.org
www.aahanet.org/index.cfm

American College of Veterinary Internal Medicine (ACVIM)
1997 Wadsworth Blvd., Suite A
Lakewood, CO 80214-5293
Telephone: (800) 245-9081
Fax: (303) 231-0880
Email: ACVIM@ACVIM.org
www.acvim.org

American College of Veterinary Ophthalmologists (ACVO)
P.O. Box 1311
Meridian, ID 83860
Telephone: (208) 466-7624
Fax: (208) 466-7693
E-Mail: office09@acvo.com
www.acvo.com

American Holistic Veterinary Medical Association (AHVMA)
2218 Old Emmorton Road
Bel Air, MD 21015
Telephone: (410) 569-0795
Fax: (410) 569-2346
E-Mail: office@ahvma.org
www.ahvma.org

American Veterinary Medical Association (AVMA)
1931 North Meacham Road, Suite 100
Schaumburg, IL 60173-4360
Telephone: (847) 925-8070
Fax: (847) 925-1329
E-Mail: avmainfo@avma.org
www.avma.org

ASPCA Animal Poison Control Center
Telephone: (888) 426-4435
www.aspca.org

British Veterinary Association (BVA)
7 Mansfield Street
London
W1G 9NQ
Telephone: 0207 636 6541
Fax: 0207 908 6349
E-Mail: bvahq@bva.co.uk
www.bva.co.uk

Canine Eye Registration Foundation (CERF)
VMDB/CERF
1717 Philo Rd
P.O. Box 3007
Urbana, IL 61803-3007
Telephone: (217) 693-4800
Fax: (217) 693-4801
E-Mail: CERF@vmbd.org
www.vmdb.org

Orthopedic Foundation for Animals (OFA)
2300 NE Nifong Blvd
Columbus, Missouri 65201-3856
Telephone: (573) 442-0418
Fax: (573) 875-5073
Email: ofa@offa.org
www.offa.org

US Food and Drug Administration Center for Veterinary Medicine (CVM)
7519 Standish Place
HFV-12
Rockville, MD 20855-0001
Telephone: (240) 276-9300 or (888) INFO-FDA
http://www.fda.gov/cvm

PUBLICATIONS

Books

Anderson, Teoti. *The Super Simple Guide to Housetraining.* Neptune City: TFH Publications, 2004.

Anne, Jonna, with Mary Straus. *The Healthy Dog Cookbook: 50 Nutritious and Delicious Recipes Your Dog Will Love.* UK: Ivy Press Limited, 2008.

Dainty, Suellen. *50 Games to Play With Your Dog.* UK: Ivy Press Limited, 2007.

Magazines

AKC Family Dog
American Kennel Club
260 Madison Avenue
New York, NY 10016
Telephone: (800) 490-5675
E-Mail: familydog@akc.org
www.akc.org/pubs/familydog

AKC Gazette
American Kennel Club
260 Madison Avenue
New York, NY 10016
Telephone: (800) 533-7323
E-Mail: gazette@akc.org
www.akc.org/pubs/gazette

Dog & Kennel
Pet Publishing, Inc.
7-L Dundas Circle
Greensboro, NC 27407
Telephone: (336) 292-4272
Fax: (336) 292-4272
E-Mail: info@petpublishing.com
www.dogandkennel.com

Dogs Monthly
Ascot House
High Street, Ascot,
Berkshire SL5 7JG
United Kingdom
Telephone: 0870 730 8433
Fax: 0870 730 8431
E-Mail: admin@rtc-associates.freeserve.co.uk
www.corsini.co.uk/dogsmonthly

Websites

Nylabone
www.nylabone.com

TFH Publications, Inc.
www.tfh.com

Boldfaced numbers indicate illustrations.

D

E

F

G

H

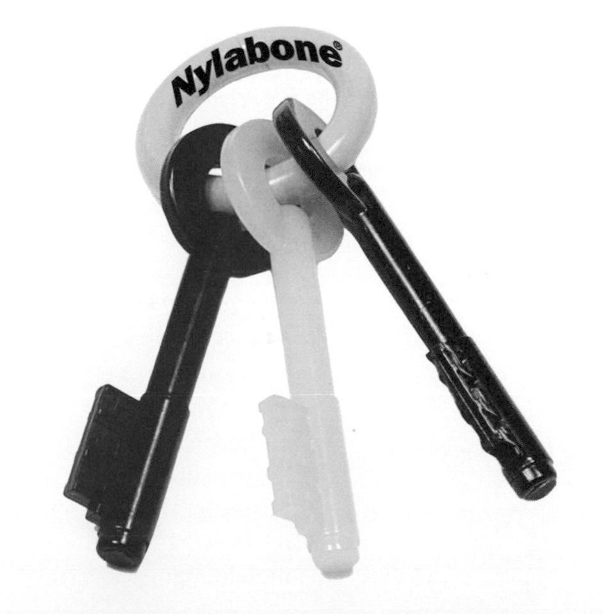

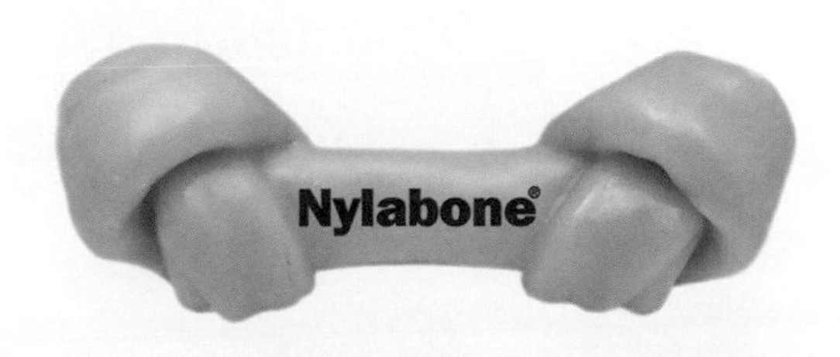
Nylabone®

U

V

W

Y

PHOTO CREDITS

Isabelle Francais: 15, 16 (top), 17, 53, 75, 99, 101, 112, 144, 150, 152, 174, 180 (top and bottom), 181, 185, 186, 191, 193

Shutterstock:
michael d skelton, Cover, 39, 85; SergiyN, Cover (Spine), 129, 131; Basov Mikhail, Back Cover, 9, 20, 138, 179; RedTC, 3; argo74, 6; Chris Pole, 8; Toloubaev Stanislav, 10, 57; MISHELLA, 12; wojciechpusz, 13, 24; FotoJagodka, 16 (bottom); Scorpp, 18, 32, 21, 34, 49, 50, 62, 78, 111; VaclavHroch, 23; Phase4Photography, 27, 56, 146; Noam Armonn, 28, 108; Quicksnap Photo, 29; Konstantin Gushcha, 30, 63, 96 (right), 192; pirita, 33; Yan Wen, 36, 86; Cheryl E. Davis, 38, 40; Tereza Dvorak, 42, 58; Lenkadan, 46, 176; Shutterstock, 52; Maksim Nikalayenka, 59; Bretislav Horak, 60; Suponev Vladimir Mihajlovich, 61, 70; Felix Mizioznikov, p 64; ItCameWiththeFrame, 66; Juice Team, 68; Joy Brown, 72, 106, 142; Iurii Konoval, 76; Viorel Sima, 80, 165, 205; objectif MC, 81, 110; ELEN, 82; Nikolai Pozdeev, 84 (bottom); Marilyn Volan, 89; Nata Sdobnikova, 90; Kovalev Sergey, 92; pixshots, 94, 125; Alexandr Ryzhov, 96 (left); turtleman, 102; Eric Isselee, 71, 104, 134, 190; Jiri Vaclavec, 113; Glenda M. Powers, 115; iofoto, 118; Bojana Korach, 120; InfinityPhoto, 122; Zdorov Kirill Vladimirovich, 124; Shchipkova Elena, 126; Dee Hunter, 128; Aksenova Natalya, 132; Makarova Viktoria, 133; Monica Wisniewska, 135; oxystel, 139; S.M., 140, 147; dough girl, 141; Lisa F. Young, 149; Giancarlo Liguri, 154; Steven Pepple, 157; Makarova Viktoria (Vikarus), 158; Erik Lam, 162; Debbie Aird Photography, 163; Troy Lim, 164; Cynoclub, 166; Shmel, 168; Liliya Kulianionak, 169; Vibrant Image Studio, 170; Mark Herreid, 171; hohotun4ik, 173; Nataliya Kuznetsova, 177; Charlene Bayerle, 182; David B. Petersen, 184; Stocker1970, 188; Gladkova Svetlana, 194; pixel1962, 196; copperman, 197; Lisa F. Young, 198; ??, 200; Serhiy Shullye, 202; argo74, 84 (top), 204; George R Gonzalez, 206

VETERINARY ADVISOR

Wayne Hunthausen, DVM, consulting veterinary editor and pet behavior consultant, is the director of Animal Behavior Consultations in the Kansas City area and currently serves on the Practitoner Board for *Veterinary Medicine* and the Behavior Advisory Board for *Veterinary Forum.*

BREEDER ADVISOR

Sharon Griffin has owned Yorkshire Terriers since 1981, and breeds and shows under the name Majestik Yorkies. She is an approved AKC, UKC, and International Kennel Clubs judge. She is a member and on the health committee of the Yorkshire Terrier Club of America and president of the Yorkshire Terrier Club of Southeastern Michigan.

DEDICATION

To Bailey, the dog who changed everything.

ACKNOWLEDGEMENTS:

Thanks to all the wonderful Yorkie owners who helped me understand this amazing dog. And thanks, as always, to Tom, who stood behind me during this adventure.

ABOUT THE AUTHOR

Sheila O'Brien Schimpf is a prize-winning journalist who lives in East Lansing, Michigan, with three dogs. One of her Goldens was a breeding stock dog who has whelped 20 puppies in Sheila's kitchen for a service dog agency. Sheila has written for *The Lansing State Journal*, BNA.com, and *Dog Fancy* magazine. Occasionally, she teaches journalism at Michigan State University. She is married and has three grown children.